Doing Ethnographies

Doing Ethnographies

Mike Crang and Ian Cook

SAGE Publications
Los Angeles • London • New Delhi • Singapore

SAGE Publications Ltd
1 Oliver's Yard
55 City Road
London EC1Y 1SP

SAGE Publications Inc.
2455 Teller Road
Thousand Oaks, California 91320

SAGE Publications India Pvt Ltd
B 1/I 1 Mohan Cooperative Industrial Area
Mathura Road, Post Bag 7
New Delhi 110 044

SAGE Publications Asia-Pacific Pte Ltd
33 Pekin Street #02-01
Far East Square
Singapore 048763

British Library Cataloguing in Publication data
A catalogue record for this book is available from the British Library

ISBN 978 0 7619 4445 4
ISBN 978 0 7619 4446 1 (pbk)

Library of Congress Control Number 2006929863

Typeset by Newgen Imaging Systems (P) Ltd, Chennai, India
Printed in Great Britain by Athenaeum Press, Gateshead
Printed on paper from sustainable resources

Contents

Preface

We hope that this book will be of use to any researcher considering the use of qualitative methods in their undergraduate or postgraduate research. It brings together a variety of disciplinary and cross-disciplinary influences from anthropology, sociology, human geography, philosophy, science studies, cultural studies, film and photography, marketing, education, heritage, folklore and tourism studies, nursing studies, rural and urban studies, postcolonialism, feminism and gender studies, gerontology, and disability studies. It does so through drawing on the attempts by two human geographers, to use combinations of qualitative methods in one's undergraduate dissertation, the other's MA thesis, and both of their PhDs in the late 1980s and early 1990s. An earlier version of this book was published in 1995. This is the finally 'finished article'. But how has it got from there to here, why are geographers writing this kind of book, how do the answers to these questions help to explain why it is the way it is and how might it be useful to others?

The earlier version of *Doing Ethnographies* was exclusively available from Mrs C. Flack in Norwich, England. You sent her £5 and she mailed it to you. It was number fifty-eight in the Concepts And Techniques in Modern Geography (or CATMOG) series published by the Institute of British Geographers' Quantitative Geography Study group. It was a very long way from being a mainstream publication. And it wasn't even a book. It was more of a booklet, a collector's item, part of an obscure back catalogue catering to a small but specialist geographical audience. This catalogue was recently bought up by a major label. Some authors were asked to update and reissue their work, now digitally remastered, for a wider audience. In 1995, you would have to have been moving in the right circles to hear about our CATMOG booklet and to get hold of an original or a bootleg copy. But perhaps that was appropriate. It had been written by two PhD students who were still doing their ethnographies. They hadn't finished them. So what did they know?

Despite these inauspicious beginnings, this early version travelled and was quite widely read, much to our surprise. It appeared in libraries that subscribed to the CATMOG series. We later borrowed and reworked bits of it for more easily accessible publications (e.g. Cook 1997b, Crang 1997a), and the feedback we got seemed mainly to be from people who had read it *after* they'd done their research wishing that they'd read it earlier. We had written it in 1993, in part because our supervisor suggested that we did so, but also in part, to make a better sense of how ethnographic research actually got done, and how it might therefore best be supervised. We were not working in a hotbed of ethnographic research. And we all had a lot to learn, even though both of us had some useful research experience at home and overseas. Ian had undertaken his Masters research into the biographies and everyday lives of four legally blind people living in a small American city, and had been supervised by Graham Rowles, whose exemplary ethnographic research with elderly people had, for many, stood out from the humanistic geography literature of the 1970s and 1980s (see Cloke et al. 2004). Mike had tried to examine the labour process in electronics firms in Malaysia for his undergraduate dissertation, and had largely taught himself how to do this. In 1993, Ian should have been writing up his multi-locale ethnographic PhD connecting the everyday lives of people working along a commodity chain between the Jamaican production and UK retailing of fresh papaya, and Mike was in the middle of PhD research using a variety of qualitative methods to examine popular understandings of national and local heritages in the UK.

Between us, we had practical experience of participant observation plus interviewing, focus groups and/or filmic approaches to research. So, because our projects had always involved participant observation, we called our booklet *Doing Ethnographies*, even though it encouraged readers to combine methods in ways which didn't necessarily involve participant observation and might not therefore meet purist definitions of 'ethnographic' work (Jackson 1985). We wanted to show how these research methods worked (together) both in principle and in practice. We wanted to work out, and pass on, what we (should have) learned from our often strange and strained experiences of getting this type of research done. Some of these lessons were specific to individual methods, but many addressed much bigger questions: about how to plan research which is intentionally unpredictable; how to take its unexpected twists and turns as signs that things may be going well rather than off the rails; how researchers could prepare to be flexible, to think on their feet, to make the most of opportunities that came along; and how their supervisors should allow and encourage them to do this. We w used to having to justify what we were doing to a mass of sceptics, c casual coffee-break conversations. Under these local circumst CATMOG booklet became a detailed justification of our choi

Our sceptics' questions were answered in its pages. We were arguing against, as much as for, a certain way of doing things. These tensions remain in the text. Readers may spot that people who worried about our lack of 'objectivity', and especially those Mike liked to call 'quantasaurs' (see Crang 1992), greatly irritated us at the time! In the decade since, however, we have mellowed, qualitative methods seem to have become a 'new orthodoxy' in human geography and, indeed, there is now talk of a backlash against them by those who bemoan the lack of number crunching skills among younger researchers (Crang 2002).

Perhaps the most compelling evidence of this new orthodoxy is the avalanche of recently published books showcasing qualitative methods in human geography research (see, for example, Blunt et al. 2003; Cloke et al. 2004; Flowerdew and Martin 1997; Hay 2000; Hoggart et al. 2002; Hughes et al. 2000; Limb and Dwyer 2001; Moss 2002; Pryke et al. 2003 and Shurmer-Smith 2002). We have recently reviewed this and other recent work for Mike's qualitative research reports in *Progress in human geography* (Crang 2002, 2003) and for Ian's contribution to *Practising human geographies* (Cloke et al. 2004). We are therefore well aware that geographers are now *practising* this, *researching* that and *doing* plenty of other things that we could only have imagined ten years ago. If only we had had access to that work then! Our research would have been so much easier to justify and to think through. Work like this is truly marvellous. So, why would we want to add our now finished version of *Doing Ethnographies* to this sagging bookshelf? How does it compare? What does it do differently? And what changes have we made? Like any text, the earlier version was a creature of its time. In the 1970s, a small but significant ethnographic tradition within humanistic geography had produced some wonderful studies of urban-social geography (see Ley 1974; Rowles 1978a; Western 1981). However, by the 1990s, these were being pushed aside by geographical readings of the feminist and 'new' ethnographic work which was helping to shape the discipline's 'cultural turn' (see Cloke et al. 2004). The earlier version was written as that turn was taking shape and, in it, we tried to draw together what we'd learned about geography's older humanistic ethnographies and the approaches from cultural studies, anthropology, sociology, feminist studies and so on, from which 'new' social and cultural geographers were drawing inspiration. Yet, although there have been important methodological and theoretical innovations in geography since that time, qualitative geography's *core* methods remain largely the same and the importance attributed to research exploring the taken-for-granted aspects of everyday life is undiminished (see Hoggart et al. 2002; Smith 2001; Thrift 2000a).

We were encouraged to work up our CATMOG booklet by two referees' reports on our proposal to Sage. Both emphasised that the discipline had changed significantly since it was written, so we'd have to flag up this new work. But they liked the old version's accessibility, its realistic portrayal of the 'complexities, challenges...frustrations, but also rewards, of research', and the 'closeness of the text to the original research projects'. They wanted the new version to retain the 'focus and tone' of the old one which, they said, they continued to recommend to their undergraduate and postgraduate students, despite the competition. However, they stressed, three main weaknesses would have to be addressed. Sage could sort out the first by making the new version more easily available than Mrs Flack had been able to make the old. We could sort out the second by updating the text to reflect important changes in information technology over the past decade (we hadn't been able to make use of email, the internet or digital recording equipment in 1993)! And we could sort out the third by updating the old text and finishing it off.

Given that *Doing Ethnographies* was first written before either of us had finished doing our ethnographies, this seemed like a good idea. Then, we had been able to build on our experience of 'conceptualising the subject', 'preparing for fieldwork', 'constructing ethnographic information' and 'analysing field materials'. But that's where we stopped. There was little about writing, and nothing about writing up. Writing that booklet had been a welcome distraction from writing our PhDs. And perhaps it showed. Very few methodological advisories are written in the middle of research projects, and understandably so. Yet, fewer still are written *by* students *for* students. That's a more positive way of framing what we did. We were 'on the job', learning our craft, and writing about it. That was what showed. Given that this was what our reviewers had liked, it therefore made no sense to rip up the old version and start again.

Mike gained his PhD two years, and Ian's was eventually awarded four years, after the first version of *Doing Ethnographies* was written. So, in the end, we did write a couple of big ethnographies. But we have also written shorter and more easily accessible papers based on them: in journal articles and book chapters roughly the same length as an undergraduate dissertation. In all of this, one way or another, we have tried to combine proper social scientific analysis with evocative writing. That's an important but tricky balancing act in qualitative research, whether you've got 80,000 or 10,000 words to play with. We've also talked quite a few undergraduate and postgraduate students through this process over the years. They have continued to surprise, educate, challenge and enthuse us with the results of their work. So, now, we have more experience of, and more to say about, writing ethnographies than we did in 1993. We are now as ready as we'll ever be to produce the finished article. Surely.

Ian Cook and Mike Crang
Birmingham and Durham

Acknowledgements

In the earlier version of *Doing Ethnographies*, we thanked Myles Gould, Steve Hinchliffe, David Ley, Sarah Whatmore, Clare Madge, James Sidaway, two anonymous referees and those others who had entered into more informal discussions with us, for their help, advice and encouragement. For this version, we would like to add our thanks to Robert Rojek, Claire Dwyer, Chris Philo and anyone else who spread, read, used and talked to us about the first version, including our students from whom we have learned a great deal. This book draws upon postgraduate research funded by ESRC studentships and a teaching assistantship from the University of Kentucky Graduate School. We continue to thank them for their support. Gratitude must also be expressed to all those who gave us the support we needed to undertake, finish, defend and get our undergraduate degrees, Ian's MA, and both of our PhDs. Gratitude, here, is long overdue to Graham Rowles, Michelle Harrison, Felix Driver, Paul Cloke, Derek Gregory, Nigel Thrift and others who cannot, and perhaps still should not, be named. Finally, we think it's important to acknowledge the responsibility of the co-author for any remaining flaws and inadequacies in this work. If it had not been for his interference this book would have been perfect.

Acknowledgement

1 Introduction

Since the early 1990s, an increasing number of researchers in human geography have drawn on qualitative methods in their work. The aim of this book is to give an introductory guide to the practice of those methods broadly referred to as 'ethnographic', i.e. participant observation *plus*, in our experience at least, interviewing, focus groups and/or video/ photographic work. The basic purpose in using these methods is to understand parts of the world more or less as they are experienced and understood in the everyday lives of people who 'live them out'. In the early 1990s, there was an established literature dealing with the poetics and politics of *writing* such ethnographies (Atkinson 1990; Crang 1992; Gordon 1988; Marcus and Clifford 1986; Marcus and Cushman 1982; Spencer 1989). Yet, far less had emerged concerning the poetics and politics of *doing* them. Historically, relatively few researchers, in their final monographs, have included detailed discussions of how their methods 'worked' in the field. And, as a result, many first-time ethnographers have found that reading these works, along with any standard 'how to' manuals, leaves them ill-prepared for the losses of 'control' and surprising twists and turns which their work can subsequently take. Although some may be drawn to the more 'predictable' and 'controllable' results which quantitative methods often promise, our intention here is to argue that with appropriate preparations, the inevitable contingencies of any ethnographic project can be productively incorporated and built upon from the very start.

This book has by no means been written as a menu of abstract concepts and methods to be learned and then applied in the field to answer tightly defined research questions. Rather, it is intended to serve as a guide to preparing for the sorts of issues and methods which have to be considered throughout an ethnographic project (with its inevitable constraints of time and money). In our experience, researchers have often been reluctant to do ethnographies because they fear that these somehow must either inevitably fail to get to the 'nitty-gritty' of a problem, or involve methods which can only be used 'properly' by rare, and unusually gifted, people. Our intention here is to argue that neither of these need be true. Drawing on both the techniques literature and our experiences of doing this type of work as undergraduate, Masters and/or PhD students, we want to demystify this approach and thereby provide a positive foundation on which others might build more 'doable' projects.

As readers may also gather as our arguments develop, another aim of this book is to dismantle the three-stage read-*then*-do-*then*-write model for academic research. We don't like this at all. Indeed, we see it as one of the main causes of qualitative research going badly wrong. You may be familiar with this model. We have certainly been advised to follow it on more that one occasion. In its purest form, it sets out research as comprising three discrete stages. Stage One (the first year of a PhD, for example) involves reading the literature and preparing a research proposal. Stage Two (the second year) is spent doing that proposed research. And Stage Three (the third and final year) is spent writing up the results of that research. Yet, qualitative researchers often find that things don't happen the way that they had planned them 'in the field' during that second stage. Those who they expect to talk to and what they expect to find doesn't happen as planned and, often, more interesting issues unexpectedly appear. So, if and when this happens, how can they salvage the situation to get their dissertation or thesis completed and handed in on time? There seem to be two main options:

(a) spend Stage Three writing up the research as if it didn't go wrong, clinging as much as possible to that Stage One proposal, or

(b) spend Stage Three reading the literature which ideally would have been read in Stage One and then, in the limited time remaining, writing up the research that was actually done.

Both of these options are the stuff of nightmares and, we argue, they're also unnecessary if an alternative combination of reading, doing and writing is pursued from the start of a project. Here, we argue, it's a very good idea to:

- agree with your supervisor to ditch that linear model as the right way to organise your work and time,
- mix up your reading, doing and writing from the start in order to gradually piece together something that's equally interesting, relevant and doable,
- undertake detailed preparations that will allow you to be ready, willing and able to deal with the unexpected twists and turns which you will inevitably experience,
- make ongoing but systematic attempts to rethink and rewrite research plans 'on the hoof' in order to understand how the project is taking and changing shape, and how some influence can be exerted over this and
- refuse to believe that you should be able to state *exactly* what your research is about (except strategically in formal proposals) because this will change as the research proceeds.

Research following the read-*then*-do-*then*-write model is, we have learned from bitter experience, almost bound to go 'off the rails' or just plain 'wrong'. In preparing for his ethnographic research on how legally blind people travelled independently through an American city, for instance, Ian spent approximately ten months reading the literature on which their mobility instruction – and therefore, he supposed, their travel – was based. Only then, after he had honed his research questions, did he arrange to meet with a blind person to see how these worked out in her day-to-day life. Having hypothesised that her travels would be limited to a portfolio of discrete, memorised routes, for instance, he asked her how well she knew them. But she replied quite indignantly:

> These **aren't** routes. These are places. These are maps and I know where I'm going. I do have to think about what I'm doing and where I am within the map.... You don't have to think. It's not a route, it's a space that I know....I **see** it in a real clear map so that at any point I know what I'm facing and, if I wanna go somewhere else, what way I've gotta turn to get there. I don't have to think because it's a map. It's a three-dimensional cognitive structure, sorta (Cook 1992: 7).[1]

This kind of description was very much unlike that which Ian had found in the blindness literature, and meant that many months of work had, to a large extent, been wasted. Subsequently, in discussing travel experiences with three other blind people, he had to go back almost to square one and he ended up addressing many unthought-of research questions which emerged out of this kind of dialogue and which had to be situated in what he had previously regarded as 'unrelated' literatures. In the alternative model that we're advocating, we can't guarantee that things won't go wrong but it's much more difficult to go 'off the rails' if you're helping to lay them, piece by piece, with those involved in all stages of your project.

This book is an attempt to provide a grounded, process-oriented view of ethnographic research. Parts of this book may be useful in preparing a research proposal, because they outline how a variety of qualitative research methods can be selected appropriately, used well and data thereby constructed analysed systematically. So, in the following pages we outline a series of issues that, we hope, will help prospective researchers to more effectively prepare for, revise and complete their research. We discuss, first, how subjectivities can be conceptualised; second, how these conceptualisations can be used to develop appropriate fieldwork strategies; third, what kinds of information or data can be constructed by using differing qualitative methods; fourth, how the consequent mass of information/data can begin to be systematically analysed; and, finally, ways in which researchers can write through this process.

Like the linear read-*then*-do-*then*-write model we oppose, our book could be read as set of issues to consider one after the other; the initial section focuses on getting ready for research, the second on constructing ethnographic information and the third on pulling it all together. However, because it acknowledges the inevitable contingencies, twists and turns of research, we prefer to think of it as something that researchers can read early on, but can also carry around and dip into throughout the course of their work. Say, for example, an amazing but unexpected opportunity to do some participant observation research came up halfway through an entirely interview-based research project. Or, say, you notice important and interesting things going on during and after your carefully planned focus group interviews that couldn't be recorded on tape. Or, say, other people turned up at your carefully planned one-on-one interview and added new dimensions to the topic in which you were interested. Or, say, you felt you had to record conversations during your participant observation research because you couldn't understand or remember in sufficient detail the nuances in what people were saying. Or, finally, say you happened to take your camera into a field setting and people started to ask you if they could borrow it to take photos of their children. If these possibilities hadn't been part of your official proposal – and maybe you hadn't read anything about them because of that – what would you do, especially if you were miles away from the nearest academic library? How would you know when, where and how to combine and do these new strands of research well? Keep to the plan? Make things up as you went along, hoping that you're doing it OK? Or reread parts of that book you brought with you to try to gain a sense of how to make the best out of your changing circumstances? Any or all of these options might be a good idea.

Section 1

Getting Ready

2 Conceptualising the Subject

I don't like the distinction between theory and ethnography. There is a saying, attributed to William James, that you can't pick up rocks in a field without a theory. Ethnography is not simply 'data collection'; it is rich in implicit theories of culture, society and the individual (Agar 1980: 23).

INTRODUCTION

In the 1970s, humanist geographers began to incorporate ethnographic methods into their research as a reaction to positivist geographers' general lack of concern with the complexities of different people's experiences of everyday social and cultural processes (e.g. Ley 1974, 1988; Rowles 1978a; Seamon 1979; Western 1981). They began to draw on sociological and anthropological traditions in which these experiences were not being treated as constellations of measurable variables but, rather, as localised, holistic 'cultures' which could be made sense of only through in-depth observation, *in situ*. Here, readings of inter-war, 'Chicago School' ethnographies as well as more philosophical works in phenomenology and symbolic interactionism were particularly important in the rethinking of people's geographies (Jackson 1983, 1985, 1989; Jackson and Smith 1984). Everyday actions were seen as the result of individuals drawing on the structures of their 'culture', rather than these structures being seen as, somehow, existing 'outside' the mundane spheres of their everyday action and knowledge. Then, as now, ethnographic research was therefore seen to be of immense theoretical and practical importance (Herbert 2000). Yet, those who appreciated the insights that ethnographies could provide have also criticised them because:

- they have invariably characterised their subjects as having a 'culture' which can be unproblematically 'read' by an apparently detached researcher,
- these subjects have been treated as pure (that is having one singular cultural identity), transparent, and knowable carriers of uncontested cultural codes,
- their 'cultures' have been seen as isolated, pure (that is not incorporating or mixed with parts of others) and homogeneous entities and

- in the face of the still-narrow 'Scientism' of mainstream academia, ethnographic researchers have had to fend off criticisms of the 'mere subjectivity' of their conclusions.

Our intention in this section, then, is to argue that, in using ethnographic methods, it is an extremely good idea for the prospective researcher to incorporate social and cultural theories which will allow her/him to take these issues into account from the very start.

THE DETACHED RESEARCHER?

In the history of ethnographic and related research, 'cultures' have conventionally been represented as independent both from the means by which the researcher gained access to and (mis)understood them, and from the ways in which they were produced, reproduced and transformed in the histories and day to day struggles of the people under study (Cloke et al. 2004; Duncan 1981). As Barbara Tedlock has written about E.E. Evans-Pritchard's classic ethnography of The Nuer (1940), for instance, in perhaps typical style he:

> ... included a seven-page first-person confessional account of the terrible living conditions and informant difficulties he experienced during fieldwork in the Sudan. In sharp contrast, the remainder of the book, written in an omniscient third-person authoritative voice, describes highly abstract, nonempirical entities, such as lineage and age-set systems, and the idealised actions of common denominator people: the Nuer do this, the Nuer do that (1991: 74).

The point here, then, is that such essentialised 'common denominators' who all 'do this' and all 'do that' – whether 'at home' or 'abroad' – have not simply been discovered in the third person by a detached researcher, but constructed out of an intersubjective research process always saturated with relations of power/knowledge.[1] If mentioned at all, these kinds of relations have usually been either consigned to the introductions, footnotes and appendices of an 'academic' text, or written as a separate account under an assumed name or by the researcher's (usually female) partner and published as a 'non-academic' text, as if one could be so easily prized apart from the other (Abu-Lughod 1990; Behar and Gordon 1995; DeVita 1992; Grimshaw 1992; Pratt 1986; Tedlock 1991).

In contrast to this masculinist scientific stance which has spuriously claimed a cool, calm and collected detachment for the heroic fieldworker, other approaches have emerged which critique this for concealing the fact that both researcher and researched are equally positioned, interconnected and involved in the changing social and cultural relations under study (Bondi and Domosh 1992; Bourdieu 2003; Conquergood 1991;

Haraway 1988; Katz 1994; Kobayashi 1994; Nast 1994; Oakley 1981; Rose 1993). The impersonal, detached account tends to suggest 'the researcher as a detached head – the object of Thought, Rationality and Reason – floating from research site to research site, thinking and speaking, while its profane counterpart, the Body, lurks unseen, unruly and uncontrollable in the shadows of the Great Hall of the Academy' (Spry 2001: 720). In reality, research is an embodied activity that draws in our whole physical person, along with all its inescapable identities. What we bring to the research affects what we get, so as Steve Herbert has put it, 'ethnographies are as much about the culture of the student as they are of the studied' (2000: 563). Ethnographies involve relationships developed between people of similar and/or different cultures, classes, genders, sexualities, (dis)abilities, generations, nationalities, skin colours, faiths and/or other identities. What's important about this is that the ways in which these relationships (can) develop have highly significant effects on the understandings which emerge from them (Cupples 2002; Nagar 1997). And the relationships that matter are not only those between researcher and researched in a traditionally ascribed 'field' setting. Others, in the academy (e.g. supervisors, examiners, referees, editors, colleagues, students), in a researcher's 'outside' life (e.g. family members, friends, children, community members) and elsewhere, have just as much, if not more, influence over the 'findings' of research (Clifford 1997; England 2001; Keith 1992; Shokeid 1997; Taussig 1992; Twyman et al. 1999). Thus, writing in a detached, scientific, third-person style rarely, if ever, represents anyone's experience of research (Richardson 2000a). If anything, it tends to mystify this experience. But the textual performance of objectivity can help researchers 'prove' to others that they are worthy of their jobs in the Scientific academy and that their projects are worthy of external funding (Bourdieu 1988; Delaney 1988; Mascia-Lees et al. 1989; Pratt 1986). In sum, whether it is acknowledged or not, it is important to understand that research on social relations *is made out of social relations* which develop within and between the multiple sites of researchers' 'expanded fields' (Clifford 1997; Cook 2001; Katz 1992, 1994).

THE PURE SUBJECT?

As much as the researcher is embedded in these multiple contexts, so are the subjects of her/his research. People experience and act in the world at multiple points, times and places and, strung together throughout their/our life courses, these experiences and actions form different biographies and self-identities. In turn, these identities are gendered, classed and coloured and, therefore, cannot be understood without understanding the histories and impacts of these and other categorisations. Moreover, while various groups have specific ethos and habits which condition what they take for granted, they/we also try both to overcome and to utilise the materials and obstacles encountered on the way. As a result, it is not enough for researchers to identify where people are (both socially and spatially) – they must also question where they/we are coming from, going to and where on these paths research encounters have occurred.

Given these various histories, a person's identity can be understood as an assemblage of thoughts, feelings, memories, ways of doing things, possessions and so forth which does not fit together in a dedicated pattern but is always a compromise, always pragmatic, always in flux and never pure (Haraway 1988; McCracken 1988a; Miller 1987). It is therefore reflected in, and reinforced by, such things as household furnishings which are chosen because they reflect and promote certain self-conceptions or are lived with because they are gifts which reflect how someone else saw them/us. People take snapshots to commemorate significant events and thereby mark what is and is not significant to commemorate, and so on. When studying people's lives, then, these can all be brought in as testimony to how people see, shape and are embedded in the world around them (Csikzsentmihalyi and Rochberg-Halton 1981; McCracken 1988a; Reme 1993; Walker and Moulton 1989). Indeed the self can be very much constituted through these material relations and objects rather than having some abstract, preexisting state (see Dant 1999; Michael 2000; Miller 1998a). In light of this, researchers should consider how the contexts in which research encounters take place can provoke memories and insights into the world views and self-conceptions of differently positioned people. Different memories may be evoked by various belongings or locales associated with different facets of people's identities (Rowles 1983), and it is also important to recognise that people live out their lives between different social locales and emphasise different facets of their identities to different people as they/we move between them (Valentine 1993a; van der Ploeg 1986). In these contexts, the ways in which people make sense of them-/our-selves and the worlds in which they/we live are often the result of discussions and debates with different groups of people as events are reported and interpreted socially through hearing about them from others, or even thinking about what someone else has said or would say about them. Therefore, not only is the place where the researcher and her/his 'subjects' meet important to any study, but also the social relations of research that are (re)arranged there. Research, we shall show, is always socially but also materially situated.

Through doing qualitative research, then, academics inevitably find that the boundaries of the pure subject must break down, as thoughts are traced back to books, to friends or relations, to newspaper stories and so on.

However, at the same time people cannot simply be expected to report all the 'facts' of their lives. In their telling, life stories involve a recasting of the past, omitting some elements, stressing others, 'forgetting' much more and constantly referring outside the frame of the research encounter. As a result, it is more than likely that within and between parts of these accounts there will be numerous inconsistencies and contradictions (Hedges 1985; Miles and Crush 1993; Pile 1993). Ethnographic research is not therefore only a matter of finding out what a spuriously pure subject might think and do but, through tracing these connections and critically engaging with these stories, it is also one of trying to get at both why this has come to be the case and what wider causes and effects this might have.

THE PURE CULTURE?

A key argument in the cultural turn literature of the 1990s was that the 'purity' often striven for in previous geographical accounts of peoples and places had been founded on the repression of connections with those in other times/spaces (see Mitchell 1995; Shurmer-Smith 2002). When deciding who to study and where to study them, researchers who believed in discrete regions or cultures embarked on self-fulfilling prophecies in which the definition of a researchable community led to findings which implied that its boundaries were secure and that it existed as a discrete entity. Doreen Massey, for instance, has argued that:

Geographers have long been exercised by the problem of defining regions, and this question of 'definition' has almost always been reduced to the issue of drawing lines around a place. But that kind of boundary around an area precisely distinguishes between an inside and an outside. It can so easily be yet another way of constructing a counterposition between 'us' and 'them' (1991: 28).

This process of active distinction, it has been argued, can go directly against the experiences of vast numbers of people (including researchers) who, while being 'placed' in both academic and popular accounts as within or outside such cultural or geographical borders and thereby ascribed discrete identities, continue to live lives very much across and between them.

To give one example, when Ian began his UK–Jamaica border-crossing PhD research, question of borders and identities were being increasingly problematised in social scientific circles. Here, researchers were attempting to tackle the relationships between the local and global power/knowledge that had given rise to variously nuanced and connected 'cultures of colonialism' (Ashcroft et al. 1989; Thomas 1994). These were seen as by no means pure nor simply situated within any cut-and-dried borders, nor were they simply black or white, male or female, 'First' or 'Third' World. So, for instance, as the black British sociologist, Stuart Hall, argued:

People like me who came to England in the 1950s [from the Caribbean] have been there for centuries; symbolically, we have been there for centuries. I was coming home. I am the sugar at the bottom of the English cup of tea. I am the sweet tooth, the sugar plantations that rotted generations of English children's teeth. There are thousands of others besides me that are, you know, the cup of tea itself. Because they don't grow it in Lancashire you know. Not a single tea plantation exists within the United Kingdom. This is the symbolisation of English identity – I mean, what does anybody in the world know about an English person except that they can't get through the day without a cup of tea? Where does it come from? Ceylon – Sri Lanka, India. That is the outside history that is inside the history of the English. There is no English history without that history (1991: 48–49).

By acknowledging and studying the histories of, and influences on, such diasporic (post)colonial cultures, popular and academic depictions of a distinct, pure, bounded and, usually, white sense of 'England' and 'Englishness' were being seriously challenged (Gilroy 1987, 1992, 1993a,b; Hall 1992; Hebdige 1990; James 1992; Jeater 1992; Jones 1988; Linebaugh 1982; Linebaugh and Rediker 1990; Rediker 1987). Studying a 'culture' could, therefore, no longer be about going 'there' and studying 'it' because 'it' would always be 'simultaneously supralocal, translocal and local, simultaneously planetary and, refracted through the shards of vernacular cultural practices, profoundly parochial' (Comaroff and Comaroff 2003: 151). Research practice, therefore, has to involve not only 'interacting with informants across a number of dispersed sites, but also doing fieldwork by telephone and email, collecting data eclectically in many different ways from a disparate array of sources' (Hannerz 2003: 212; Marcus 1998; Miller and Slater 2001; Parr 2002).

You don't only have to be studying cultures of (post)colonialism for these arguments to make sense. No 'culture' can legitimately be ring-fenced from large-scale, political and economic processes because the global is not 'out there', intruding annoyingly on the study, but is always 'in here', only existing through variously connected localities (Giddens 1984; Knorr-Cetina 1981a; Marcus and Fischer 1986; Morley 1991; Rosaldo 1989; Thomas 1991). Even if nothing seems to link your home 'culture' and that of the people you want to study, the research itself will have to be negotiated via networks of *(im)possible* connections (e.g. travel infrastructures, referrals, etc.) which enable contact to be made in the first place (Dwyer 1977). Moreover, if that contact leads to a fully fledged ethnographic research project taking place, you might – as is customary – attempt to develop 'shared imaginations' with your informants, a process which itself creates 'a space beyond the immediate confines of the local' (Marcus in Gustavson and Cytrynbaum 2003: 254). In sum, it is necessary to challenge the stereotype of ethnographic research involving a researcher's immersion in, and eventual understanding of, a 'pure', 'local' 'culture' (Jackson 1983). This is not only politically suspect but also practically impossible: *unless*, that is, you want to study others' attempts to *create* a 'pure culture' (Cloke et al. 2004; Mitchell 1995). Thus, it is important to note, the 'research communities' that we talk about throughout this book are as much fashioned as they are found through the process of researching them (Law and Urry 2004).

'SUBJECTIVE' CONCLUSIONS?

All of the above may well leave prospective ethnographers somewhat nervous about admitting the positionality and partiality of their knowledge. Unlike their colleagues claiming to use more 'objective' methods, they may feel that they cannot be so rigorous or exacting, or draw equally valid conclusions. This is, however, far from the case. If we scratch the surface of what is often said about such 'objective' methods, they have much more in common with their 'subjective' counterparts than many would like to admit. While scientific methods classes, for example, often:

> ...tell parables about objectivity and scientific method to students in the first years of their initiation,...no practitioner of the high scientific arts would be caught dead acting on the textbook versions. Social constructionists make clear that official ideologies about objectivity and scientific method are particularly bad guides to how scientific knowledge is actually made. Just as for the rest of us, what scientists believe or say they do and what they really do have a very loose fit. The only people who end up actually believing and, goddess forbid, acting on the ideological doctrines of disembodied scientific objectivity enshrined in elementary textbooks and technoscience booster literature are non-scientists, including a few very trusting philosophers (Haraway 1988: 581).

We might therefore say that the task for *all* researchers is to recognise and come to terms with their/our partial and situated 'subjectivity' rather than aspire to an impossibly distanced 'objectivity'. Once this is done, 'subjectivity' is much less a problem and much more a resource for deeper understanding.

Ethnographic research reveals, and is often undertaken to question, the erroneous neatness of distanced, abstract, theoretical understandings of social, cultural, economic and other processes (see Miller 1998b, 2000) because societies are always messier than our theories of them (Mann 1986). Thus, as Alan Hedges has argued:

> There are very few golden rules and certainly no magic formulae for cutting through to Truth – if indeed there is any single monolithic truth, which is not typically the case. Human beings are complex, ambivalent, inconsistent creatures; not even the brightest and best organised of us lives in a sharp-edged world where we have all consciously and consistently sorted out our attitudes and beliefs on all conceivable subjects. It is a mistake to assume that there is a pristine Platonic reality under the muddle of our public utterances to which really sharp research tools can cut unerringly through. Underneath the mess of language lie a mess of thought and a tangle of behaviour. If our research tools cannot recognise ambivalence and inconsistency as real and important, they will not help us to a very profound understanding of human thoughts and behaviour (1985: 85).

An ability to engage with, rather than withdraw from, this 'real world' messiness is seen as perhaps the most valuable contribution ethnographic research can make. But ethnographers cannot take a naive stance that what they are told is the absolute 'truth'. Rather, research must involve the struggle to produce *inter-subjective truths*, to understand why so many versions of events are produced and recited. It is the ways in which people make sense of the events around them, and render these 'true' in their own terms, that is most revealing about how their/our lives are embroiled in larger social, cultural, economic and political processes. Therefore, stories told in the research encounter are not simply to be regarded as means of mirroring the world, but as the means *through which it is constructed*, understood and acted out.

Under these circumstances, however, readers may wonder how ethnographers can validate their truth claims? How can they ensure that their research is thorough, rigorous, systematic and convincing? For us, the answers to these questions lie in trying to undertake research which is theoretically sampled, saturated and adequate. Let us define these concepts:

- *Theoretical sampling:* although sounding like a term straight out of the positivistic canon, this refers to the means by which a researcher decides who should be approached to take part in her/his work. In place of the random sampling of statistical research, this approach involves gaining selective access to appropriate groups of people who may be concerned with, and/or involved in living through, the research problem and encouraging them to teach the researcher about it from their various perspectives. Therefore, it is not the sheer number, 'typicality' or 'representativeness' of people approached which matters, but the quality and positionality of the information that they can offer (Geiger 1990; McCracken 1988b).
- *Theoretical saturation:* researching the lives of every member of every interest group may not only be impractical but also unnecessary

because there usually comes a point in the research process where the range of arguments which can be made concerning a particular matter has been made. Here, researchers often find that the accounts they/we are told begin to have the same ring to them and that 'you have heard the range of stories that people within the community have to tell you about their experiences and explanations of what is happening to them' (Burgess 1992a: 209). This is the point of *theoretical saturation*. Within any interest group, only a relatively small number of discourses may be used, in various combinations, to explain certain events, attitudes and so on. These will have been picked up, modified and shared through conversations with other interest-group members and through access to other sources of information. Therefore, once the point of saturation has been reached, this may either be the time to get stuck into the analysis of these discourses or to seek out viewpoints from another, differently positioned group.

- *Theoretical adequacy*: ethnographers have been encouraged to understand the various contexts of their studies, and their similarities and differences with others (Schutz 1967). Therefore, library visits are vital in order to search for *other* researchers' interpretations of similar situations, as well as more general theoretical concepts within which a study could be situated. The main idea here is that, for a researcher to have confidence that her/his study has been rigorous enough, she/he must have sought out and explored the tensions and commonalities between multiple perspectives on the research problem, i.e. hers/his and other people's.

We have found that these three concepts can help to turn worries about the 'mere subjectivity' of ethnographic research into a sense of rigorous subjectivity. As ethnographers, we don't have to try to be 'objective' or 'unbiased' in our work. This misses the point entirely. The truth-claims of ethnographic research must be gauged on their own terms. We do not believe in being defensive on this issue because there is virtually no other way of studying the vital interrelationships between subjectivity and the kinds of wider social, economic and other processes we have mentioned. Rather than being a source of weakness, the always already positioned and intersubjective nature of ethnography can be seen as a strength out of which more rigorous understandings can be built. But, as we argue later, this means that considerable attention needs to be paid to tailoring *combinations* of research methods which are appropriate to specific research topics.

SUMMARY

Throughout this chapter we have argued that the conceptualisation of subjectivity is of profound importance at all stages of an ethnographic project. It is important to acknowledge that, first, researchers cannot claim to (have) isolate(d) 'local' cultures from more 'global' political, and economic processes because the latter are never simply 'out there' but, rather, are always 'in here', constituting and being constituted by variously connected 'localities'. Second, they/we can not make similar claims to (have) isolate(d) either 'presents' from 'pasts' or 'individuals' from the 'societies' in which they/we live and learn. Third, prospective researchers should take account of this in all stages of their research project, not only by tracing such connections as necessary but also by recognising that the resultant enquiries will inevitably be both partial and positioned within a particular web of interdependencies whose horizons will define the limits of possible interpretation (Clifford 1986).

3

Preparing for Fieldwork

Quite unlike its pristine and logical presentation in journal articles – 'the reconstructed logic of science' – real research is often confusing, messy, intensely frustrating, and fundamentally non-linear (Marshall and Rossman 1989: 21).

INTRODUCTION

In this chapter we set out in detail the kind of preparation which we feel is necessary to avoid the pitfalls of the read-*then*-do-*then*-write model of research. The main issue here concerns the 'surprises' which emerge when deduction and induction, data and theory, collide, by accident and design (Comaroff and Comaroff 2003; Willis and Trondman 2000). For us, the most important issue is how researchers can set up and deal with these surprises. As we argued in the introduction, organising work via the read-*then*-do-*then*-write model can engineer big surprises as researchers move from the reading to doing stages. This is not perhaps the best way to experience the most fascinating aspect of ethnographic research, i.e. what you don't expect to discover. However, we argue, by dispensing with that linear model and, instead, mixing up reading, doing and writing from the very beginning of a project, surprises are still encountered but they're often much smaller, easier to respond to and should help to shape research that's simultaneously interesting, relevant and doable. Below, then, we build on the considerations outlined in the previous chapter to think through the more practical aspects of starting a research project. Before thinking about the kinds of detailed relationships between ideas, literature and methods which have to be outlined in research proposals, we argue, it's important to have cast a preliminary research net, initiated access to appropriate people and places and thought through the role of language, power relations and ethics.

CASTING YOUR NET

As a first step in any ethnography, it is important to develop early contacts in the organisation/industry/community/area in which you are interested to find out what research may be possible within the constraints of access, time, mobility and money available for 'fieldwork', and to undertake methodological, theoretical and linguistic preparations accordingly. Here, it is a good idea to:

- talk about what or who you plan to study with friends, family members, fellow students or faculty members (Tillman-Healy 2003),
- contact appropriate governmental and non-governmental organisations, community groups, campaign groups, religious organisations and the authors of relevant academic and other articles (see Dowler 2001),
- place advertisements in the personal columns of appropriate local/national newspapers or special-interest magazines, place posters on community notice boards and/or phone local radio stations to air your plea for participants and/or
- try mail-shots in the place you intend to study, email individuals and groups identified through targeted web surfing, blog reading and/or through taking part in internet chat room discussion (see Gatson and Zweerink 2004; Hine 2004; Hoggart et al. 2002: 292–95).

Whoever you contact, always outline the project you have in mind, look for contacts who might be of further assistance, identify the 'gate-keepers' who may be most sympathetic to your project and arrange to meet with them.

As a general guide, one of the most important tasks to work on at the start of a project is that of developing a wide network of contacts loosely based around the germ of your project. Moreover, once contacts have been cultivated, you can ask who else might be worth talking to about the topic in hand: ask for an address, a telephone number, an email address or an introduction and try to snowball contacts on from there (Cassell 1988). Ian's ethnographic research on a Jamaican papaya farm, for instance, resulted from the development of a complex web of contacts involving a professor known by his supervisor who played tennis with a managing director of one of the 'Big Four' British supermarket chains who arranged an interview for him with its trading and marketing directors. Also, letters he sent to each of these chains' trading managers outlining the project and asking to meet with them to discuss their exotic fruit sourcing and marketing practices led to contacts subsequently being developed in the HQs of two of the other chains which, in turn, led to introductions to the people responsible for buying their exotics and, via them, to executives working for the companies which supplied them. Still other contacts were made through his office-mate whose partner was doing research in Jamaica who, in turn, introduced Ian to one of his colleagues who had met the farm manager and his friends on a previous visit there. Although this had not been his cynical intention at the time, when the introduction was finally made to this farm manager, these discussions with people he knew and, by and large, trusted probably made Ian seem a somewhat accepted part of an already known community rather than a completely unknown and difficult-to-place stranger. This, it must be stressed, is a far from unusual research tale and illustrates how projects often come into focus through this kind of networking (see, for example, Davies 2003; Keith 1992).

In these initial stages, you might also consider the need for research permits and visas needed for any overseas fieldwork. These are not needed for all countries. When Ian did his research in Jamaica, for instance, British citizens did not need any sort of visa to spend up to six months in a country in the Commonwealth Caribbean and this was one of the reasons he decided to do the bulk of his 'fieldwork' there. However, in some cases researchers may have to apply for a research visa perhaps six months to a year in advance with no guarantee of getting it. It took Mike an unexpected seven months to get a research visa for Malaysia, for instance, and the delay threatened to stop the research project altogether. If an overseas destination is vital, then such practicalities must be taken into account at an early stage. Our advice is to start off by contacting other researchers who have recently conducted fieldwork there, and ask their advice about official and unofficial procedures. When the former routes seem too difficult to negotiate, researchers often end up weighing up the pros and cons of entering their chosen country on a tourist visa (Sidaway 1992), a processes which raises some thorny political and ethical issues about who should control what kinds of research get done by whom and where.

Casting your net widely in the early stages of an ethnography, then, is vital. This process may be more influential in determining the shape of your research than any theoretical minutiae pored over in the academy. As we have said, ethnographic projects do not emerge in the form of pristine hypotheses to be tested later 'in the field' but require a fusion of knowing what is interesting, relevant and doable. Detailed research projects will eventually come together this way, but not without time, effort, imagination and, to mix metaphors, a willingness to see things – at least at the start – in a relatively soft focus.

INITIATING ACCESS

Earlier, we argued that research *on* social relations is *made out* of social relations and that, given the geographical aspects of identity politics, the subjects and sites of ethnographic encounters are intimately related. Thus, we argue, it is important early on in a research project to think about issues of access to social groups you wish to work with/in and/or the spaces in/between which you could conduct your research. Perhaps the stereotype of research is that it has to be 'all new': going boldly where you have not been before. However, for many researchers, projects develop out of already-existing memberships of social groups and/or access to particular spaces. First- or second-hand experience of an issue both 'out there' in the 'real world' *and* 'in here' in academia often provides the spark and motivation for ethnographic research projects (e.g. Saltmarsh 2001). Here, it is important to acknowledge, the 'expanded field' of academic research is already at work. Students may already have been working at a restaurant during the holidays and been concerned about working conditions, food contamination and food marketing; they may have been looking after their friend's children for a number of years and asked why it was so difficult to get a child in a pushchair around a city centre; they may have been to a number of music festivals and wondered what produced that fleeting sense of community they often felt with so many strangers in a field; they also may have come across related literatures during their degrees, and may wish to bring these 'outside' and 'inside' interests together in their research (see Cook 1997b).

The examples above have direct connections to the students' lives but, as we argued in the previous section, researchers' involvement in diverse social networks can mean that access to apparently distant groups and spaces can often be only a few steps away. Workplace ethnographies, for example, can start with jobs which students already have but also with the *kinds* of jobs or job training for which employers would expect them to apply. Thus, the early stages of a research project could begin by scanning a local newspaper's 'Situations Vacant' columns, enrolling with an employment agency, enrolling on a training course, asking a friend or family member to put in a good word with their employer or contacting previous employers to see if they have any vacancies for a tried and trusted worker. Indeed, with the financial difficulties experienced by many undergraduate and postgraduate students alike, one advantage of taking on such work is that it can double as a means to earn much-needed cash (Crang 1994).

In contrast, if a researcher's interest is in studying domestic or leisure activities such as household labour, TV watching, shopping activities or membership of particular social clubs, political/campaign groups or subcultures, then she/he must somehow negotiate access to their appropriate spaces. Although the aim, at this stage, may be to gain access to a single place – village, neighbourhood, festival site and so on – ethnographies can also cross-cut such places. Here we are thinking of work such as Gill Valentine's (1993a,b) research on the management of multiple sexual identities by women in a lesbian community who lived their lives somewhat differently within and between various settings such as the local high street, their homes, workplaces, bars and clubs (see also Taylor 2004). Moreover, when setting up interviews or group work especially,

the researcher may also be involved in creating a space in which participants are free to talk about the research topic. Again, much of the same
types of advice apply as with seeking initial contacts, but even in the best
organised study no one ever achieves a 100% response rate. One of the
more nervous and dispiriting times during a research process is when you
receive a steady stream of rejections to initial enquiries. All that can be said
is that if you keep trying, sooner or later something will give somewhere
and this phase will pass. This situation is much the same whether mailing
potential interviewees or seeing 'gatekeepers', and it is important to keep
this in perspective. Rejections should not be taken personally – you are
seeking to inconvenience people so their rejections are hardly surprising.
You may be able to improve the proportion of favourable responses a little
by remembering this and being sensitive to the constraints and pressures
on potential respondents (McCracken 1988b; Stewart and Shamdasani
1990). Perhaps the main point to keep in mind here is to follow up your
ideas and contacts, but always to think about a second, and perhaps a third,
point of access in case one or the other closes up as the work progresses.

Setting out to take these first, often tentative steps, it is important to
note that this is where the 'fieldwork' starts. The processes through
which particular people and/or positions are found make for good ethnographic 'data' because they are likely to involve 'gatekeepers' assessing
aspects of your identity which are considered (in)appropriate for them
(see Mountz et al. 2003; Thornton 2000). Much can depend on how you
can be placed or positioned by these early contacts – especially if they are
government officials who will assess your proposals and have the power
to grant or to deny access to an entire country. It is therefore necessary
to consider how you portray yourself and your research to these and
every other 'gatekeeper'. To give an example of this process, when
preparing to undertake some interviews in electronics firms in Malaysia,
Mike encountered great difficulties in contacting workers. The firms were
surrounded by barbed wire, the workers were suspicious of the motives
of anyone who wanted to know about their jobs and he came to realise
that many Malay women were suspicious of the motives of Western men.
Many were also worried about the consequences for their employment
and for their reputations, given the local meanings associated with being
seen to rendezvous with a man, unaccompanied. Mike therefore worked
via the contacts of local academics with the Malaysian Trade Union
Congress, but found even these people very cautious. At his wits' end
after a stony meeting with the Deputy President of the local branch,
Mike produced his research permits from the Prime Minister's Office
that, if anything, added to his problems. He tried the ploy that he was a
student and was thus no threat to anyone. This also did not appear to be
working, but in the process of digging through his wallet to find

something that would prove his status, he came across his UK Labour Party membership card. The Deputy then began to take interest – which was an improvement – so Mike showed it to him. The Deputy then read out loud from it the statement that, at the time, was printed on every card, 'To secure for the workers by hand or by brain the full fruits of their industry and the most equitable distribution thereof that may be possible upon the basis of the common ownership of the means of production, distribution and exchange, and the best obtainable system of popular administration and control of each industry or service', paused, and then said, 'That is possibly one of the most beautiful things I have ever seen written'. Unexpectedly, then, this aspect of Mike's identity, once expressed, opened a number of important doors for his research.

In the process of gaining access, researchers usually endure days or weeks of doubt and frustration before, as in the case above, becoming quite suddenly overjoyed when things somehow work out, sometimes better than could have been planned. But, in terms of the time that this can take, this can be very unpredictable, particularly in the initial stages of forming contacts. It may take a couple of weeks to arrange a first formal meeting with someone in a company, for example, who may then refer you to another employee. If this meeting takes just as long to arrange, you could have spent a month on just two interviews. Therefore, we suggest that attempting to establish as many contacts as possible helps to increase the speed of access, both in the event that one meeting falls through or that a 'gatekeeper' proves uncooperative or uninformative. What will tend to happen is that, as more contacts are established, you will begin to get multiple suggestions for further contacts and it will become easier to know who to contact and how. Thus, in later stages of your work, the problem may be less of an inability to see people and more one of being overwhelmed by possible contacts. So, on the one hand, it can be a good idea to stagger different stages of your work so that everything does not happen at once but, on the other hand, some comparative research can be aided by studying what different people are doing over the same period of time. We would therefore suggest that a good deal of thought be given to how the research is likely to occupy time in the field in order to most productively use it. That said, we have never got responses or access according to any preplanned schedule. So, again, perhaps the best advice here is to prepare to be flexible.

TALKING THE TALK

In the process of casting your net and of initiating access to the people and places you wish to study and/or work with, issues of language will inevitably surface. You may notice differences in the ways in which you and your contacts tend to talk, in your styles of written and spoken language and/or in how you use often taken-for-granted bodily gestures in communication. Those planning to undertake a significant part of their research in a second (or third, etc.) language may expect to encounter such differences. Those with a multi-lingual background may already do so as a matter of course (Marcus 1998; Temple and Young 2004). But those working in their first and only language may also (perhaps unexpectedly) have similar issues to tackle. Given that the goal of ethnographic and related qualitative research is to understand something meaningful about the lives of other people, the language(s) within and between which this understanding develops requires some detailed thought. When preparing for fieldwork, two main questions need to be addressed in this respect. First, to what extent should the researcher's linguistic competences or 'pure' research interests decide where and with whom their research is best undertaken? And, second, how effectively can they then usefully translate meanings from the language(s) used by their research participants into those that they and their likely audiences like to hear?

We argued in the previous chapter that researchers' projects often develop and are shaped through (im)possible connections. What we want to argue here is that linguistic competences, capabilities and opportunities are important elements of this process. One of the reasons why Ian undertook the overseas research for his PhD in Jamaica, for instance, was that he was fluent in only one language: English. While he was initially keen to learn Spanish in order to increase his options for overseas research, this had been ruled out in supervision because of the tight deadlines for the completion of PhD theses in the UK. One of his priorities in the early stages of his research was, therefore, to find out from supermarket buyers what English-speaking countries in the 'Third World' they got their tropical fruits from, year-round. Jamaica was the only country, at that time, which fitted the bill. Please don't think that this story has been told in order to argue that allocating limited research time and resources to learning a new language may often be unnecessary.[1] In many specialist academic fields (here we are thinking, in particular, about area studies), language learning is expected and incorporated into (in)formal research 'training'. And many researchers enter academia with already-existing multi-lingual skills gleaned from previous schooling, travels, family life and other experiences. The point we want to make is that, in order to make decisions about where and with whom a research project should be undertaken, equal attention should be paid to practical issues like researcher's linguistic abilities and opportunities as to more theoretical issues like where and with whom a literature review suggests a project might best be done. These issues of language and theory are clearly connected. George Marcus, for example, has suggested that anthropology's move towards studying and theorising transcultural worlds has coincided with its recruitment of more transcultural researchers who have 'fluency in more than one language and who are at home, or at least familiar, with several culturally distinct places through their autobiographies' (1998: 247). So, the question becomes, how could you make the most of your abilities in this respect?

Whatever language(s) in which a research project is conducted, there will inevitably have to be some kind of translation between the language(s) that the researcher learns to use in 'the field' and that/those which she/he should use when presenting her/his findings to academic and other audiences. When the results of qualitative research are published and its research participants are quoted, what is often exciting for readers is that sense that we are gaining an insight into the lives of other people as described in *their* 'own words'. But because this aspect of language is so often made invisible – as if translation from one language into another is a technical, data-handling exercise and does not, therefore, need to be discussed – questions of precisely whose words they are and whose insights they represent are rarely asked (Borchgrevink 2003). As readers of such work, Bogusia Temple and Alys Young (2004: 163) argue, we should wonder:

> What language was the data collected in? At what stage were the interviews translated and transcribed? What translation and transcription issues were there? [An interview]...quote could be from a woman speaking English or it could be from an interview in another language that has been translated, presumably by the researcher. What is the researcher's relationship to the interviewees...?

Most of our discussion of transcription is presented in the next chapter. Here, however, we need to pay more attention to the role of translation in ethnographic and related qualitative research.

Shirley Ann Jordan (2002) argues that three strands of translation are woven through any ethnographic research process. The first consists of those translations made, over time, in field-setting encounters where both researcher and researched try to make sense of the other's ways and lives, there and then, in their own terms. The second consists of those made by researchers in order to communicate this sense-making in terms which can be understood by audiences elsewhere who weren't there, then. And the third consists of those made by members of those audiences as they attempt to make sense of these accounts in *their* own terms. Here, as you may imagine, there is an awful lot of room for 'meaning [to be] lost and invented' (Hoggart et al. 2002: 260). Translation can rarely, if ever, be a straightforward technical exercise of matching 'conceptual equivalence[s] across languages' (Temple and Young 2004: 165) because languages are rarely, if ever, structured along parallel lines and expressions of meaning are multi-dimensional, taken for granted, contextual and only partly 'linguistic'. In field settings, it is important to appreciate that 'almost any utterance in any language carries with it a set of assumptions, feelings and values that the speaker may or may not be aware of but that the fieldworker, as an outsider, usually is not' (Philipps 1960 in Temple and Young 2004: 165). What the fieldworker brings into this translation, however, are her/his own set of assumptions, feelings and values. And, if a translator is also involved – as Mike found out when a Malaysian Trade Union official helped him on a couple of occasions – yet another set of assumptions, feelings and values becomes part of the process.

What translation produces, therefore, are hybrid, in-between forms of cultural understanding in which choices have been made about whether and how to hide and/or highlight the failures of fit between one language and another (Twyman et al. 1999). Temple and Young (2004) illustrate this point nicely in their discussion of the choices that can be made when translating British Sign Language (BSL) into written English. These two languages by no means work along parallel lines because:

> BSL in common with other sign languages is not grammatically structured in a linear subject-verb-object structure. Rather it is a topic-comment language in which inflection is produced through facial expression, visual orientation, movement and spatial location. It is thus possible to produce complex multi-layered expression in what may seem to be a very short sign utterance but which in fact corresponds to an awful lot of English words and long sentences (2004: 166).

So, should the translation of BSL into written English involve turning these very short, multi-dimensional topic-comment expressions into much longer, one-dimensional subject-verb-object expressions? This is the neat option: undertaking an apparently direct translation from one language to another. However, other translations are possible and can, themselves, make important points about the topic under consideration:

> It is interesting that in his work as a deaf academic who uses BSL, Ladd (2003) often chooses to self-consciously represent the translation act in the English rendering of data originally produced in BSL. (Typically he 'translates' the BSL into atypical English grammatical forms with added contextual information and extensive use of ellipse and phonetic play). However, in doing so he is not simply demonstrating the problems of language equivalents.... He is also using the strategy of making translation visible to make Sign Language visible through drawing attention to the structural differences of signed and spoken/written languages and celebrating the failure of fit between the two (2004: 166–67).

The politics and practicalities of translation (and, it must be said, transcription[2]) are, therefore, intimately connected. So, it is worth asking, how can these thorny linguistic issues be dealt with earlier on in the research process, as you are trying to put things together?

First, it may be sensible to develop a linguistic self-reflexivity from start to finish of a project, because a researcher's (and her/his translator's) language(s) and world view(s) will shape her/his/their findings just as much as those of the researched (Borchgrevink 2003). When difficulties in establishing shared meanings become apparent during field work, these will need to be described in the researcher's field note book, as will subsequent encounters in which, hopefully, these meanings become clearer (Jordan 2002; Twyman et al. 1999). Moreover, to extend this reflexivity to include the role of translators, one extra duty should be added to their job specification. Temple and Young (2004: 170) argue that translators should be treated as 'key informants rather that as neutral transmitters of messages'. Thus, not only could you, perhaps, ask your translator to interview people and transcribe and/or translate the recordings, but you can also ask her/him to take part in (tape recorded?) discussions with you about how they were and could be interpreted (see also Borchgrevink 2003; Twyman et al. 1999). Second, this means that research methods may need to be adopted and adapted so that the contextual meanings of words can be better appreciated. For instance, a project that was initially going to comprise only interview research might usefully be complemented by participant observation because, 'The solutions to many of the translator's dilemmas are not to be found in dictionaries, but rather in an understanding of the way language is tied to local realities, to literary forms and to changing identities' (Simon 1996 in Temple and Young 2004: 165; see also Jordan 2002). Given that qualitative (and other) research involves *informal* participant observation anyway (e.g. hanging around, waiting to meet people etc.), all that may be necessary is to plan to keep a participant observation style research diary (see later) detailing relevant conversations, observations and so on which take place 'off the record'.

POWER, KNOWLEDGE AND ETHICS

As our discussion of language briefly showed, research is always bound up in issues of power/knowledge and is, therefore, inherently political. Many writers have argued that this is something that the researcher should tackle head on, rather than simply deny through sheltering behind the traditional veil of 'objectivity'. Yet, the energy that researchers have to direct at tackling the immediate problems of getting through each part of their work may mask how she/he has also struggled through these in contexts of unequal power relations. Among the 'Third World' peoples usually studied by ethnographers, for instance, Jarvie has argued that 'many people would not tolerate the white stranger snooping around were it not that he [sic] belongs, as far as they are concerned, to the powerful white society which they hesitate to brush with' (in Cassell 1988: 93; Clifford 1992). Also, where researchers are suspended between differently powered groups, their/our roles and responsibilities may have to be compromised (Wade 1984); and, in situations where more powerful elites are being studied, on the one hand they/we may be seen as a threat through having the power to open out these people's lives for ridicule or ruination by other groups (Cook 1993; Johnson 1992)[3] yet, on the other, these are also the people who usually have the power to bar the researcher's access, or stifle what they say through research contracts (Bradshaw 2001; Cassell 1988). So, in terms of gaining access, not only must the significance of the researcher's position and apparent intentions be considered but so too must her/his responsibilities over how the people being researched will be represented in any account produced, how this will be circulated and the impact that this might have on their lives in the future. As Michael Taussig has insisted, researchers in the Americas, and we would argue elsewhere, have a responsibility to ask themselves 'who benefits from studies of the poor, especially from their resistance? The objects of study or the CIA?' (1992: 52; Katz 1994; Sidaway 2000b; Tedlock 1991).

We therefore believe that it is vital for the prospective ethnographer to consider whether the community in question might resent and/or suffer badly as a result of having such a 'viper in its bosom' (as Mike was described, half-jokingly, by some Civil War reenactors).[4] This issue has become particularly sensitive, and the tradition of the archetypal white, male, middle-class, Western, heterosexual, able-bodied researcher study-ing and pronouncing upon his poorer and/or less powerful 'Others' has been strongly critiqued from various quarters. As members of various subaltern groups have made their presences increasingly felt in academic and popular debates, dominant white (mis)conceptions of black people, male (mis)conceptions of women, middle-class (mis)conceptions of working-class people, Western (mis)conceptions of non-Western people, heterosexual (mis)conceptions of homosexual people, non-disabled (mis)conceptions of disabled people and so on have been persistently highlighted, researched and challenged (Oliver 1992; Tedlock 1991). What may be seen in the academy as rigorous scientific accounts often seem ludicrous and/or happenstance to those whose lives they describe. But these experiences become far more than 'funny stories' when researchers' initial impressions produce tragicomic misunderstandings that then shape others' research in, and government policy relating to, the same people and/or place (see Smith 1999; Torgovnick 1990). For a many oft-studied peoples, then, 'research' may be 'the dirtiest word...[their] vocabulary' (Smith 1999: 1). What therefore need to be questioned are researchers' precise motives. Are 'we':

- indulging in a heroic mission to 'make the world a better place' for 'them',
- hoping to discover a 'true' or new self via a detour through the 'Other' and/or
- jumping through a hoop to get or keep a degree or job?

As a result of these questions being so repeatedly asked, dominant representations of the research process as a cool, scientific, non-exploitative process have *themselves* begun to appear quite ridiculous (Abu-Lughod 1990; England 1994; Mascia-Lees et al. 1989; Moore 1988; Oliver 1992; Schrijvers 1991; Smith 1999).

In this light, a number of suggestions have been made regarding what and how research might be set up in order to be more sensitive to the power relations in such work. Researchers could:

- work 'with' rather than 'on' people and frame questions 'according to the desires of the oppressed group, by choosing to do work that "others" want and need' (Mascia-Lees et al. 1989: 33; Schrijvers 1991),
- shift perspective to undertake work which will 'expose the colonisers, the powerful, the affluent, who cheat, mistreat or oppress the colonised, powerless, and poor peoples of the world' (Cassell 1988: 90; Douglas 1976; Nader 1974; Punch 1986; Thomas 1993; Wax 1980),
- combine these approaches in studies which develop 'insights and knowledge into global relations among people diversely located and vying for power' (Gordon 1988: 21; Marcus 1986, 1992; Marcus and Fischer 1986),
- 'turn the question away from Others, especially poor and powerless Others, and onto ourselves and our own quite violent practices whereby we figure ourselves through the creation of objects of study' (Abu-Lughod 1990; Agar 1980; Katz 1994; Taussig 1992: 38), and/or
- study 'our own' cultures, cease taking them as some universal benchmark and problematise their values (Bourdieu 1988, 1990a; Strathern 1989).

None of these approaches, separately or even in combination, will necessarily solve the problems outlined here. However, the prospective researcher is advised to read around these debates, discuss them with sympathetic colleagues and members of research communities and have them in mind at all stages of her/his work.

As well as dealing with the politics of knowledge by thinking through more personal and situated ethics in your research process, you may also be required to submit a formal set of Research Ethics during the early stages of your research. Ian had had to gain 'Human subjects approval' to undertake his MA research in the USA in the late 1980s, but the formal consideration of ethics has only recently become a common requirement for UK researchers. Increasingly an 'ethical review' of your proposed research may have to be written for assessment and approval by internal and/or external assessors before your 'field' research can formally start. The UK's Economic and Social Research Council (ESRC), for example, provided a very short list of three minimum 'ethical considerations' to be outlined in applications for PhD studentships:

- honesty to research staff and subjects about the purpose, methods and intended and possible uses of the research,
- confidentiality of information supplied by research subjects and anonymity of respondents, and
- independence and impartiality of researchers to the subject of the research (ESRC postgraduate guidelines 2004, para 6.44, Research funding guidelines 2003 para 22.2).

However in the last year this has expanded to 37 sides of Research Ethics procedures and guidance (although that has only increased the substantive issues covered to 6 bullet points – see Box 3.1).

Box 3.1: 'Ethical Considerations' to be Included in ESRC Funding Applications

- Research should be designed, reviewed and undertaken to ensure integrity and quality
- Research staff and subjects must be informed fully about the purpose, methods and intended possible uses of the research, what their participation in the research entails and what risks, if any, are involved. Some variation is allowed in very specific and exceptional research contexts for which detailed guidance is provided
- The confidentiality of information supplied by research subjects and the anonymity of respondents must be respected
- Research participants must participate in a voluntary way, free from any coercion
- Harm to research participants must be avoided
- The independence of research must be clear, and any conflicts of interest or partiality must be explicit

Source: ESRC Research Ethics Framework (2005: 1).

Other bodies may provide lengthier lists and have more formal procedures for evaluating whether they are met.[5]

On many levels, such lists of considerations appear sensible and well intended. However, they also often seem to rest upon questionable assumptions about how research should be organised, how it can be done well and how institutional politics affect how ethical standards are assessed and monitored in different places (Bosk and de Vries 2004; Gordon 2003; Marshall 2003; Plattner 2003; Punch 1986; Thrift 2003). One assumption, for example, appears to be that the research process is divided up into stages (e.g. read-*then*-do-*then*-write) where 'ethics' must be 'sorted out' before starting 'fieldwork'. Throughout this book, however, we draw upon examples of 'ethical' research in practice that turn around every one of even the ESRC's older minimalist three-point list of considerations. In terms of the first, we have experience of situations where being 'honest' with the people involved in our research may have been 'unethical', and where such 'honesty' was extremely difficult when the purposes, methods, uses and risks of research were changing as projects proceeded. When research changes as you do it, yesterday's honesty can often become tomorrow's apparent lies. In terms of the second consideration, we have found ourselves in circumstances where confidentiality was very difficult to maintain and, indeed, where research participants have insisted on not having it. Finally, in terms of the third consideration, we have already questioned whether research can or should be 'independent' or 'impartial' when we live in a world where gross inequality and injustice is all around us. Indeed, it must be acknowledged that many researchers are drawn to issues precisely to tackle inequalities and injustices (Cloke et al. 2004; Scheper-Hughes 2004).

It is important to point our here, then, that challenges to establish, maintain and/or revise your ethical stance will not only come from within academia. Rather, they may also have to be negotiated between the various locales of your research. Ian, for instance, has written about the ethical challenges presented to him by the papaya farm manager ('Jim') and his friend the sugar farm boss ('Tim') who had introduced Ian to him. Both had been extremely hospitable, both to Ian and to Michelle another English PhD student working in the area. Following Michelle, Ian had rented a room in Tim's Great House in the neighbouring valley to Jim's farm, and Jim had subsequently asked Ian if he would like to look after his brother's house on the farm while he was away. Tim, Jim, their families and friends also invited Ian and Michelle to parties and on fishing trips and, when he couldn't get to Kingston with Michelle in her car, he relied on them for lifts. So, what did he owe them back? As he has written elsewhere:

> I got to know Tim and Jim very well through my research, both as people from whom I learned a great deal about fruit farming in Jamaica, and as people who

I would hang out with socially. But, as my research progressed there over a period of six months, the hospitality and frankness which they had initially offered became increasingly punctuated by their anger over the 'brass-necked' nature of what I was doing. What, they argued, gave me the right to swan into their lives, look closely and critically at their finances, business methods, family lives, and, perhaps most sensitive, ways of dealing with their increasingly impoverished workforces and then fly away and write about this as if I didn't equally owe my livelihood to the ugly means of exploitation I obviously saw in theirs? Given that, at that time, my parents had been running their own business for 32 years..., their most disturbing question concerned whether I would even *consider* researching how they had made their money off other people and then speak about it critically in an academic arena. And, although much of this line of argumentation could be seen as tactical – their playing off what they saw as my 'misplaced socialist idealism' against what they knew about my family background to persuade me where my ultimate loyalties should perhaps lie – I could not deny that they had a fair point and this was something which, if these ideals were to remain somehow intact, I would have to deal with in my work (Cook 2001: 114–15).

But this was not all. 'Jim' also became concerned that, once published back in the UK, Ian's research could provoke a consumer boycott of his fruit. And did Ian know who would suffer the most if this happened? The farm workers he spent so much time talking to and seemed to care about the most. This situation therefore led to an ultimatum, presented when Jim was giving Ian yet another lift to Kingston. After pulling off the road for a 'chat' about Jim's concerns, they ended up agreeing that, in order for Ian to be allowed to continue his research on the farm, he would have to anonymise the fruit. These two challenges, about writing about them and about writing about it, both had to be met. Even though 'Jim' didn't remember making the first challenge (as Ian found out years later after bumping into him at an 'ethnic food fair' at Birmingham's National Exhibition Centre), Ian included discussion of his own family and family business in his PhD and in subsequent publications (see Cook 1997a, 2001; Cook et al. 1998). Having done this, he felt that he could more justifiably write about Jim's family and business, still appropriately anonymised of course. Second, a decade after this research was done, when Jim's farm was no longer supplying that fruit to UK supermarkets, and after two of the intermediary companies had gone out of business or been sold off, Ian felt that he could begin to say that he worked on a *papaya* farm, and show how the fruit itself made a difference to its trade (see Cook et al. 2004a,b).[6] Naming it in print in 2004 could not do any harm to the people he cared about, surely, so Ian felt that he was free of that in-car promise.

In sum, then, perhaps we need to think in terms of two kinds of research 'ethics'. First, there are those with a capital E that comprise the broad and fixed principles that might help to shape our plans when research proposals and 'ethical reviews' have to be submitted. And, second, there are those with a lower case e that feed into and emerge from the smaller, everyday encounters tied together throughout the research process. These are a messier, ongoing, impure, continually updated set of ethics that develop over time and through experiences. These result from situated decisions and ongoing debates about how we each should act in a world where behaving ethically often doesn't seem to be the foremost consideration shaping other people's actions. Few, if any, of us can act like a saint who is able to go into and emerge from their research unscathed by ethical wrongdoing. Doing 'the right thing', or knowing what the right thing is in the first place, is not always straight-forward or apparent. Indeed, at the end of a process full of countless uncertain, failed and/or successful attempts to act properly with respect to all of the others involved in your research, you are likely feel that, despite your best efforts, your ethics have been compromised; that they are, in fact, quite grubby, and that, if you had been a better person (or at least got more sleep), you would have been able to do a better job. We have certainly felt all of this. And this is surely normal.

SUMMARY

In the previous chapter, we argued that in order to undertake ethno-graphic and related qualitative research, it is necessary to have a critical, conceptual, geographical understanding of the (inter)subjectivity of researchers and researched, and the groups (e.g. 'cultures') they may be seen to be part of. In the next chapter, we outline the practicalities of a variety of approaches to undertaking qualitative research which you may wish to adopt during the kind of intensive 'fieldwork' that usually gets done later on in a project: for example, when the event that you've been waiting to happen eventually takes place, when you have to make that overseas trip or when a systematic series of interviews finally gets arranged. This chapter has outlined the 'doing' that, we argue, should be done alongside reading and writing from the very start of a project. Specifically, we have tried to encourage readers to recognise and make the most of the skills and opportunities that they already have, and could usefully develop, by:

- starting off with a topic that's deliberately in soft focus,
- considering wider issues such as visa restrictions and linguistic geo-graphies that could limit choices of where and with whom research could be undertaken,
- casting their nets widely to see what and who they might be able to 'catch' where,

- testing out existing and new contacts to see what doors may be open, closed or ajar;
- trying to gain permission and/or referrals to others who may help them to locate and to gain permission to work with people and communities who are beginning to seem appropriate for the study and,
- thinking carefully about the formal and practical E/ethics through which they should try to do the 'right thing' by themselves and others who become involved in, and (may be) affected by, their research.

This is practical advice that, we believe, can enable prospective ethnographers to avoid the pitfalls of the read-*then*-do-*then*-write model of research. Putting together a doable research project, with its formalised methodology, should result from reading, doing and writing taking place alongside one another, being informed and critiqued by one another, so that that project can change and take shape from the start.

Section 2

Constructing Ethnographic Information

[T]raditional ethnographic 'pretences' about detached observation and scientific method reveal anxiety about the uncontrollable messiness of any truly interesting fieldwork situation (Conquergood 1991: 182).

INTRODUCTION

In this section, we treat ethnographic methods as ways of studying a variety of communities. We do not propose a comprehensive list of 'approaches' – Renata Tesch (1990) listed some forty-three of these – but hope to give a flavour of those which might be adapted, altered and/or combined to fit various purposes and situations. As we said in the introduction, we concentrate here on four of the most commonly used face-to-face approaches to social research: participant observation, interviewing, focus groups and video/photographic work. Each of these will be discussed in a chapter which is broken down to cover gaining access, roles, contexts and materials and how you might construct information from the method. We do not mean for this list to be prescriptive of what should be adopted and combined in your work: ethnography is, after all, defined as participant observation *plus* any other appropriate methods/techniques/etc. including statistics, modelling and/or archive work *if they are appropriate for the topic*. There are lessons in each that are relevant to all. Moreover, we don't believe that the approaches outlined below should be treated as formal methods to be applied *after* the preparations outlined in the previous chapter have been undertaken. A lot of what we described there will involve using a lot of the skills described below. So, what we would strongly suggest is that the dynamics and benefits of each method be kept in mind as the possibilities for research unfold, so that appropriate methods cannot only be formally proposed but also flexibly adopted when the need or opportunity arises.

4 Participant Observation

Nothing is stranger than this business of humans observing other humans in order to write about them (Behar 1996: 5).

Historically, ethnographic research has developed out of a concern to understand the world-views and ways of life of actual people in the contexts of their everyday lived experiences. Participant observation is the core means by which ethnographers have tried to do this. Perhaps the best single phrase description of this is 'deep hanging out' (Wogan 2004). In its basic form it can be described as a three-stage process in which the researcher somehow, first, gains access to a particular community, second, lives and/or works among the people under study in order to grasp their world views and ways of life and, third, travels back to the academy to makes sense of this through writing up an account of that community's 'culture'. But, straightforward as this may sound, when considering using this method it is vital to understand the key tension suggested in its oxymoronic title. To be a *participant* in a 'culture' implies an immersion of the researcher's self into the everyday rhythms and routines of the community, a development of relationships with people who can show and tell the researcher what is 'going on' there and, through this, an experience of a whole range of relationships and emotional states that such a process must inevitably involve (Hunt 1989; Wax 1983). Conversely, though, to be an *observer* of a 'culture' implies a detached sitting-back and watching of activities which unfold in front of the researcher as if she/he wasn't there, a simple recording of these goings-on in field notes, tallies, drawings, photographs and other forms of material evidence and, through this, a striving to maintain some form of dispassionate, 'scientific' objectivity (Fyfe 1992; Maranhao 1986; Tedlock 1991).

Like many other writers, we argue that to talk about participant observation should not be to separate its 'subjective' and 'objective' components, but to talk about it as a means of developing *intersubjective* understandings between researcher and researched (Crapanzano 1986; Dwyer 1977; Spencer 1989; Tedlock 1991). Moreover, it is important for the researcher to think not only about how she/he becomes 'immersed' in the community under study, but also about how she/he and, variously, *they* are immersed in other communities outside – which may be based around geopolitics, banking, the media, mass consumption, sports, leisure, friendship, family, etc. – and how this affects the ways in which the research process develops. In this section, such development is discussed in terms of the ranges of researchers' potential access to, and roles within, certain communities, and how various types of information and understandings can be actively constructed, represented and contextualised for use in the subsequent stages of analysis and writing up.

ACCESS

We have already dealt with many issues that impact on initiating access to study areas, but it is worth noting that for this method there are some particular considerations. Much of the discussion on participant observation focuses around how researchers can, where possible, take on already existing subject positions in the communities which they study or, where it is not, construct new ones. For instance, given that it is rare for researchers to be given enough time and/or money to develop a professional skill in preparation for their study, some labour processes are difficult topics for participant observation research. Unless researchers have spent some years qualifying and working as plumbers, nurses, accountants or pilots, for instance, although they may be able to observe such work, it is extremely unlikely that they will be able to *participate* in it without anyone noticing their inability to solder a joint, administer a suppository, keep double-entry books or land a 747. You could, however, and there is a whole genre of these studies, do an ethnography of *'becoming a'* certain professional – be it plumber, nurse, accountant or pilot by attending the training courses and so forth (see for example Mike's material later or Crang 2000, or Hochshild's 1983 study with trainee airline stewardesses) – with the additional possibility of thus financing your studies (Katz 2001: 457). In other cases, researchers may have spent a significant portion of their lives working in a particular profession and then, for whatever reasons, have gone (back) to college to do research which builds on this.

In the case of professional spaces, then, perhaps the nearest the relatively unqualified researcher can get is to apply for perhaps more easily accessible jobs in the same spaces – as a plumber's mate, hospital porter, or clerical assistant – and to participate and to observe at this level. Alternatively, the researcher can search for already established positions in which participation in, and observation of, professional lives by outsiders is a legitimate role. Sarah Thornton's (2000) academic background, for example, meant that she was qualified to enter the advertising profession. She was therefore able to do her ethnography 'on the job'. Similarly, when undertaking preparatory research with supermarket fruit buyers, Ian found that like any other university graduate, he could have been suitably quali-fied to apply for one company's three-month graduate placement scheme. With its purpose being to allow potential recruits to watch and to question employees already doing this work, and eventually to try it out for them-selves, this was tailor-made for participant observation research.[1] In this respect and, again, in the early stages of the research, it may be a good idea to find out if similar kinds of access may be possible into a particular pro-fession or company. Otherwise, you could ask or volunteer to tag along as a researcher who might occasionally 'help out' as a driver, translator and so on. Such a role can have the benefits of providing the researcher with a legitimate occupation, new contacts and the chance to give something back to the community under study (Ley 1988); yet care must also be taken to prevent this role from swamping the research (Wax 1983).

Contrary to its traditional image, then, participant observation research is not always a matter of spending a year or two living in an isolated community in some remote part of the world. Many of us live segmented lives, embedded in different networks of family, leisure and work. Thus, most 'communities' formed within these networks are spatially dispersed, and many are occasional or intermittent. Therefore, if you are interested in studying a 'community' that comes together in different places and at different times, then the constant 'immersion' suggested in many anthropology texts will not be necessary or possible (Hannerz 2003; Radway 1988). Here, it may be 'normal' to be doing participant observa-tion on some days of the week and 'ordinary' work on another. Mike's participant observation work with an historical reenactment group, for instance, involved meeting them for 'musters' on separate weekends in fields near York, Bradford and Yeovil. The 'community' was thus spatially dispersed, temporally intermittent and his work involved studying a small but important part of certain individuals' lives. This was neatly illustrated by the following exchange between two of his informants:

Amy: I never understand it; you talk to these people at musters and you
    would never believe they could hold a responsible job.
Gav: That's because you have never understood the switch off effect. You see
    these people on the 5 weekends a year when they are completely out of
    control (Mike's field notes 22 July 1993).

In this and most other experiences of participant observation work, boundaries between field and academic experiences become blurred. Often the days back in the academy will have a profound effect on your views of the field, and vice versa. Mike certainly found this in that while he was join-ing in with the activities of reenactment groups, the 'normality' of the activ-ity was never in doubt. However, the moment he returned to the office, there were constant jibes about his 'hessian underpants', doing everything '...as a Tudor' and the 'sad weirdoes' whom he was both studying and supposedly becoming like. He found it extremely difficult to 'forget' this when he went back to the next reenactment, and this illustrates the importance of adopting different identities in the academy and in 'the field' and attempting to understand and to build on the tensions between these (cf. Madge 1993).

Academic and 'field' identities can feed off each other informatively, and uncomfortably. In one ten-day period, for example, Mike found himself attending postgraduate classes on 'how to do ethnographies' where he learned about trying to adopt customs, play roles and fit in with locals, *and* reenactment classes where he learned how to adopt customs, role play and fit in with the mis-en-scene (see Crang 2000). Moreover, after explaining his project as a 'group ethnography' to a few reenactors around a fire one evening, he noticed that they went off and asked their 'head archer' Pete what this meant. Pete, he later found out, was a graduate in social anthropology. This brought very close to home, the multiple ways that researchers position and present themselves to different people and how they interpret the researcher's presence. Indeed, Mike's research experiences even forced him to reflect on whether he could claim his academic knowledge was different, or superior, to that of the people he studied.

ROLES AND RELATIONSHIPS

In terms of gaining access to particular places and communities, it is not only who the researcher contacts that is important, but also how she/he explains the project to them. The ways in which she/he presents aspects of her/his self in the process of negotiating access is particularly important in participant observation, although what we say here is also relevant to the development of relationships with informants using other methods. Here, the matter of to what degree the researcher's questions and roles should be overt or covert has to be breached at an early stage. When they first meet, for instance:

- What should the researcher tell any 'gatekeepers' about exactly why she/he wants to become part of a community's life?
- If you gain permission from someone 'senior' or important, can you assume that everyone else will know what you are doing and agree to your persence or be happy with it (Mandel 2003)?
- Should she/he immediately divulge the intricacies of her/his project to initial and later contacts or wait until relationships have been developed in which such revelations may more easily be made?
- Will community members care very much what they are?
- Will they (mis)understand the language the researcher uses, and vice versa?

- Is it likely that a researcher will or should have the same purpose at the end of their fieldwork as at its beginning?

After a number of initial enquiries with contacts in the field, the researcher will have had the chance to hone her/his 'purposes' in order to properly word any formal or informal application for access. In these early stages, the researcher may simply want to enquire what constitutes the community's everyday activities. Later, once this has been established, a general idea of what the research might eventually be about or a watered-down version of the question(s) perhaps already set out in an academic research proposal will often suffice. In terms of what these questions might be, there is often a marked difference between what the researcher tells her/his academic supervisors and colleagues that the research is about and what she/he tells various 'gatekeepers' in 'the field'. Yet we do not mean to make a distinction between the former necessarily being the real reasons and the latter being their more tactical versions. While deception can and does occur (both researched and researchers can be guilty of this), it is important to recognise that research projects have multiple audiences and are changing entities in time and space. Thus, multiple versions of the same project get fashioned for funders, supervisors, colleagues, friends, family and the various people with whom we do our research. None of these versions need necessarily be *the* 'true one'.

In his fruit research, for instance, the main question that Ian wrote for his research committee went as follows:

> Given that many authors have argued that the global food economy functions through connecting, maintaining and often deepening extremes of wealth and poverty, overnutrition and malnutrition, and so forth, and that this has been regarded as 'obscene' by many of them, how can such an 'obscene' system operate through the everyday actions of people who, I assume, do not see themselves as 'obscene'?

Later, once it had been decided to settle on addressing this question in the context of a commodity system linking the retailing of a tropical fruit in the UK and its production somewhere in the 'Underdeveloped World,' and when the time came to start making contacts in the UK fruit trade, the project was rejigged in some letters as:

> Given that there has been a significant increase in the amount and variety of exotic fruits being sold in British supermarkets over the past ten years or so, I'm trying to find out why and how this has happened;

and in others as

> I'm treating the commodity systems of fresh fruit as social systems stretched out over massive expanses of time/space, and am trying to find out how they are co-ordinated on a day to day basis from farm to shelf.

Each version of what he wanted to do was 'true' and, as he met others elsewhere in his 'field', other explanations were offered, often grilled, and elaborated upon as appropriate.

To complicate this picture further, not only do researchers and their projects have multiple audiences, but they are also bound to change as they proceed. As projects develop over time through encounters in a number of connected but dispersed locales, researchers can become – in effect – different people (see Saltmarsh in Cloke et al. 2004, 366–67). First, taking on the role of 'the researcher' means that you will very likely behave in ways that might feel and be seen under other circumstances as quite odd. Do you 'normally' spend your time hanging around with strangers, watching what they are doing, trying to take part in it, asking them to tell you about their lives and going round the corner to scribble bits of what they say in a notebook? Or, indeed, do you 'normally' spend your time with middle-class academics trying to sound clever and competent? We certainly didn't (and maybe, just maybe, still don't). Second, the process of meeting people we might not normally meet, learning first-hand about lives that may be very different from our own and living between different worlds can have quite profound effects. Researchers should not expect to emerge unaffected by such encounters. Finally, not only do researchers have to worry about the goals and ethics of their academic work, but also about how to get on with the people they are working with in a personal, everyday sense (see Ahmet 2003). It is not unusual, for example, for researchers to emerge from their work with new and unexpected friends – and other relationships (Cupples 2002; Tillman-Healy 2003). Researchers' changing relationships and identities are, of course, wrapped up in changing research processes. If it is apparent to those researchers work with that they and their projects are somewhat in flux (sometimes radically so: see Shurmer-Smith 1998), it should not surprise researchers if they get labelled in multiple, changing ways (Butz 2001; Paerregard 2002). Roles, relationships and understandings in ethnographic research projects tend to be partial, contingent and subject to change for all those involved.

All this change may seem exciting and/or daunting. But there are some useful guidelines to follow when thinking about how to behave 'in the field'. According to Joan Cassell (1988: 97), for instance, the researcher:

> ...should adopt a role or identity that meshes with the values and behaviour of the group being studied, without seriously compromising the researcher's own values and behaviour...[and] not...inventing an identity; we all have several,...but...the most appropriate one can be stressed.

For those following the advice to begin research projects by taking advantage of close contacts they already have through family, work and other networks, this may happen as a matter of course. As a doctor's wife, for instance, Cassell (1988) had a ready-made identity that allowed surgeons to discuss issues such as malpractice suits, patient billing or the costs of education with her just as they might with any colleague's wife. More distant contacts can also be developed by researchers belonging to diasporic and other wider communities. Lorraine Dowler (2001), an American catholic of Irish descent was able to undertake an ethnographic study of a Belfast community where members of the Provisional IRA lived after contacting a local catholic priest to ask for help with finding a family with whom she could board. Finally, even when useful 'lines of identification' have been established, they can be subject to change. Jean Morrison, a white Scottish woman undertaking research in rural Botswana, for example, found that:

> Attitudes towards me shifted as I moved from being seen as young and rather anomalous in terms of gender identity during the first period of fieldwork, to being seen as more clearly gendered during the second period (when I was obviously pregnant), and even more so during the third trip (when I was accompanied by my nine-month-old daughter) (Twyman et al. 1999: 316; see also Cassell 1987).

It is unusual for researchers and researched to have absolutely nothing in common with, or no location within the world views of, each other. But it may not only be aspects of a researcher's personal identity that (unexpectedly) provide the connections. Some researchers have found that activities such as photography, for example, can provide a readily understood reason and purpose for their presence in certain places at certain times. At tourist sites, weddings or historical reenactments, for example, someone hanging around taking photographs will not stand out from the crowd, as would a person asking questions and taking notes. Indeed, because those present often ask about the photographs being taken, the former may be an excellent entree to the latter (see chapter 7; Cohen et al. 1992; Collier and Collier 1986; Schwartz 1989).

It is important to recognise that while these 'lines of identification' may be useful, possibly multiple and can develop some depth over time, they may also be fleeting, limited and (unexpectedly) subject to change (Narayan 1993). However long they spend living and working in their subject community, most researchers will simultaneously feel that they are like *and* unlike the people they are working with, that they belong 'inside' *and* 'outside' that community (Kneafsey 2000; Mullings 1999; Valentine 2002). Take Tony Whitehead's (1986) account of his initial research experiences in a rural Jamaican community:

> I am a black American who grew up in the rural South to impoverished sharecropper parents. Regardless of the upward mobility I experienced, when I went to Jamaica I still perceived myself as one of the little people (i.e. lower status)

because of my experiences as a member of an ethnic minority in the United States.... With such a self image in tow, I was shocked when the people [there] began referring to me and treating me as a 'big', 'brown', 'pretty-talking' man. 'Big' was not a reference to my weight but to my higher social status. I was aware of the West Indian correlation between skin colour and social status, but I was not prepared for the personal experience of my lightness of skin colour being associated with higher socioeconomic and moral status.... More embarrassing than bothersome were the references to how 'pretty' I talked, a comment on my Standard English speech pattern (1986: 214–15).

What is often strange, and perhaps interesting, to researchers are the ways in which they get 'placed' in these ways, because this can often provide insights into the world views of the people under study (see DeVita 1992; Murphy 1992; Pollner and Emerson 1983; Rapport 1993). Researchers' skin colours, nationalities and (apparent) religious affiliations, for example, can often mean they get '(mis)placed' by their respondents in unexpected and enlightening ways. Take Robina Mohammed (2001), a Pakistani Muslim by birth who was brought up in Britain and undertook her PhD research with Muslim women in the UK. She found that her skin colour, and related (mis)conceptions about her identity and beliefs, made some of the women she worked with refer to her as 'one of us' (2001: 108). Given that this was not always a sense of belonging that she, herself, felt this gave her a sometimes dubious access and authority to research and represent British Muslim experience. Ian's experience as a white British male PhD student working with and interviewing mostly black Jamaican female farm workers was quite different. What came up in (in)formal conversations were rumours of wealthy white men like him seeking out women like them because they were sex tourists or because they were looking for someone to take back to the USA or UK as a domestic worker.[2]

In terms of deciding how to settle on particular presentations of the researcher's self and project, then, there are no easy answers because, to a large degree, these can be outside the researcher's control. Many aspects of her/his identity inevitably end up being played off against each other in various contexts as her/his appearance, ideas, intentions, feelings, politics, ways of doing things and so forth (have to) change through the experience of setting up and seeing through the project. Through initial conversations and particularly through sustained periods of interaction, researchers can, first, learn which aspects of their identity allow them to be more or less acceptably placed in the world views of both their key informants and the community under study and, second, thereby establish how any common ground might be found. Some questions to think about here, then, are as follows:

- If the researcher is expecting the people she/he lives and/or works amongst to be frank about their opinions and experiences, should the researcher do likewise in order to foster the development of a genuine intersubjective understanding?

- Should the researcher step back, at least for a while, observe, ask innocent questions, and be careful what they reveal about themselves?
- How long should she/he spend skipping between different members of the community before relationships can emerge in which researcher and researched develop the trust necessary for both to 'open up' to share (often private) experiences and frankly argue out the issues which each thinks are important, both in the community and more widely?
- If the researcher comes to form an opinion about the people she/he has been working with, should she/he present this to them to see whether this gels with their experience, or should she/he preserve the perhaps delicate nature of the relationship by keeping quiet until either the closing stages of their fieldwork or, indeed, the writing up stage when it can, perhaps, be most carefully worked out and handed back for comment?
- Having promised confidentiality to her/his informants, can the researcher ask questions of members of one fraction based on information gleaned from members of another (Johnson 1983)?

All of these are questions of practical ethics, and most researchers make uneasy and improvised compromises about such issues as their research progresses. Some find themselves in situations where they are trusted with extremely private and/or damaging information which they feel should not be written about, even in the most carefully anonymous account (Stacey 1988). They can also feel shocked, disgusted or threatened by some of the opinions that certain community members hold dear and/or act upon (and, no doubt, the opposite may also be true, e.g. Keith 1992; Nast 1994). At the same time, though, it is not uncommon for people under the researcher's gaze to feel self-conscious or threatened knowing that anything they say may be 'written down and used in evidence against them'. It is a good idea to keep in mind the fact that few people, including the researcher, are ever 100% (dis)honest, earnest, flippant, sure what they think, consistent in what they say across all contexts or anything else. And, it can take quite some time before the researcher comes to understand these kinds of subtleties and to respond to them appropriately. First, second and third impressions can often be wrong because members of the research community may well be just playing on their expectations of the researcher's expectations to wind her/him up, to provoke a reaction and enjoy themselves at her/his expense (Taussig 1987; Whitehead 1986). You should always be suspicious, then, of why you understand what you understand within the contingent, intersubjective, time/spaces of your field work (Crick 1992).

Whatever role the researcher ends up adopting, communities are extremely unlikely to be so homogeneous that to understand them from *one* perspective is to understand them from *all*. So, the question becomes to what extent the researcher can/should try to gloss over these divisions by attempting to get on with everyone. For many, the ideal stance is that of 'an intelligent, sympathetic, and non-judgmental listener' to all of its members (Cassell 1988: 95). Yet, there can be problems here because this approach can, in practice, make the researcher stand out in that few, if any, members of a community take up such a role themselves. On this note, Jacqueline Wade (1984) has argued that:

> To present oneself as an unalterably 'neutral' character in the course of the sub-jects' life events courts an impression that the (researcher) is gullible, amateur-ish, inane, or uncommitted (or some combination of these) and, thus, unworthy of subjects' attention and time. Furthermore, such a stance could convey to subjects that the (researcher) has, in truth, a negative regard for their inner workings, thereby potentially causing inimical involvements in future areas of field relationships (1984: 219).

At the same time, an entirely partisan, single-focus stance would surely be a case of poor *theoretical sampling*. How could you critically understand the meanings of a particular situation or problem if you didn't study the perspectives of differently positioned people who struggle over these with each other in the course of their everyday lives? In many cir-cumstances, however, this even-handedness may be impossible and/or undesirable. If you are working on issues where unequal power relations are structuring what you are trying to study, opting for a role of 'partisan observer' may offer you political and ethical purchase on the situation and with the respondents. Paul Routledge's (2002) work on tourist development in Goa is a case in point. He made the most of his whiteness and ability to emulate a Western businessman to overcome local NGOs' learnt distrust of, or at least distaste for, researchers whose impartiality meant they offered little in return for the help that locals gave. He then took part in actions with these NGOs which involved him in quite deliberate deception and, indeed, in illegal activities such as breaking into development sites. He posed as a tourist agent to interview developers, in order to uncover their illegal activities. And he used his academic credentials to write up his find-ings for a popular highbrow magazine. Routledge's work violates nearly all the standard 'ethical considerations' we outlined in chapter three. But it was more important to him to honour his obligations to these NGOs. However, in playing out multiple roles as researcher, collaborator, activist and publicist, he also acknowledges the frisson of danger and transgression in such work, as perhaps a guilty pleasure, that appeals to another side of his identity, irrespective of his collaborator's needs.

Traditionally, the assumption with participant observation research has tended to be that the researcher befriends and establishes empathy and rapport with people in her/his research community. While we certainly think this is part of the process, it seems to set a normative model that is not always, or often, realistic or helpful. These are nearly always friendships with a purpose. Thus, if we want to participate in people's lives and expect them to be honest with us about their thoughts and feelings:

- Should we also do likewise or bite our lips when this might mean that rapport may be broken?
- Should we simply agree with whatever people in our research communities say or do, and even join in, so as not to sever access to their 'real' lives?
- In a subtly worded or more straightforward way, should we challenge them to justify themselves?
- Can we justify not being honest with all of them all of the time?
- Do we expect (all of) them to be totally honest with us all of the time?

As we stress throughout this book, there are no easy or final answers to such questions. All we can do here is to raise these issues and suggest that they may only be precariously resolved at any given point in a research project. Once access to a community has been negotiated, the researcher can hardly if ever simply 'blend in' via an uncontentious process of 'role-playing'.

With so many factors being played off against each other in the field, then, any researcher's first stab at participant observation is almost bound to take unpredictable twists and turns which are alternately fascinating, disturbing and challenging in both academic and personal senses (Crick 1992). And research roles and relationships can get even more complicated and difficult to control if/when:

- they find themselves to be the latest in a line of researchers to study the community, meaning that they may have to live up to expectations based on other people's behaviour (Pratt 1986; Shostak 1981),
- partners and/or children have accompanied them into the field, meaning they are inserted into generational structures and seen as parents or, if they pay others to care for children, inserted into class structures as upper- or middle-class employers (Cassell 1987; Cupples and Kindon 2003; Price 2001; Rosaldo 1989; Schrijvers 1993; Shurmer-Smith 1998; Tedlock 1991),
- their work is undertaken as part of a team including other researchers, translators, and others with different identities, abilities and connections (Barley 1984; Douglas 1976) and/or

- their work is part of a broader (non)governmental initiative which can (dis)advantageously place researchers as representatives of an (un)known and/or (dis)trusted organisation (Katz 1994; see Twyman et al. 1999 for all of these together).

The complexity of the role-playing and relationship-forming core of participant observation may look, to someone who has never tried it out, like far too much to worry about. However, as Steve Herbert (2000) argues, prospective ethnographers will rarely be complete novices in dealing with the issues raised. Most of us will have had at least some experience of living in/between a number of locales and 'social scenes', of trying to gain access, understand, fit into and develop relationships within new locales and 'scenes' and of having to maintain and/or sever ties with old locales and 'scenes'. 'A good ethnographer', Paul Cloke et al. (2004: 170) argue, is therefore 'someone willing and able to become a more reflexive and sociable version of him or herself in order to learn something meaningful about other people's lives'. Could this be you?

LANGUAGE IN CONTEXT

In the previous chapter, we discussed the ways in which researchers' linguistic abilities could influence the planning of research in its early stages. Here, we want to concentrate more on contextual, face-to-face, 'in the field' language issues. Here, even if the researcher is familiar with the (official) language they expect their 'research community' to speak, it is likely that it will have a local, improvised, slang and/or creolised version. So, even the most proficient speaker will not necessarily be identified as an 'insider' by the way she/he uses it. But this is not necessarily a bad thing as trying to sound too much like and 'insider' may be incompatible with a role of well-meaning 'outsider' (Whyte 1955). Thus, there may still be plenty of room for awkward and (partially) misunderstood discussions. In some conversations, the researchers may find that they can understand only a few sentences, phrases and/or words and have to guess what the other person meant in order to continue the conversation. And this is a process that is likely to be gone through by both parties. Sometimes the potential for misunderstanding may seem so great that researchers go through periods of not wanting to talk to people they are working with for fear of being damagingly misunderstood (this was Ian's experience on the papaya farm, at least). Often it is the case that such communication breakdowns can be advantageous in that they render previously unnoticed processes apparent (Agar 1986; R. Thomas 1993). And sometimes they don't. For example, Ian often had problems understanding what 'JD', one of the participants in his blindness research, said and meant. This was, first, because he had trouble understanding JD's very strong Kentucky accent, second, because JD had a habit of starting off his responses to Ian's questions by mumbling and using words which Ian could make little or no sense of and, third, because JD invariably finished off his often incomplete sentences with a coarse, exhaled laugh. However, Ian came to the conclusion that this communication problem could be largely ignored because 'what I can understand is fab anyway, and the words he mumbles are the ones he doesn't care about much anyway – i.e. they are the precursors to his "real" responses – as if he is "warming up"' (Cook 1992: 94). Whether undertaking research in your first, second and/or other language(s), and whether you are or are not employing a translator, the main point that we want to make here is that language use varies by geographical and interactional context. This therefore means that whatever preparations you have made, there will always be some language-learning to do 'in the field'. If you are working in your first language, for instance, it may take considerable time to understand the kinds of 'abbreviations and technical terms' as well as 'esoteric gestures, movements and behaviours' habitually used by members of your research (Cassell 1988: 98). In her work with surgeons, for instance, Joan Cassell found that this contextual language-learning took 'more than a year' (Cassell 1988: 98).

Choosing to work somewhere because you won't have to learn another language is often, therefore, not as straightforward in practice as it may seem in principle. Although a Jamaican academic working in the UK had told Ian he would have no problems in her home country because people spoke English there, he quickly found out that the English that he and the farm workers spoke were often very different. If he had been more circumspect about this advice and undertaken some linguistic research, he would have found out that the language spoken in Jamaica is Jamaican English (or, simply, 'Jamaican').[3] Jamaican, in turn, is not a discrete language but is, rather, a *linguistic continuum* comprising 'overlapping "lects", or specific modes of language use, (which) not only contain forms from the major languages "between" which they come into being, but forms which are functionally peculiar to themselves' (Ashcroft et al. 1989: 45). Linguist Mervyn Alleye (1988), for example, lists eight different Jamaican versions of the Standard English phrase 'He is eating his dinner': from the most 'African' version – *î a nyam î dina* – to the most 'English' – *hi iz iitin hiz dinner*. Jamaican speakers move along this continuum, adjusting their talk to fit the linguistic context they are in (Ashcroft et al. 1989: 45). The English that Ian spoke was therefore located at the far end of this continuum, and he was trying to have conversations with farm workers who were unused to speaking with people in his linguistic context. This was just the tip of a linguistic iceberg. The historical–geographical circumstances through which

Jamaican developed mean that, for instance, words long dead in Standard English – like *'quitter* (pus) in a wound – a word... which the OED traces no later than 1689 in this sense' (Cassidy 1961: 4) – are still alive in Jamaican, while some familiar words in Standard English can have unexpected meanings. So, for example, when Ian was told by a fruit packer that she had loudly berated the farm's foreman because she was 'ignorant', she was not attributing her actions to her lack of experience, knowledge, awareness or education about the situation (the Standard English meaning). Rather, as he later found out, 'ignorant' is 'a malapropism for *indignant'* in Jamaican (Cassidy and Le Page 1982: 234), and means 'to become angry, to consciously assume an attitude, especially in combative circumstances where the dignity of the ignorant is in question' (Cooper 1993: 185). This made much better sense, under the circumstances.

If the researcher has the time, sustained interaction can allow language skills to be improved and misunderstandings to be resolved. And, if she/he has the equipment and the money, it may be an idea to tape-record some or all conversations and have them professionally transcribed so that they can be slowly pored over later to decipher the subtle nuances of the interactions and to get at how inter-subjective understandings developed out of such dialogue (this is what Ian tried to do). Whatever gets planned and turns out to be the case, it seems reasonable to suggest again that the language(s) of any research project are best learned in the classroom and in the 'field' and that (informal) participant observation of language use *in context* can improve our understandings of other people's lives.

CONSTRUCTING INFORMATION

However researchers work out their access and involvement in research communities, they must somehow be able to leave with detailed information upon which they can base their theses, dissertations and other accounts. For participant observers, the core data that they generate is that which fills their *field diary* or *notebook* and, in a similar vein, their letters, emails and other correspondences 'home' (see Emerson et al. 1995; Sanjek 1990). Kept, at worst, every few days, the purpose of a diary or notebook is to:

- keep some kind of record of what the researcher learns, day by day, about the people and places under study,
- try to make sense of the ways in which (mis)understandings develop, and research takes shape, in/between various research settings and
- provide the kinds of detailed descriptions which can allow the eventual readers of their thesis, dissertation or other account(s) to imagine being there, standing in their shoes, understanding things in the ways that they did, then and there.

As we have already begun to suggest, it is a good idea for *all* researchers to keep such a diary throughout their research process, whether or not they are formally doing participant observation work. Interactions at 'home' with supervisors, fellow students, bank management, research council officials, journal referees and editors, etc. can have as much, if not more, of an effect on how the research 'turns out' as can encounters with members of the official, 'out there', research community. All of these encounters can usefully be noted.

Paul Cloke et al. (2004: 201–04) suggest that prospective ethnographers could usefully combine six layers of description, moving from observation, through participation to self-reflection. Below, we borrow their headings and provide an idea of the kinds of questions that go with them:

(a) locating an ethnographic setting
   - what country is it in?
   - is it in the north, south, east, west, centre or a combination?
   - is it a city, town, village or other setting?
   - where in that larger setting is it located?
   - what is the background and character of that setting?
   - how could you describe your setting's location so readers can picture it?

(b) describing the physical space of that setting.
   - what size and shape did that setting have?
   - what were its main physical characteristics?
   - how would you describe them so that readers could picture them?
   - could you find or draw maps, do some sketching and/or take photographs?
   - (how) did this physical setting change?

(c) describing others' interactions within that setting.
   - who were the people, and other 'actors', present in that setting that day?
   - what did you see them doing and hear them talking about?
   - how did they appear to be interacting with one another?
   - how could you describe this so readers can imagine being there?

(d) describing your participation in interactions in that setting.
   - where did you locate yourself in that setting that day?
   - who introduced you to whom and how did they describe what you were doing?
   - how did you see, hear and get involved with what was going on?
   - what did you learn from talking and doing things with the people there?
   - how did your participation change over time, and in other settings?
   - how could you describe this so readers can imagine being in your shoes?

(e) reflecting on the research process
- what were your first impressions and how have they changed?
- what did you divulge to whom about your work and how did they react?
- how did you think you were being placed by the people you worked with?
- how did your research team (if you had one) work and fit in?
- what effects did this seem to have on the way the research could be done?
- how did your initial findings match your expectations?
- what language problems did you have, and how did you deal with them?
- what were the 'surprises', big or small, that needed further investigation?
- did your powers of description, photography etc. capture enough?
- (how) did the ways you did your research change people's behaviour?[4]
- how was your research taking shape and what control did you have over this?
- how did you change your questions, methods, etc. as a result of these questions?
- how would you rewrite your methodology as if you had known this would happen?

(f) self-reflections
- how did various aspects of these research encounters make you feel?
- how appropriately did you think you behaved in these encounters?
- (how) did you (try to) please everyone, including your supervisors?
- (how) did you (try to) do the right thing *and* get that research done?
- (how) did people question your motives or behaviour in the field?
- how did you respond to this and what effects did this seem to have?
- how did you deal with your emotions in your fieldwork?
- how did you have to manage your 'self' in the field, and how hard was this?
- how and to whom did you let off steam, and how did they respond?
- if you felt like giving up, what kept you going?

We are not providing this list for readers to copy down and go through heading by heading, question by question in *their* research diaries. Rather, we suggest that this *sort* of list could work like an interview checklist (see later) where the researcher writes down, in advance, what they think they should cover in an interview but a) not necessarily in that order and b) not necessarily keeping only to those questions if other interesting and relevant issues unexpectedly come up. So, for example, rather than writing his participant observation notes in separate layers, Ian just kept these layers in mind when writing stream-of-consciousness notes which, he felt, better set out and allowed him to think about the emerging connections between different aspects of his work (see Boxes 4.1 and 4.2 for raw and processed excerpts from these

Box 4.1: An Excerpt from Ian's Research Dairy: on the Papaya Farm[a]

Saturday 30 May 1992

Too bored with myself last eve to write anything, despite the importance of it being the first six days of diary stuff. Yesterday, I traipsed off to the packing house at about 9.30 (probably after an hour or so of reading and sorting out tapes and forms – actually, it's probably unreasonable of me to expect those keeping diaries for me to remember what [illegible] the day before if I can't), stood by the end of the packing house cool [illegible] to see if [redacted] and/or [redacted] were there. As I did this [redacted], at the other end of the table with Hyacinth (I think) was looking at me, calling me over. So I went. She asked me how come I had not given her the watch and pen? She lived in [redacted]? So I said something like "OK. I was going to ask you" and suggested that we talk about it in the canteen. As we walked over, I told her that I had meant to catch her yesterday but didn't [illegible] on her own. If I asked her in a group, I didn't want others asking me for a watch, too. As we sat down, I unzipped the small pocket of my pouch (which formerly held the small microphone which I broke) and took out the watch. Having given the others the choice of watches, this was the remaining one – a kind of square chunky LCD watch whose face and strap were fashioned after army camouflage (not desert storm) and the watch face had 2 [illegible] bars to supposedly protect it from the brutality of war, ie

Anyway, I was a little embarrassed about this watch – I thought it was easily the most hideous of the 6(5?) before showing it to anyone in the packing house, and then nobody chose it – even after I gave it to [redacted] the day before when [illegible] was showing, the [illegible] and I couldn't [illegible] it: she [illegible] it back when [redacted] had double bypass – why the badly chosen [illegible] pens

[a] Here, all proper names have been blanked out in an attempt to preserve the anonymity of those involved.

Box 4.2: Box 4.1 Later World-Processed for Analysis.110

Annotation
This typed version of the hand-written notes above could not contain the sketch of the watch above (see Pfaffenberger 1989), but literally took months to type up when Ian returned home. It does, however, contain pseudonyms for the people and places involved in an attempt to preserve their anonymity. When making notes anonymous, it is a good idea to draw up a table of real names and their intended equivalents, and to refer to this at all stages of your analysis. It is probably better to analyse your diary and interview materials with the real names in place – in order to avoid the constant distraction of having to translate from one to the other when making sense of your materials – and to then substitute the pseudonyms at a later stage.[a] See later for a discussion of the (time/space) diaries mentioned in the first sentence that were kept by 'Cerene' and five other packing-house workers who lived in 'Ibrox', along with their supervisor and the manager of the farm. In this excerpt, these watch-related encounters were important to note because none of the workers involved possessed a watch or a pen to note in their diaries the times when certain things/events happened, so Ian gave them one of each. This giving led to a number of unexpected reactions which had to be noted down because they had an effect on the research process as, here and elsewhere, Ian by no means blended in to 'observe' the day-to-day workings of the farm's packing-house unnoticed.

––––––

Saturday 30 May 1992
Too bored with myself last eve to write anything, despite the importance of it being the first big day of diary stuff. Yesterday, I trooped off to the packing house at about 9.30 (probably after an hour or so of reading and sorting out tapes and forms – actually, it's probably unreasonable of me to expect those keeping diaries for me to remember much from the day before if I can't), stood by the end of the packing bench looking around to see if Emilie, Lana, Gloria and/or Pru were there. As I did this Cerene, at the other end of the table with Vivette (I think) was looking at me, calling me over. So I went. She asked me how come I had not given her the watch and pen? She lived in Ibrox? So I said something like 'OK. I was going to ask you' and suggested that we talk about it in the canteen. As we walked over, I told her that I had meant to catch her yesterday but didn't find her on her own. If I asked her in a group, I didn't want others asking me for a watch, too. As we sat down, I unzipped the small pocket of my pouch (which formerly held the small microphone which I broke) and took out the watch. Having given the others the choice of watches, this was the remaining one – a kind of square clunky LCD watch whose face and strap were fashioned after army camouflage (not Desert Storm) and the watch face had 2 thin metal bars to supposedly protect it from the brutality of War, i.e. (sketch of watch). Anyway, I was a trifle embarrassed about

Box 4.2: continued

this watch – I thought it was easily the most hideous of the 6(5?) before showing it to anyone in the packing house, and then nobody chose it – even after I gave it to Gloria the day before when hers was showing the wrong time and I couldn't mend it: she gave it straight back when Baldwin had done the business – using the badly chosen fine fibre tip pens...

[a] NB under circumstances where failure to maintain anonymity may be life-threatening, this approach is a terrible idea (see Dowler 2001).

notes). Separating out the different types of description for inclusion in his thesis would, he thought, be better done later. Mike's attitude was similar, except for the fact that he chose to tape-record his notes. This was partly for the same stream-of-consciousness reasons that shaped Ian's. But tape-recording was also necessary because of the circumstances in which Mike was working. Doing participant observation research on historical reenactments meant that he could not openly make notes during the day, and writing by torch-light in a tent meant even he could not read his writing the next day. In Jamaica, Ian had a house with lights to go home to each day, although to many it might look as if he wrote his notes in the dark (more about this later). For a brief discussion of writing versus typing research notes, and the issue of anonymity, see the annotation in Box 4.2.

In practice, noting observations of, and participation in, the daily lives of a research community should involve both trying to describe things in breadth (e.g. to make sense of an event, and everything and everyone apparently involved in it, from beginning to end) and trying to focus in on what seems most important (Emerson et al. 1995). Novice participant observers have described the initial stages of this process as full of 'the angst of not knowing what to write down, what ought to be written, what's the most important part of a conversation, an observation, an event... (and) the feelings of drowning in "data" and not knowing where to start' (Bennett in Bennett and Shurmer-Smith 2001: 255). So, more 'comprehensive notes' are the kinds written towards the beginning of period of participant observation, where it can be important to get a broad sense of the 'scenes, characters... roles... patterns and regularities, rhythms and routines, dominant discourses and ways of seeing' in/of a particular setting (Cloke et al. 2004: 198). These temporal and spatial regularities can, indeed, help to structure field notes (e.g. you could describe journeys through the spaces of your 'field', and sequences of events in/between different places: Emerson et al. 1995). Having to write these kinds of notes can force researchers to attend to mundane happenings which they might otherwise bypass, to question their preconceptions of what is important for people living and working in a particular setting, and to note and question when, where and why everyday time–space rhythms and routines get disrupted (Wolfinger 2002: 91–92). Given what we wrote in chapter two, readers might imagine that researchers would get to a point of *theoretical saturation* in these notes, when they found themselves writing the same things over and over again. Once this point has been reached, they might imagine that more 'targeted notes' would be written as the relative importance of events could then be better appreciated. But, perhaps unsurprisingly, this two-stage model of note-taking is more ideal than likely. Writing comprehensive notes – i.e. about everything everywhere – is an exhausting and impossible task. Thus, the targeted note-taking of some activities in preference to others inevitably takes place from the start of a period of participant observation. This means that researchers often 'jump the gun' with some issues, miss out others that later turn out to be important and, therefore, end up working back and forth between comprehensive-style and targeted note-taking throughout their research process.

Given the difficulties in undertaking and noting participant observation work, it is often the case that a considerable amount of field noting gets devoted to 'self-reflections'. Indeed, as Cloke et al. (2004: 197) argue, for 'many researchers, this self-reflective, soul-searching, worry-writing may comprise the majority of their fieldnotes'. The reasons for this are that, first, participant observation involves researchers plonking themselves into unfamiliar situations, and often staying for long periods of time. As Pam Shurmer-Smith has written, 'Ethnographic research should transform the researcher and it certainly is not for people who are unwilling to take risks with their selves' (in Bennett and Shurmer-Smith 2001: 260). Taking such risks can make researchers more self-conscious and anxious than usual because new professional and personal identities are coming into being, often with difficulty, and often with the help of this self-reflective writing (for the self in field notes and for the self and others in correspondence with close friends, partners and/or family). Second, participant observation research can often be an intensely lonely, boring and/or frustrating process. Many researchers try to cope with this through over-copious note-taking which, itself, can become an obstacle to, or displacement activity for, doing fieldwork (Magolda 2000).

It is extremely important to point out here that ethnographic note-taking can take a considerable amount of time. One estimate is that each hour of participant observation requires two hours of note-taking (Burgess 1986) and that notes from six months of fieldwork can amount to tens, or hundreds, of thousands of words. Therefore, field-note writing should not be something you imagine you'll do in your 'spare time' (Crang 1994). Rather, writing times and places should be factored into the organisation of all of the other work you plan to do 'in the field'. Here, it is important to be able to note things down when they are fresh in your mind because, even eight hours later, your recollections may have blurred. This means that time and space must be put aside not only after, but *during*, periods of participant observation to *quickly* jot things down that can be elaborated upon later. This kind of behaviour can, however, have effects on your roles and relationships in 'the field'. If your writing function is known by community members, it is likely to become a distinctive part of your identity because you are observing, writing things down and forming opinions about 'them' (Jackson 1995; Miles and Crush 1993). Joan Cassell (1988), for instance, found that the surgeons she worked with were perturbed to see her continually taking out a notebook and pen to jot down what they were saying and doing. So, she has written:

> Eventually, I put [it] away... and carried 3″ x 5″ cards in the pocket of my white coat or operating room scrub suit; I took as few notes as possible, scribbling a few words every once in a while on the white cards, using them as mnemonics for each night's session at the word processor (1988: 96).

For similar reasons, many researchers make sudden and frequent trips to the toilet to write these quick notes in private – symptomatic of the so-called 'ethnographer's bladder'. But it can be the case that even those 'sessions at the word processor' may have to be concealed. Take Elspeth Robson's account of her 'secret' note-taking in Nigeria:

> I had my own notebook computer and portable printer as research tools. In a situation where even university professors were dependent on unreliable sec-retaries, ancient typewriters, and poor stationary supplies I felt it politic not to flaunt my high-tech equipment (1994: 38).

It is not, therefore surprising that many ethnographers end up becoming twitchy about these notes. According to the anthropologists interviewed by Jean Jackson (1995: 51), while these notes somehow pre-served their experiences of being there doing that research, they could also be the source of personal and professional embarrassment because 'some of them look pretty lame... stupid or puerile' and, if made public, would allow 'people... [to] see you in a state of intellectual undress'. This is one of the reasons why a lot of field-note writing is hidden from other people's views. It's also why Ian has had little trouble coming to terms with the fact that the writing in his field notebook is so illegible, sometimes even to him. He didn't want anybody else to be able to read it, except for the times he copied bits out neatly in letters to his supervisor.

Finally, we have to say that in whatever ways a research community accepts and involves the researcher in their lives, if they have been told more or less what she/he is 'up to', this is unlikely to be forgotten even when the researcher thinks that she/he has successfully 'blended in'. Michael Keith (1992), for instance, found himself in the following situation:

> Having at [one] time spent several nights with [one] pair of [police] officers we had got to know each other 'reasonably well' (an oxymoronic phrase?). We had got on well, finding some issues of common interest, though my usual reserve topic of conversation, football, was of no interest on this occasion. This had not stopped us going out drinking together outside work hours. Apart from the football, the routine facets of male bonding in a gendered research methodology were readily present.
>
> However, getting onto politics was a big mistake. Some interests might have been shared, but politics clearly were not and in the early hours of the morning silence followed a disagreement that was capped with the comment: 'So what are you going to do once you have finished with us then? Write up your horror stories about the brutality of the police in London in a book then or just put them in stories in one of those left wing newspapers?' (1992: 554–55)

This begins to raise issues of the politics and ethics of participant observation notes. So, we have to ask, is it possible and/or desirable to try to inject a sense of fairness into the ways in which we represent other people and their lives? Under what circumstances might research participants deserve a right to reply? We would draw your attention to three examples of how this has been treated. First, Graham Rowles' (1978a) ethnography of an ageing community in a North American city contains one chapter written by one of his informants about his relationship with Rowles the researcher. Second, Paul Willis' (1977) ethnography of working-class 'lads' in a UK secondary school setting contains an appendix comprising a transcript of the conversation that Willis had with them after they had read a draft of his book. And, third, Katherine Borland's (1991) efforts to involve her research participants in shaping her accounts of their lives led her to have difficulties with one (her grandmother) who strongly objected to being characterised as 'proto-feminist' in an early draft. After a series of exchanges and redraftings, both researcher and researched settled on a mutually acceptable text (see also Duneier 2001). These kinds of approaches may be 'ethical' because they give relatively poor and powerless people who are usually the subjects of academic research a long-denied chance to have a voice in the ways in which they are portrayed. However, what if the people in your research community are more powerful and more used to controlling representations of their lives and actions (see Bradshaw 2001; Cook et al. 1998)? We would not imagine, for instance, that Paul Routledge (2002) would have offered the organisations he worked against a right of reply to, or an opportunity to settle on a mutually agreeable version of, his work! What these and all of the other issues discussed in this section show, therefore, is that there can be no simple and unproblematic 'collection of data' in the field. To give that impression (at least in writing that's supposed to have a discussion of 'methodology') would be misleading, to say the least. As we have tried to emphasise throughout this book, research on social relations is made out of social relations, and these are as much created as they are found through the research process.

5 Interviewing

Is it really 'enough simply to buy a tape recorder, invest in a suit and tie or a smart dress, write some letters, prepare a semistructured questionnaire and seek out some research subjects'? (Cochrane 1998: 2123).

Along with participant observation, interviewing has been a primary means through which ethnographic researchers have attempted to get to grips with the contexts and contents of different people's everyday social, cultural, political and economic lives. As a means of gleaning information from conversations within and between various research communities, interviews can range from the highly structured (akin to questionnaire survey in which the researcher asks predetermined questions in a specific order), through the semi-structured (where the researcher and participant(s) set some broad parameters to a discussion), to the relatively unstructured (akin to a friendly conversation with no predetermined focus). These approaches have, in turn, been allied to various types of research project involving, at one extreme, the generation of numerical 'data' from one-off visits to tens, hundreds or thousands of people which are then *statistically* analysed and, at the other, the recorded conversations between a researcher and the handful of her/his research participants which unfold over a number of visits which are then transcribed and *discursively* analysed. Not surprisingly, the literature discussing interview techniques has been torn between treating interviews as ways in which the 'detached scientific observer' can *'collect'* relatively 'unbiased data' from her/his interview 'subjects', or as ways in which the researcher and researched together *construct* intersubjective understandings.

Like all of the other approaches discussed in this book, interviewing can by no means be treated as a separate method because all social research involves learning through conversation. So, like participant observation, 'interviewing' can be thought of as a formal *and* an informal research method. It is therefore worth reading about it even if you don't plan to formally do it. As we have already begun to show, apparently 'separate' methods can end up blurring into one another in research practice.

In Ian's experience, for instance, the interviews on which his MA dissertation were based were sometimes like participant observation with a tape recorder switched on (see Rowles 1978a, b), and those for his PhD research included questions which arose through his participant observation work (see Murphy 1999). This is only the tip of our blurred methodologies. We have also both been involved in interviews with individuals that have ended up being group interviews (see chapter 6) because other people were (unexpectedly) present and joined in with the conversation. And other interviews we have conducted also became exercises in filmic interpretation (see chapter 7) because they involved looking at interviewees' photograph collections and asking about who was in certain pictures, why they had been taken and so on (Becker Ohrn 1975; Collier and Collier 1986). It is worth pointing our that these combinations are almost bound to happen if an interview is arranged in the right time and place, when and where these events, people and things are close by and easily referred to.

As far as interviewing is concerned, the key questions asked by novice researchers usually concern the nuts and bolts of arranging and conducting them. For example:

- How on earth do you approach (almost) complete strangers and persuade them to talk to you about their thoughts, feelings and actions?
- How do you decide how many interviews you would like to arrange with the same person and how do you fill these up?
- Once such meetings have been arranged, what sort of questions should you ask so that you can get at the information and stories you are interested in without embarrassing or offending your interviewees, or yourself, in the process?
- And, in asking such questions, how do you decide what is and is not any of your business?

These questions have to be thought through each time you approach potential research participants for 'initial interviews', i.e. those approaches:

- you might make to various 'gatekeepers',
- you expect or want to be just one-off meetings with particular people and/or
- you hope will become the first in a series of interviews with the same person over a period of time.

All such encounters require some care in setting up and seeing through. As with participant observation and group work, this is a matter of making compromises between what it takes to gain access to, and to maintain contact with, potential research participants and what it takes to continue addressing your research concerns. Most researchers are wary of saying or doing something that would make them (or other researchers) *persona non grata* for subsequent interviews with the same or other people in the communities under study. But, they also want to find ways of asking questions which they believe are important to their projects, but which may prove difficult, awkward or embarrassing to their interviewees. Thus, the issues relating to research roles and relationships discussed in the previous section are also relevant here. Do you want to be, and/or get, treated as collaborator, nuisance, threat or oddball by your interviewees? How easy is it to bridge any apparent cultural differences between yourself and your interviewees (see Herod 1999)? And what do you do about those half-felt and difficult-to-articulate power relations that appear to be permeating these encounters (Bennett 2000)?

MAKING ARRANGEMENTS

When setting up initial interviews, many researchers feel most comfortable going through a reasonably formal, businesslike procedure which goes along the following lines. When a good contact is suggested from whatever source, get her/his postal address, phone number and email address. Then write a letter (because this should be more difficult to ignore than an email) including:

- details about yourself (e.g. as a PhD student), your institutional affiliation and what your research is about,
- who and/or what suggested that she/he be contacted as someone who has important knowledge about this subject,
- the fact that you would therefore like to talk with her/him at a mutually convenient time and place,
- that you would like to record the conversation,
- that everything said would be treated, if necessary, in the strictest confidence,
- that all efforts would be made in the final text to mask her/his identity and
- that you will telephone shortly after she/he receives the letter to arrange a possible appointment.

Then, in the couple of days after sending the letter, or longer if these are overseas posts:

- telephone the person,
- remind her/him of your letter,

- ask if she/he would mind talking with you and
- try to arrange a meeting at a mutually convenient time and place.

Once this is set, telephone her/him again a day or two before the meeting to confirm that she/he will be able to attend. On the day of the meeting, try to dress in such a way that will allow you to close some of the distance that may exist between yourself and your interviewee, and turn up early. Then, in the few days after the interview, write and thank the person for her/his time and remind her/him of any names, addresses, data, references and so on which she/he may have promised to supply you with during the interview, and perhaps suggest that a follow-up interview might take place some time in the future (Fetterman 1989; Thomas R 1993). Most researchers find an hour to be sufficient for a single interview. This is usually long enough for some rapport to be established and to enable the discussion of a range of issues, and short enough to be 'user friendly' for most interviewees.[1] At some point in this process, perhaps after the person has agreed to meet you, the ideal duration of your intended meeting needs to be raised. With Ian's meetings with fruit executives, for example, he felt that they would not feel inconvenienced if he asked for half and hour of their time. When these meetings took place, however, they invariably went on longer, often because of the homework that Ian had done beforehand (see later) that gave his interviewees the impression that he was knowledgeable as well as curious and was not, therefore, wasting their time. Equally if it is clear the interviewee has a tight schedule, do not jeopardise a good contact by outstaying your welcome and make sure you prioritise issues you most need to cover.

As part of this protocol, careful consideration should be paid to when and where these interviews take place. Sin (2003: 306) has argued that 'Writings on the theory and practice of interviewing have largely neglected the specifics of settings and activities.' So, as we argued in chapter 1, it is important to understand how various facets of people's identities are very much immersed in/between the different spaces and places of their lives. So, in Ian's initial interviews with three of the four people who took part in his blindness research, the fact that these took place in their homes became important to the outcome of his research because the home provided a form of reference and reminder for both interviewer and interviewee alike. As stories were elicited about each person's day-to-day life in that place, illustration and corroboration could easily be made through reference to objects near at hand. Moreover, arranging an interview in such a meaningful place for an interviewee can provide a basis for asking questions which do not always have to rely on what she/he says, such as 'Why have you arranged this room in this way?', or 'Have you kept photographs of your family?'

When arranging meetings in such a manner, then, the selection of an appropriate time and a place must be considered at an early stage. If you have a preference, it is a good idea to state this in your introductory letter. However, particularly if you suspect that your potential interviewee might have a problem with this, always suggest an alternative and/or negotiable time and place to meet. Whatever the case, it is important to bear in mind that the ability to arrange meetings with appropriate people in appropriate places can have an important bearing on the outcome of your research. As Andrew Herod has argued, for instance, any amount of reading that a male researcher may have done in order to focus in on a particular research topic may be wasted because:

> many women understandably are often reluctant to invite unknown men into their homes [so t]his can pose problems for male interviewers conducting research into, for instance, the economic geography of industrial homework since the overwhelming majority of homeworkers are female (1993: 309).

Similarly, in Ian's case, the importance he attached to interviewing legally blind people in their homes meant that although he gained valuable insights from his male participants, he had (a largely unexpected) difficulty in involving women in his study. His first, female participant initially agreed to take part but later withdrew saying that she was very busy, that she gave her husband priority in her free time and that if Ian was to visit her house he was in danger of being attacked by her Doberman. And a second female participant would only be interviewed on the university campus or at home over the phone. Therefore, although he was aware that there were important differences between the experiences of legally blind women and men (Asch and Sacks 1983), he was not able to explore these in any great detail. Thus his understandings were very much of male blindnesses, albeit differentiated by age, class, levels of visual impairment, biography and so on. Again, as we have argued throughout this book, such compromises will inevitably get made between what may be significant and what is feasible as a research project takes shape.

Having so far talked only about interviewing people in their homes, it is important to acknowledge that this is by no means the only place where an interview can or should take place. Not only is it highly possible that your research project will not have a domestic focus, but you (as well as your research participants) may also feel nervous or vulnerable in the presence of a stranger in such a private space. For instance, just as many women are not keen to invite strange men into their homes, many female researchers are reluctant to interview strange men alone in their homes.[2] There may also be issues to consider about privacy for respondents interviewed in households where the presence of other household members may mean that one partner's view may dominate the other's. Equally, children may not wish to discuss some things in front of their parents (or vice versa). Thus, separate interviews could reveal domestic tensions, differences of opinion and address things kept private from the other household members (Valentine 1999). A compromise for researcher and researched alike may therefore be to arrange interviews in a more public space which the latter's life also flows through, such as a place of work or leisure. Interviewing people in these locations, first, may enable interviewer and interviewee to feel more at ease in each other's company. Second, such an arrangement also acknowledges that most people's lives are stretched between a number of different locales that can serve as references and reminders of different aspects of their identities. In many circumstances, interviewing people outside the most obvious places may be a good thing. For instance, a worker may be more willing to talk outside rather than inside their employer's building or, in an organisation's office, people may foreground the role of that organisation and downplay other issues you want to talk about. These settings and their apparent effects on the conversation that takes place there may well be worth noting, participant observation-style, in a research diary or could, perhaps, be spoken into the recorder after the interview. Mike chose the latter option that, again, shows how different methods – and forms of data construction – can effectively blur into one another in research practice (see Elwood and Martin 2000).

Having said all of this, it is also worth pointing out that interviews need not involve sitting and talking in a *fixed* setting. Given both the nature of certain research questions and the practicalities of arranging meetings, there can be considerable room/necessity for invention here. Interviewing 'on the move' can enable people to situate and recount complex and fluid events and memories which might otherwise appear to have taken place in more or less separate places, communities and lives (Anderson 2004; Hitchings and Jones 2004; Kusenbach 2003). As part of his blindness research, for instance, Ian arranged to accompany three of his research participants on a walk along one of their well-trodden paths through the city in which they lived in order to ask them, in this kind of 'travelling situ', how they negotiated these spaces. Similarly, Graham Rowles (1980) interviewed an elderly woman in his car as they drove along the roads of her childhood.[3] Rowles' story was at the back of Ian's mind when, after discussing how distracting conversations can be in cubicles in busy open plan offices, he and one supermarket fruit buyer agreed that the best place for their research interviews to take place was in the latter's car travelling to and from work and/or to or from his various visits to stores, depots and suppliers. However, when this failed to materialise and their meetings took place in his office cubicle and were interrupted by phone-calls, unexpected visits from various reps and so on, this was far from disastrous as they provided first hand-access to the very stuff of his daily business and were, again, an unplanned blending of participant observation and interviewing. Finally, with the increasing use of email, chat rooms and message boards, 'interviews' can now be conducted not only with people who might otherwise be difficult to find and expensive to meet in person but also, perhaps, with people who might be more forthcoming (or dishonest) if they didn't (initially) have to meet a researcher face to face (see Gatson and Zweerink 2004). In his research on fruit and jam production in New England, for instance, Lucius Hallett (2001) found that his interviewees welcomed the opportunities that email interviews afforded them. With interviews conducted over a period of days or weeks, his interviewees were able to take their time to answer his questions carefully and in detail and he felt that this considerably enriched the quality of his data.

PREPARING A CHECKLIST[4]

Once an initial or one-off interview has been arranged, it is common for this to be conducted in a fairly formal manner in which, before it commences, the researcher has done a certain amount of background reading, has set out a clear agenda of issues to be covered in the meeting and then uses this as a *checklist* which she/he then tries to steer the conversation through in whatever order. This, it has been argued, serves to ensure that the researcher always meets her/his objectives in each interview, that there is some equivalence across them and that interviewees are, to a certain extent, allowed to raise their own issues for discussion and potential inclusion in the researcher's continually modified checklist of questions (Burgess 1992a; Ostrander 1993). In particular, this approach has been put forward as vital, first, to 'corporate interviewing' where researchers are often spared only perhaps an hour with busy executives to find out about their company's decision-making processes and/or changing involvements in different markets (McDowell 1992b, 1998; Schoenberger 1991, 1992),[5] and, second, to life history work where a broad knowledge of events and institutional structures which are likely to have had an impact on a person's life-course can also be an advantage (Lawson 2000; Miles and Crush 1993).

So, how, where and why can/should background research be done for such interviews? Erica Schoenberger (1991) has suggested, for instance, that in corporate interviews it is necessary to know about a firm's business strategies, relationships to its markets, production technologies and methods, labour relations and the behaviour of its competitors. In the early stages of such a project, it is not unusual for researchers to have picked up on an issue that has gained prominence in the financial press and/or national or local media that is directly related to their academic interests. Most such issues can be further traced through back-copies of newspapers and magazines that are held in many local authority and/or specialist libraries, and/or from annual reports, market surveys, various kinds of corporate literature and articles in the trade press. Annual reports are usually available for reference in local business libraries and/or can be obtained directly from the companies concerned, who may be able to send backdated as well as current versions if requested. Market surveys, corporate literature and trade press articles, though, can take some time to hunt down as insider knowledge is often needed to find out what is relevant and available. When starting out on his 'corporate' fruit research, for example, Ian found that extremely useful places to visit were the City Business Library in London, and the Jamaica Promotions Corporation (JAMPRO) Library in Kingston. By simply going up to their counters and stating what business he was interested in, he was directed to sections containing various market surveys, feasibility studies and statistically laden reports covering levels of fruit production, consumption, imports and exports over a considerable period of time.[6] Furthermore, after initial interviews with UK fruit executives in which he specifically asked what trade journals they referred to, he was directed to publications and, with one company, to a file of articles on exotics which they had kept and allowed him to photocopy on the machine in their office. Moreover, with these same people, he also asked if they had gained their information about these fruits from any particular books, asked to see them and copied down their titles in order to order them through the interlibrary loan system. And, finally, with the help of both his friends and the executives who he met, he also collected and read the exotic fruit recipe leaflets that each supermarket chain had produced for distribution in their stores. So, again, rather than being a discrete stage of his research to be conducted *before* doing his interviews, much of this reading was, and could only have been, done as the interviews progressed over a period of eighteen months or so.

According to Schoenberger (1991), such background preparation is essential for making the most of the limited time which executives are often willing to set aside to talk with researchers. She has argued that through being able to ask knowledgeable questions and to have an understanding of a trade's technical terms, researchers can:

- reassure their interviewees that they understand the issues thereby encouraging more open and detailed answers,
- invite responses as they would usually be worded in the office, rather than asking questions in such a way that interviewees have to translate their responses to approximate the researcher's language and frame of reference,

- be more able to spot and question any issues which the interviewee may either have glossed over or contradicted her/himself over,
- ask specific questions about their competitors' strategies in similar markets to encourage a detailed comparative approach,[7]
- build the kind of detailed problem-solving questions into the interview which executives may be accustomed to dealing with in their daily work and
- use this knowledge as a form of power to redress, at least partially, the usual imbalance which favours an interviewee who either is, or likes to appear, 'accustomed to being in control and exerting power over others' (1991: 182; see also Cochrane 1998; McDowell 1992a).

In other scenarios, though, particularly if interviewees may be more used to being in the position of supplicant when faced with a typical middle-class, university-educated, researcher, this background knowledge needs to be used in a much more subtle and hesitant manner in order to redress power imbalances which may well be skewed in the other direction.

ASKING THE 'RIGHT' QUESTIONS

As with the other approaches discussed in this book, in interviewing the initial research encounter can be an anxious time for both interviewer and interviewee alike as each has to carefully weigh up the other before, during and after the conversation. The questions to consider here are as follows:

- What is each prepared to reveal about themselves through their questions, responses and responses to responses?
- How are these questions and responses likely to be received?
- And what is motivating the other to take part in the research?

Whoever you interview and whatever preparations you have made before doing so, if it is your first time, you are likely to find your initial interviews rather stressful. So, instead of encouraging a conversation through which the expected issues on your checklist (as well as the unexpected ones which emerge in the course of the conversation) can be easily threaded, you may end up nervously going through your list almost as if it were a questionnaire. To prevent this happening, it is a good idea to prepare to ease into the conversation by remembering to:

- exchange pleasantries,
- introduce yourself,
- ask where you should sit,
- confirm the topic of the interview,
- explain why you want to talk to her/him about this issue,

- go through a standard ethics protocol (if you have decided to use one, see McCracken 1988b: 69),
- ask if she/he minds you recording the interview (you can emphasise here that note-taking is slow and distracting and that taping conversations minimises the risk of misunderstanding and misquotation, but do not be surprised if she/he is reluctant to be recorded) and
- remind yourself to do these things by writing them down as instructions at the top of your list.

To begin the interview proper, it is a good idea to ask a *prepared* first question as a means to combat any nerves that you may have at the start of the meeting. Then it is usually better to introduce your checklisted issues more 'naturally' into the flow of the conversation. And outlining key phrases, questions, 'facts' and so on can help to flesh out some of your questions and responses, and may encourage your interviewee to take you more seriously.

These early stages of an initial or one-off interview should not be arranged solely to combat *your* nerves, however, as those of the interviewee must also be taken into consideration. As Grant McCracken has written:

> Whatever is actually said in the opening few minutes of the interview, it must be demonstrated that the interviewer is a benign, accepting, curious (but not inquisitive) individual who is prepared and eager to listen to virtually any testimony with interest. Understandably, [interviewees] are not keen to reveal very much about themselves, or to take a chance with an idea, if there is any risk of an unsympathetic response. [Interviewees] must be assured that the potential loss-of-face that can occur in any conversation…is not a grave danger in the present one. …It is better here to appear slightly dim and too agreeable than to give any sign of a critical or sardonic attitude (1988b: 38).

Your questions will usually need to be of a non-threatening kind, then, and the standard approach is to begin by employing so-called 'grand-tour' questions (Spradley 1979). These ask the interviewee to outline the general characteristics of the place and/or social networks which she/he is involved in and which you intend to research. Through asking simple 'what?', 'who?', 'where?' and 'how?' questions about what you're interested in, the basic grounds for your conversation can be established. Given that the main aim of interviewing in ethnographic research is to allow people to reveal their own versions of events in their own words, it is important to get people to recall what they know of events and activities. Then you can ask follow-up questions in such a way as to encourage and to critically question these recollections in order to get at the 'whys' and 'wherefores'. The aim with a lot of interviewing is to get at the 'long stories' of events, decisions and so on, and to bypass the short, snappy, conventional, rehearsed versions that may normally suffice when interviewees are asked about these things (Katz 2001).

When your interviewees are answering your questions, then, it is worth remembering that the stories they are telling are often *not* simply made up on the spur of the moment. Many will have been told, retold and refined on a number of occasions, in a number of places and with a number of different audiences. Therefore, instead of taking them at face value, it is important to ask questions that encourage their elaboration. So, for instance, to establish how your interviewee has become, and is, involved in the situation under discussion, you can ask questions which refer to what she/he has stated such as 'What do you mean when you say...?', 'Why did you do that and not something else?' or 'How did you get involved with those people?' and so on. In order to ask critical questions without appearing to criticise, you can ask questions such as 'Is it true that...?', 'What do you think about the critical coverage that this issue has recently had in the news – did you see the piece about...?', or 'How does this relate to what you said earlier about...?', and so on. In order to get beyond blanket statements about a subject, always ask for examples and, where possible, for examples of when/where this affected the person directly. Finally, if you think that you have asked an inappropriate question, simply apologise and/or say '...or is that none of my business?'

On top of these different forms of (hopefully) non-threatening question, you will also need to develop skills of keeping a conversation going. Many of these will be familiar to you from holding everyday conversations. But, you might have to be considerably more attentive than usual, and this involves a great deal of concentration, focus and effort (Dunn 2000). You will, for example, need to pay close attention throughout an interview to what the person is saying in order to ask follow-up questions. You may therefore need to listen, talk and continually scribble on your checklist:

- crossing off issues discussed in sufficient detail,
- highlighting issues your interviewee skated over but to which you would like to return for elaboration and
- jotting down one-word reminders of issues that aren't on your list but which also seem to need further elaboration.

Even when your interviewee has offered the elaborate explanations you are looking for, it is worth checking that you understand them. So, as part of the conversation, it is often worth trying to put what they have said into your own words and asking them if your understanding is right. If they say yes, then you can more confidently cross that issue off your list. Initial or one-off interviewing therefore involves a constant moving back and forth between conducting a conversation and scribbling on a list. Researchers have to keep sufficiently close to it so that they interview members of their research communities about the same things. But they also have to allow unexpected issues to come into these conversations and to be elaborated upon where relevant. In practice, this means that researchers not only have to concentrate hard on trying to understand what interviewees are telling them, and on trying to get them to elaborate where their accounts are a bit thin or difficult to understand, but they also have to deal with interviewees' wanderings and pauses. When interviewees start to go off at an apparent tangent to your checklist-related questions, you might feel the urge to nip them off in the bud. This may not be a good idea, though, because this is how unexpected perspectives and insights often become part of the conversation. Conversely, when your interviewee appears to have finished an account, or pauses in the middle of one, you may consciously have to stop yourself jumping in with new questions. It is often a good idea to allow such pauses to go on a little longer because your interviewee may simply be thinking about the question and/or about her/his first attempt to answer it before having another go (Burgess 1992a; Stewart and Shamdasani 1990). At the same time, though, such silences may simply be the result of your daft, ridiculously wordy, inappropriate or otherwise awkward question. So, if and when you consider a silence to have become overly long and you cannot think of a question relating to what your interviewee has already said, this may be the time to introduce a new theme from your list. Finally, there is the issue of the awkward and/or critical issues you might like to raise, the ones that you imagine may make your interviewee uncomfortable. Here, the advice is that, unless she/he broaches them earlier on in the conversation, leave them to the end. This is because, either she/he may feel that you have understood enough about the rest of her/his work or life to more sympathetically see those issues from her/his perspectives or, if she/he does take your questions about them as 'unsympathetic' and becomes less co-operative, at least the 'cooperative' dialogue will already be recorded.

Interviewing can, as we have said, be both intense and mentally exhausting. This intensity, often combined with nervousness, can lead to what we would call a 'panic-interview'. This is where a researcher tries to make sure that they cover everything on their checklist before the allocated time for the interview is over. And it's not surprising that this happens. The balance between being relaxed enough to let a conversation meander in its own directions at its own pace and being professional enough to make sure that you find out everything you wanted to know is difficult to establish. This may, after all, be the only meeting your interviewee agreed to, and you know that it has a fixed time limit. With experience, you might get a better sense of how many points a checklist should contain for, say, an hour-long interview. By accident and then design, however, we have found that there is another option. Ian made a point of preparing checklists which covered all of the issues he wanted to bring up with his fruit trade interviewees, regardless of whether it might be possible to cover them in the single 'thirty-minute' meetings arranged. Not surprisingly, as their allotted times were stretched and eventually had to come to a close, there were still a number of issues that he had not had time to ask them about. So, he asked if it would be possible to arrange another meeting to discuss them. This was invariably possible and he was, therefore, able to undertake relaxed but thorough interviews. The ability to listen carefully to the recording of the first meeting, and to flesh out his checklist accordingly, was an additional bonus. But what if your time slot isn't limited to thirty minutes or an hour? What if an interview can go on for much longer? How long can you concentrate for? This is where mental exhaustion can become a problem. Under 'normal' conversational circumstances, you might get excited or bored by what someone has said, or let your mind drift on to other topics (nice shoes!), the practicalities of getting where you have to go next, that kind of thing. To be frank, this can happen in research interviews too, particularly after a certain amount of time has elapsed. Sometimes, there may simply be too much to take in, your concentration gets stretched to its limits and you find yourself switching off and checking that the recorder is still on, so you can listen carefully to what the person is saying at a later date. At this point, the interview should probably have ended already, and should certainly end soon. We have found that hour-long meetings, and no more than two of them in a day, are plenty to deal with. Ian's plan to do eight diary interviews a day for two weeks solid was, therefore, a sound idea in principle, but a terrible idea in practice (see page 80).

Next, it is important to appreciate that many interviews which end up being quoted in academic texts have not been fully transcribed (see later), complete with questions as well as answers, mumblings, misunderstandings, repetitions, embarrassing ideas, directive questions, warts and all. This is often because of the prohibitive amount of time it takes to do this, but also because researchers often fall foul of wanting to tidy up what is already regarded by many as an overly 'subjective' and messy approach to constructing knowledge. The resulting neatness and order of such representations in the published literature can therefore serve as another means of making the first-time interviewer feel somewhat inadequate as she/he bumbles through her/his checklist. But, while it may be extremely counterproductive to ask a barrage of *directive* questions (i.e. those which imply that you have already made up your mind about the answer, e.g. 'how badly do you exploit your workers?' or 'you must really enjoy living here, right?'), blurting out one or two of these accidentally in the course of an interview is not a disaster and may even lead to interesting responses. Other accidental or deliberate floutings of the rules can also lead to interesting insights. Any researcher new to a particular cultural scene may, for instance, not have the right cultural competence or cash to dress appropriately (McDowell 1993). Robert Thomas (1993) has talked about the conservative, navy blue suit that he routinely wore to interview corporate executives for his research. When he visited one company, this became an issue because, he has written:

> I found that I stood out like a sore thumb by comparison to the pullover sweaters and slacks which were the norm. ...several times...people chided me for dressing too much like a consultant – a comment that was tantamount to an insult (1993: 93).

Rather than this being a problem of 'biasing' his information ('away from what?' should always be the question), his accidental flouting of a dress code drew attention to its importance in that environment and therefore opened up a potential line of inquiry that might otherwise have been missed. Other researchers, instead of trying to minimise this kind of reaction, have played it up deliberately seeking to do the 'wrong' thing in the 'wrong' place among the 'wrong' people in order to disrupt taken-for-granted rules and assumptions, and to try to understand their intricacies and influences (Fusco 1994; Garfinkel 1984; Giddens 1984, 1991). Whatever the case, though, it is vital to understand that, as mentioned already with respect to participant observation, there is no ultimately 'neutral' scientific identity that the researcher can attain. Rather, to a large extent an interview style appropriate to your topic and to the people you talk with will emerge over a period of time through self-critical experience (Rowles 1978b).

SERIAL INTERVIEWS

Perhaps the main disadvantage of initial or one-off meetings is that they can only scratch the surface of an interviewee's life. This is not only because of the limited time available for rapport to be established between interviewer and interviewee and for stories to be told, but also because the place where the interview occurs will be one of many in which that person's identity has been immersed throughout her/his life. The limits of these encounters therefore need to be taken into account when considering what you want to get out of any interviewing you plan to do. Serial interviews (aka. 'interview series') are an alternative worth considering. These comprise a number of interviews with the same people over a period of time. Their intention is usually to:

- try to get at the taken-for-granted aspects of a person's life history and everyday life through researcher getting to know her/him very well (e.g. to understand unspoken bodily and imaginative adaptations to the aging process: see Rowles 1978a,b) and/or

- follow people's lives as they relate to the topic under consideration (e.g. the experience of a backpacking holiday during and after the event: see Desforges 2001).

The main difference between a series of multiple interviews with the same people and a range of single interviews with many more is that after repeated visits with the same person over a period of time, the relatively formal interviewing style discussed above can dissolve. Here, interactions can become much more like informal conversations. Both parties can feel more able both to reveal their often undecided, ambiguous and contradictory feelings about the matter in hand and to challenge each other about them in an atmosphere of mutual respect and trust. Serial interviewing is therefore much more about understanding people's lives in *depth* than in breadth. Both this 'atmosphere', and the depth of understanding that it can provide, are the most valuable aspects of this approach.

Most interview series are proposed to potential interviewees at initial meetings, which can be very much like one-off interviews. Here, you would need to go through the same protocol for arranging a one-off interview and, at that meeting, you would need to outline your research interests and find out if your interviewees would be willing and able to take part in the series. Thus, you will need to explain to them:

- why this research will require a *series* of meetings,
- how long you would like this series to go on for,
- how much time it will be necessary to set aside for this,
- what each session will hopefully involve and
- that your interviewee has the right to withdraw from the series at any time without any need for justification.

As Jacquie Burgess et al. (1988a,b) have argued about the convening of serial focus groups (see chapter 6), this approach provides a clear structure for researcher and researched alike in which clear parameters to the research encounter are established. What this means is that, first, the researcher can plan in such a way as to produce a more or less set amount of ethnographic data with which to work. And, second, this should enable an easier withdrawal from the research relationship for both parties.[8] Even after setting out the purposes and organisation of a series at an initial meeting, though, it must be realised that the commitment which is required by both parties, not to mention any anxieties that interviewees may have about promising to attend repeated meetings with such an inquisitive stranger, may mean that getting people to agree to take part is more difficult than gaining consent for that first meeting. Again, the advice here is to try to be sensitive to the reasons why some will turn you down while others will not, and to try to gain some appreciation of the positionality, partiality and intersubjectivity of the knowledge which may be gained from those who *do* agree to get involved.

One of the most important considerations when setting up serial interviews is that, depending on the time and resources available to you, the numbers of participants and meetings involved have to be set off against one another. To get an impression of what these numbers can turn out like, take the following examples:

- Ian's research with legally blind people involved four participants, one interviewed on three occasions as part of a pilot study and a further three interviewed on ten occasions for the main body of the research,
- Graham Rowles' (1978a) research with elderly people involved five participants who were interviewed on an unspecified number of occasions,
- Steve Pile's (1991) research with dairy farmers involved six participants who were each interviewed on twelve occasions and
- Anne Oakley's (1981) research with impending mothers involved fifty-five participants who were each interviewed on four occasions.[9]

When weighing up how many participants you want to recruit and on how many occasions you want to meet with them, what is usually sacrificed in terms of a breadth of experiences is more than made up for in terms of a depth in understanding. This 'depth' potential of serial interviewing has two major attractions for researchers. First, it can allow, at least in part, a dismantling of the hierarchy of knowledge between researcher and researched which is often at work in questionnaires and other 'initial' interviews where both parties by no means participate in the construction of knowledge on an equal footing (Herod 1993; Oakley 1981). And, second, serial interviews can also enable research encounters in which there is sufficient time, space and trust to plumb the depths of people's taken-for-granted biographies and life worlds in order to study actions and feelings which, if they ever reached the light of day in an initial interview, might be difficult for either party to enunciate or to reflect upon in any sustained and detailed fashion (Rowles 1978b).

To elaborate on this first 'attraction', a number of writers have criticised traditional accounts of interview methods because they advise researchers to develop a rapport with their interviewees which is sufficient to elicit responses whist keeping the 'necessary social distance [which] ensure[s] that she/he does not "bias" the outcome of the interview by interjecting personal opinions or values' (Herod 1993: 309). Researchers interested in conducting both 'one-off' and serial interviews, then, have been instructed to employ a number of tactics that can minimise this 'bias' ('away from what?' should *always* be the question). One important question here has been how to react to the very common and awkward situation where interviewees ask questions back. Anne Oakley has pointed out how such advice has often gone along the following lines:

> 'Never provide the interviewee with any formal indication of the interviewer's beliefs and values. If the informant poses a question...parry it.' 'When asked what you mean and think, tell them you are here to learn, not to pass any judgement, that the situation is very complex.' [Or,] 'If he [sic.] (the interviewer) should be asked for his views, he should laugh off the request with the remark that his job at the moment is to get opinions, not to have them' (1981: 35).

Oakley was writing as a feminist researcher involved in often intense and highly revealing interview series that followed a number of women through the latter stages of their first full pregnancies and into the few months after they gave birth. To her, this advice seemed morally reprehensible because it meant that her interviewees' questions 'such...as "Which hole does the baby come out of?", "Does an epidural ever paralyse women?" and "Why is it dangerous to leave a small baby alone in the house?" should be fobbed off' (1981: 48). So, at least in these kinds of situations, where interviewers may be in a more powerful position in society *vis à vis* their interviewees, she has argued that they should not only *admit* that they contribute their own ideas and feelings into such conversations, but that they are *morally obliged* to do so as part of a necessary dismantling of the traditionally hierarchical and exploitative research encounter (see also Berger 2001). For these reasons, then, researchers who are (or become) concerned with such ethical/moral issues in their work may feel more at ease interviewing relatively few people on a number of different occasions in order to try to develop such relationships.

The second attraction of serial interviews is that they can allow time for researcher and researched alike to begin to think about, explore and make sense of the contradictory, inconsistent and taken-for-granted natures of their everyday lives. In response to questions during a one-off interview, most interviewees will not come up with fully formed concepts, stories and arguments (unless, that is, they are highly rehearsed: a situation which can be the case if she/he is accustomed to talking about her/himself). They are unlikely to make perfect sense. The stories people tell about their lives are usually pieced together, put forward, argued with, transformed and retold in different versions in the multiple contexts of their biographies and everyday lives. Serial interviews can therefore allow you the time and the opportunity to flesh out these concepts, stories and arguments, to help to make them fuller and more understandable. These kinds of explanations are not usually forthcoming after repeated questioning on the same issue in one meeting. Rather, they emerge through dialogue with the researcher that develops over a number of visits. Stories that don't quite hang together because of apparent contradictions or problems in remembering specific details, are often revisited at subsequent meetings after both interviewer and interviewee have had a chance to reflect on them. Moreover, serial interviewing can allow sufficient knowledge and trust to be developed for both parties to speculate on, and to discuss, what the more deeply rooted/routed reasons for thoughts and actions might be.

This potential move from rehearsed and/or quick explanations to thoughtful introspections and sensitive and intersubjective explorations of interviewees' taken-for-granted lives is one of the great strengths of serial interviews. As has been amply illustrated in the ethnographic work of geographers such as Graham Rowles (1978a,b, 1980, 1983) and David Seamon (1979; Seamon and Nordin 1980), as well as in more theoretical work such as that of Anthony Giddens (1984, 1991) and Nigel Thrift (1983, 1995, 2000b, 2004), a great deal of what researchers might like to know about other people's lives is unlikely to be noticed by them or easily put into words. Like walking, driving or swimming, so much is learned through more or less instruction and/or osmosis, with more or less thought and/or practice, to eventually become something that we can just 'do' (Highmore 2004). In his ethnographic studies of 'ageing in place', Rowles (1983) described different types of 'insideness' that his elderly research participants seemed to have derived from living in the same place for many years. There was, for example, the elaborate bodily knowledge of the physical dimensions of known spaces which allowed them to be negotiated with minimal thought and effort, and the ways in which place and personal identity were intimately entwined through everyday emotions evoked, for example, by widows or widowers living alone in the house previously inhabited by them and their significant others. Ordinarily, he found, these were issues that they rarely, if ever, stopped to think about or discuss in detail.

It can often require a considerable amount of introspection and speculation to begin to put these kinds of 'knowledges' into words. But this is a process that can be encouraged through appropriately designed interview series (often involving participant observation's combination of talking to and *doing things with* research participants). Both as a non-threatening start to a series and as a way of getting an impression of how a person's everyday life may be rooted in and routed through various places, times and social relations, it is often a good idea to begin with a general discussion of her/his 'life story'. As a first interview, this does not have to involve as much homework or to be as analytical as, perhaps, a corporate interview. Rather, researchers can simply encourage their interviewees to talk about themselves both in terms of the more 'factual' aspects of their biographies – where and when they were born, what their parents/guardians did for a living, where and when they went to school, what they did subsequently and where and so on – as well as their reasons for, and feelings about, them both at the time and perhaps more recently. At this stage, the interviewer's task can be little more than that of:

- asking very general questions in order to get the person talking, e.g. 'Where were you born?', etc.,
- occasionally putting aspects of these stories told back to her/him as questions, e.g. 'Do you mean that, after you did that, you moved straight away to live there, or did you wait a while?',
- asking follow-up questions when certain details are mentioned but not explained, e.g. 'Who was she?', 'How did you meet her?' or 'What is this (unknown object/term)?',
- inviting speculations about paths not taken, e.g. 'Why did you choose to do that rather than something else?' and
- asking to see any objects, texts and/or photographs (see chapter 7) which would help to illustrate these stories.

In taking this approach, then, researchers should not only be able to 'break the ice' and to get to know interviewees in a relatively non-threatening way, but should also be able to encourage the telling of a wealth of stories which both parties will be able to refer back to in subsequent discussions when trying to make sense of other issues.

This attempt to make sense of how the person has lived her/his life into/through the issue(s) you are interested in can be followed up in sub-sequent meetings either in the longer term by concentrating on how they make sense of events and issues through their biographies and life-histories (Geiger 1986; Gluck and Patai 1991; Holland 1991; Miles and Crush 1993; Personal Narratives Group 1989; Portelli 1981), or in the shorter term through meetings which focus on her/his present everyday life. Here, to encourage detailed discussions of activities that will often be very much taken for granted, a number of other tactics can be employed to bring these out. Many researchers, for instance, have asked their participants to keep activity diaries over a period of time in which they are asked to record various mundane details of their everyday lives. Here, narrative accounts based on these diaries may provide fascinating insights, but asking people to keep them is a lot to ask and many are reluctant to do so because they may feel intimidated by the task or simply don't have the time. To make things a little easier, the researcher can promise to provide her/his participant with a set of tables on which to record certain details about their activities each day. In both his blindness and fruit research, for instance, Ian asked his participants to fill out tables with the following headings:

Time of day	What did you do?	Where did you do it?	How did you get there?	Who was with you?

Once filled in, in practice, often by researched and researcher together,[10] these kinds of tables can then be used as a *basis for discussions* of the taken-for-granted aspects of a person's everyday life.[11] And these discussions can be based on quite simple questions which:

- ask for *explanations* of the whens, whats, wheres, hows and with whoms of the person's day,
- encourage comparisons with other diary days and/or with other, perhaps more distant, times and places in her/his life and
- ask about her/his feelings about such routines and relations.

Thus, for example, as this kind of interview series progresses from an initial biographical discussion through, say, a week of daily activity diary meetings,[12] a *relatively* non-threatening, non-hierarchical research relationship between researcher and researched can develop. Here, both parties may well come to feel comfortable making debatable arguments and connections between aspects of various accounts made and can try to *understand* any apparent inconsistencies and contradictions in them rather than seeking to distinguish between the 'true' and the 'misguided'. Interviewees can often develop sufficient confidence to express themselves without fear of criticism, to disagree with the researcher's interpretations as they surface in discussion and, if the researcher allows it (which they should), to play a much greater role in shaping the course of the research. Finally, towards the end of a series, time can also be set aside to reflect on the development of their research relationship and its (un)resolved misunderstandings (Delph-Janiurek 2001).

As far as the structure of such a series is concerned, it is important to tailor this to achieve some kind of balance between the general issues in which you are interested and the more idiosyncratic biographical and everyday contexts in which these will have been embedded and interpreted throughout the courses of your participants' lives. Moreover, as mentioned earlier, such considerations should also include making decisions over where and when these interviews should take place in order more easily to approach certain aspects of a person's identity/life. Another advantage of serial over one-off interviews, then, is that the former can be scheduled to take place *in and between* a variety of relevant times/places. Ian's blindness research, for example, was intended to understand legally blind people's apparently different abilities and willingness to travel independently (i.e. using a white cane or dog guide). Thus, his formal methodology included interview series with one set of people who were asked to keep one set of diaries. Nine out of the ten meetings were in his interviewees' homes, but the tenth was 'on the move'. These meetings were organised as follows:

- *Meeting 1:* here, each person was asked to talk about both his[13] general biography and how his history of blindness fitted within it.
- *Meeting 2:* here, each was asked to describe the extent of his day-to-day travels with reference to a map of the city in which he was living.
- *Meetings 3–9:* here, each was asked to keep an 'activity diary' for a one-week period which outlined where, when, why, how and with whom he travelled. Here meetings were held on every day of the diary week.
- *Meeting 10:* here, Ian accompanied each person on a familiar journey through the city asking general questions and, at various points, stopping to ask where they were and how he knew.

In contrast, in his fruit research, the concern was to study the relationships between the everyday lives of farm workers, farm management and their suppliers and markets. Thus, a different and more complex series of diaries with a variety of people was seen as appropriate. This involved asking:

- six farm workers, their supervisor, and the farm manager to keep 'activity diaries' like the one above for two weeks,
- these workers also to keep 'money diaries' recording their incomings and outgoings (both in cash and in kind) over the same period,
- the farm's supervisor to keep a 'labour allocation diary' recording who was at work, on what days, and between what times (records which were already being kept for payroll purposes) as well as what he had told each person to do each day, where they had done it, and why he had given them those jobs at those times,
- the manager to keep a 'communication diary' in which he was to record his day-to-day contacts with suppliers, shippers and European and North American markets and
- one UK supermarket fruit buyer to keep a 'papaya diary' during the six months that Ian was working on this fruit farm, in which he would keep a record of any decisions he had to make concerning the sourcing and marketing of the fruit being grown there.

Except for this last case, Ian's aim was to then use all of these diaries as the basis for daily tape-recorded 'interviews' about the matters noted in them. As you might imagine, such a massive set of diaries detailing the everyday connections between these different people's lives could not be fully constructed. Ian found that it was difficult to conduct research between groups of people who wanted/needed to keep their activities somewhat hidden from others, who were somewhat suspicious of his motives and who were (or claimed to be) too busy to fill out the forms and/or to find time to discuss them with him every day. And the 'papaya diary' was never written because that UK supermarket had a huge executive clearout while Ian was in Jamaica (see chapter 4, footnote 1).

There are lessons to learn here, then. First, depending on the circumstances and the aims of your research project, a whole variety of diaries can be used to structure, at least partially, an interview series. But, second, getting a 'complete set' in a more complex series can often be a problem not only for the kinds of reasons mentioned above but also because, for instance, you and/or your interviewee(s) may be unable to attend part of a series due to illness or problems of transportation, or you may find that it is difficult to coordinate daily interviews of unpredictable durations with more than a handful of participants at a time. Ian, for instance, found that the eight diary interviews he had planned per day on the fruit farm were extremely draining and difficult to manage. Two, or perhaps three at a stretch, would have been plenty. We could put our usual positive spin on this, and say that such messiness and unpredictability is perhaps to be expected and, indeed, may provide many interesting insights into the issue(s) being studied. But it has to be said that it may also be stressful and counterproductive, and result from over-ambitious and unrealistic research planning. We (now) therefore think that anyone telling themselves that 'This is what my research demands and I'm going to do it, even if it kills me' should really fight that feeling.

CONSTRUCTING INFORMATION

In all kind of interviews, if you are more interested in the ways in which your research participants have told their stories and described their feelings than in the nuts and bolts of the who, where, what and how (many) are described in these accounts, it is vitally important that a recorder is used to pick these up. The reasons for this are numerous:

- constantly scribbling down phrases and other notes can be very distracting both for the interviewer and interviewee and may disrupt what could otherwise proceed as a fairly normal conversation,
- the researcher's memory, even straight after such a conversation, is unlikely to be good enough to remember the intricacies not only of what was said but of how it was said, and comparing notes taken afterwards with actual transcripts often reveal important differences between what the researcher remembers being said and what was actually said (particularly if you are not interviewing someone in your and/or their first language) and
- many researchers find it mentally exhausting to listen very closely to everything that their interviewees say, so it can often be a relief to

know that if your attention wavers you can still listen to the recordings at a later date.

As we have argued already, ethnographic data is *constructed* intersubjectively and, in interviews, this simply means out of conversations between researchers and people comprising their research communities. If these are casual and/or 'off the record' conversations, the researcher will need to note anything relevant or interesting about them in their research diary. If they are recorded, then s/he will need to transcribe them. Either way, it is important to point out that *these notes and transcriptions are the data that's constructed*. The dialogue itself is not data until it gets put to paper.

Whether or not you record an interview, it's always a good idea to make extensive notes as soon as possible after the meeting. Sometimes these are necessary when, listening to the recording soon after the interview (always do this!), you realise that you either had an equipment failure and there's nothing to transcribe, or where loud background noises mean that there will be important gaps to fill in the eventual transcript. It's also the case that, if the transcript is to be 'the *best possible record* of the interview' (Dunn 2000: 73 emphasis in original), anything relevant that the tape recorder could not pick up needs to be written down as soon as possible. As Kevin Dunn has put it:

> If an informant points to a wall map and says: 'I used to live there', or if they say: 'The river was the colour of that cushion,' then the tape recording will be largely meaningless without some written record afterwards (2000: 72).

And, of course there's more to non-verbal communication than pointing:

- What about the location where the interview took place? Was it out in the open where others could see you talking, or were you taken (or did you ask to go) to a more secluded place to talk?
- What about the ways in which both you and your interviewee spoke? Did you and/or they seem bored, excited, agitated, sarcastic, whatever at certain points in the conversation?
- What about body language? Did either or both of you hunch over and talk quietly at certain points so others nearby could not hear or, at others, lean back to make a loud comment that everyone else could hear?

All of these issues, and plenty more besides, contribute to the intersubjective understandings that develop in interviews, so they need to be noted (and reattached to the transcripts of recorded interviews – see chapter 8). Participant observation and interviewing should, therefore, not be considered as separate methods. A good interviewer has to know how to write a good research diary.

Constructing interview data is not as straightforward a process as you might hope it to be. For a start, it is often the case that the ideal social environment to encourage an interview may not be the same as the ideal acoustic environment to record one. To illustrate this, we return to Ian's work on the farm. On his first visit, he tape recorded the guided tour he was given by Jim, the farm manager. This was effectively an interview 'on the hoof' and was a fabulous 'show and tell' introduction to papaya farming. But, after transcription, the 'data' that ended up on the page looked like this:[14]

> *[In the packing house] You know, with [another farm] and myself shipping some, sometimes we're sending fifteen tons. {pause} You know. . . . Yeah. . . . three and a half thousand boxes a day. And that fills, pretty much fills the cargo allocations on the Jumbo.* Really? Yeah. *It's a lot of {indecipherable – loudening tractor noises}.* OK. {tractor noise} So what's the relationship between [the other farm] and [yours] now? *Well, basically, just because I used to work there before..* Yeah . . . *and, we sell to the same markets, you know {we climb into his six-wheeled buggy and he starts it up – very loud} that's how I {indecipherable buggy noise} ..* when I talked to them, there was a lot of {sounds like 'vibrations'} between.. *Yeah, yeah.* Um. . . . *Yeah, yeah.* It's not, actually, you're sort of straight competitors. *No no, not at all. {long loud buggy ride where only words such as "I", "yeah", "um" and "and" can be heard, if anything – 1 minute 50 seconds. Stops and talks in patois with* **a woman}** *.. better, one a you go go tell, uh, se, wan boy dem..* **{Someone} gan aready sir.** *Who you sen message wid?* **Wid me daata.** *Oh. {pause and wind noise – in the fields now.} To get the hermaphrodite, we have to plant a, what we do, we plant three trees..* Right . . . *and, after about eight, nine, weeks when they're about three foot tall. . . . Yeah. . . . You see like at the end of those rows – they start flowering. And by the shape flaw-, flower, that's how we determine the sex.* OK. Are they grown {Walkie-talkie fuzz interrupts}, are they grown from seed..? {indecipherable but short walkie-talkie message received} ..or are they grown from seedlings? *From seeds.* From seeds, OK.

Finding it difficult to transcribe interview recordings because of intrusive background noise was by no means an unusual experience for Ian. In his PhD and MA research, he came away with recordings interrupted by, among others:

- a rumbling air-conditioning unit in a dorm room,
- the engine and radio noise in a moving car,
- a rainstorm and an overhead fan in a kitchen,
- constantly tweeting birds,
- a dog panting and repeatedly dropping a stone at his feet on a ceramic tiled floor and
- the wind allowed to blow through farm buildings to keep workers (and their interviewer) cool.

Background noises like this are inevitably going to end up on most recordings. They are, after all, part of the 'atmosphere'. But, many aren't the kinds of noises that you would even notice in an interview, or they're not the kinds that you might imagine would later cause you trouble. And there will always be other noises that you may know will cause you trouble when transcribing, but you record the interview nonetheless.

So, how can researchers attempt to come away from their interviews in assorted locations with recordings that both retain some of that atmosphere but also maximise the sound quality of those conversations?

- first, this can simply be a matter of learning how to best use the equipment you have, for example, in terms of microphone placement (e.g. sheltering it from the wind with your body),
- second, if you know for example that an air-conditioning unit may make an interview difficult to transcribe, you could ask your interviewee to turn it off,
- third, if these noises are too distracting, you might have to decide whether to continue with an interesting but acoustically suspect interview or to suggest that it could be continued and/or repeated at another time and/or place and
- fourth, you could buy or borrow higher quality recording equipment.[15] Adjustable recording levels (to enable louder and quieter speakers to be heard in the same detail) and stereo recording capabilities (to help pick out voices in three-dimensional space) can make a noticeable difference.

None of this advice, however, will address *all* of your potential recording/transcribing problems. Transcription is always hard on the ears. Whatever equipment you have used and however carefully you have arranged it, you are likely to later find yourself sitting at a computer:

- straining to listen to parts of a conversation (even in 'stereophonic space'),
- turning up the volume to hear them better and
- then getting deafened by a noise you may not have remembered being there.

This may not always be from a pneumatic drill or a juggernaut. Mike's experience of transcribing focus group discussions (see later) recorded using a flat-bed microphone set on a table around which everyone sat is a case in point. As he found to his shock, these microphones use tables as sounding-boards, so 'every cup of tea put down (got)... magnified to ear-shattering proportions' (Crang 2001: 218).

Whatever the problems with background noise in an interview, it is important to point out that in order for there to be something to transcribe at all, you must have taken your tape recorder (or other device) out of your bag and made sure it is switched on and is working. To help ensure this, it is essential:

- *before each interview*, to check that your batteries are fully charged, including any that power a detachable microphone, that you have spares (Ian once had to nip out to a shop in mid-interview because he had forgotten to pack them) and that you have extra blank tapes (or equivalents) should the interview go on longer than expected,
- *at the start of each interview*, to get your recorder out (Ian always tried to carry his recorder into meetings in his hand, after forgetting to take it out of his bag once), and ask permission to use it, put it in the right place to record both what you and your interviewee say, check that the microphone is fully plugged in to the correct hole (we have both suffered from this one), that the 'record' button is on while the pause button is off, that the tape/disk/memory card has been placed inside the recorder the right way round and that the spools are actually turning, the record symbols are one etc., before the interview formally starts,
- *as the interview progresses*, every now and again to check that your recorder is still recording (by subtly glancing at hopefully still-turning spools, lights representing recording levels, etc..) and
- *immediately after the meeting*, to listen to the tape/file to see if recording has been successful (if you discover that it has not, you will be able to write much more detailed notes of what you can remember being said straight away).

This may sound like rather patronising advice, but *all* researchers who have used tape and other recorders have their own embarrassing stories to tell about 'lost discussions' when they somehow managed to bungle this 'simple' operation. Nerves can make even the most experienced researcher ham-fisted and forgetful at the start of an interview.

Recording an interview requires a great deal of concentration, then. But transcribing one requires much much more. Like note-taking in participant observation, it should 'preferably [be done] on the same day as the interview' (Dunn 2000: 73), but not in your 'spare time'. If you have reasonable typing skills, you should expect the *full* transcription of a one-hour interview to take between six and ten hours (focus group discussions can take longer). Transcription is, by and large, a tedious task that has to be chipped away at. Mike, for example, has never been able to manage more than a two-hour session at the keyboard before needing to lie down (see Crang 2001). So, when you are planning your research, it's important to realise that a one-hour tape-recorded interview, with related participant observation style notes, and proper transcription (in two-hour sessions with breaks) will involve between one-and-a-half to two days of hard work. If you're doing your research 'by the book', then, how many interviews should you plan to do in a week, a month, a year? Making time for an interview *and* its transcription is essential. Nothing is more disheartening than putting transcription off until a later 'stage' of your research and then finding yourself sitting in front of a computer with dozens of tapes to slowly grind your way through over the coming weeks and months. There is, it seems, no easy option as far as the labour of transcription is concerned. But, there are ways to minimise the stress.

Some researchers deal with this situation by doing partial transcriptions, i.e. typing up only the quotations they think they might use in their write-ups. This 'quote-hopping' should be resisted, however, if you wish to avoid accusations that (your) qualitative research is not methodologically rigorous. We have not even begun to discuss formal analysis yet. There, we hope, you will see what we mean. Another reason for resisting the urge to quote-hop is that interview data is *intersubjective*, it's always *made out of dialogue*. Take, for example, the following extract from one of Ian's MA interviews with JD that were mentioned earlier. Just before the conversation quoted below took place, Ian had been surprised to learn that JD had been diagnosed as 'legally blind' after decades of living with his visual impairment and not worrying about it 'one bit'. Nevertheless, JD's official diagnosis meant that he was sent to 'Hines', a residential 'rehabilitation' centre near Chicago, to 'relearn' how to do everyday tasks as a blind person. So, Ian asked him:

Ian: What did you think of Hines, then?
J.D.: I liked it. . . .
Ian: So, do you think you learned a lot of useful things there?
J.D.: Yeah, see I already did all the cookin' anyway before I went to Hines (laughs)!
Ian: You what?
J.D.: I said I did all the cookin' here.
Ian: You did it anyway?
J.D.: Yeah.
Ian: OK, so..
J.D.: ..I do all the cleanin', laundry and everything myself.
Ian: So, are you saying that they were teaching you things that you could do anyway?
J.D.: Uh huh [yes] (laughs)!
Ian: OK, so I guess it was easy then.
J.D: Yes, it was easy for me, cause I was. (laughs)!
(Cook 1992: 99).[16]

Ian's understanding of JD's 'rehabilitation' was therefore constructed here, without doubt, in dialogue. In the process, Ian put words into JD's mouth: something that should be frowned upon, in principle at least. Here, the researcher was by no means 'collecting data' from the researched! No interviewer does, even when faced with the interviewee's most rehearsed stories. Transcription must therefore involve typing up, 'warts and all'; not only what interviewees say but also what interviewers say (however much the latter may be tempted to tidy up their language appear more coherent and professional). Most importantly, though, transcribing things this way, and being able to quote such dialogue in finished works, shows the evidence upon which empirical arguments are based.

Transcription can be made quicker and easier if you have access to a transcription machine. If you have used a cassette recorder, you put the headphones on and your tape in. Then you can play, rewind and fast forward it using the foot pedal, which leaves both your hands free to type. Each time you take your foot off the play pedal, it rewinds the tape a little so you can double-check what you've typed and make sure everything is joined up properly. It's also *designed* for transcription, so its motors and heads are less likely to burn out than those on your domestic tape player or walkman. Transcription is often part of secretarial work, so check with people you know who might be able to lend you one. Also, please note that some machines are made for standard cassette tapes and others are made for micro-cassettes tapes. You can also get similar transcription machines that play from multi-media memory cards, and packages of software and foot pedals that allow you to configure your computer to play audio files back with a pedal linked through either a USB or a firewire port. So check the compatibility of your recorder and any transcription equipment and software you might borrow. If you are lucky enough to have someone else to do your transcribing – check the compatibility of *your* interview equipment with *their* transcription machinery. You can also get annotation software that allows you to label and work directly with segments of audio, without transcribing them, on your computer (for instance using the freeware Transcriber[17]). Recent developments in voice-recognition software offer an alternative technique for transcription. Here, after teaching it to recognise your voice, you should be able to sit in front of your computer with your headphones on, and repeat the conversation to which you're listening into a microphone. Your words should then appear on the screen for correction, notation, annotation, whatever – though our experience suggests that this in the end does not save much time.

Finally, if you have the money, the right contacts, and/or are desperate for help to get through that pile of tapes, you may consider getting someone else to do some or all of this for you. While Mike has done all his own transcription, Ian was able to apply for extra funds to pay others to do at least some of the transcription for his MA and PhD research. While this option may save considerable time and therefore be no bad thing, two criticisms of this 'second hand' approach are that the researcher:

- gives their transcriber access to conversations that they promised would be anonymised and treated in the strictest confidence and
- misses out on the detailed internalisation of what was said that laborious typing can bring (Crang 2001; Dunn 2000).

However, if you want someone else to do some or all of your transcription, there are a couple of relatively simple procedures you could follow to tackle these issues:

- insist that your transcriber agrees to maintain the confidentiality of these conversations, and the anonymity of those taking part (you could also inform your interviewees that you may want to do this) and
- as soon as you get a new transcript back from your transcriber, read it through while listening to the tape and correct any mis-hearings, add annotations and revise notations (this can be time-consuming, as there may be a lot to do here).

Following the latter route, Ian felt that his interview materials had been handled sensitively by professional transcribers used to making such assurances. Indeed, one insisted on annotating the transcripts every time she heard him including snippets of information he had promised to keep confidential in other interviews she had transcribed. Moreover, by the time he had produced the second draft of each transcription, and then repeatedly read through each transcript in the process of formal analysis, he could not imagine knowing their contents any better.

To finish, we want to point out that whoever types up your transcripts, it's essential for their labour to involve standard filing and notation work. What exactly should be typed onto transcripts so that you can file them and make it easy to later go back to the original tapes to check things? And what about the shorthand notation that could indicate the pauses, interruptions, guessed words, other elements of your participant observation notes etc. that a *full* transcript should contain? As far as filing is concerned, it is important to make sure that:

- *each tape* (or equivalent) has written on it an identification number, the name(s) of the individuals or groups interviewed (singly or in groups), the interview number (if it is part of a series), the interviewer (if interviews are done by different people), the translator (where appropriate), the date, time and place of interview, and its duration,
- *the transcript of each tape* (or equivalent) starts with the same information, in order to allow a return to the original recording later on, where necessary, when formal analysis is being undertaken and
- at regular points in the transcript, the number on the tape counter (or equivalent) is included so that, if and when a recording is later revisited, the exact point in the conversation being checked can more easily be found.

And, as far as notation is concerned, a number of writers have provided detailed lists that can be used to add detail to a transcript (see Dunn

2000: 74; Fine 1984; Silverman 1993: 115–43). Many researchers appear to find this sort of thing useful, and it is worth checking these lists out. But Mike often found many of them 'to be overkill for the level of detail I needed' (Crang 2001: 219). So, if you are going to use (parts of) these lists and/or make up your own notation, make sure that you write them down, use them consistently and explain to your reader what they mean.

6 Focus Groups

It is certainly true that the same people might say different things in individual interviews than they would in a group discussion, but that does not mean that one set of statements is distorted and the other is not (Morgan 2001, in Hollander 2004: 632).

Earlier, we argued that ethnographers should be reluctant to consider the participants in their work as pure and isolated sources of data. Rather, it is important to understand how people work out their thoughts and feelings about certain matters in *social contexts*, i.e. on the basis of interactions with other people whom they learn from, react to, misunderstand, resist and so on (cf. Schrager 1983). Focus groups are hence a key means through which researchers can study these kinds of processes by setting up a situation in which groups of people meet to discuss their experiences and thoughts about specific topics with the researcher and with each other. Such groups can provide forums for the expression and discussion of the plurality of sometimes contradictory or competing views that individuals and groups hold and can become 'spaces of resistance' in which participants can 'explore and enable...[their] social agency and collective knowledge production' (Hyams 2004: 106). However, it is important to realise that there are many places where many people are not used to, or encouraged to contribute ideas to, 'debate' or to challenge ideas from those in authority (Kong 1998). Focus group research can therefore be immensely valuable, but is fraught with difficulties.

Focus group work has two genealogies in contemporary social science. The first is from psychotherapy (cf Bondi 1999; Burgess 1999; Oliver 2003). Here, in a series of meetings, group members explore their own personalities and identities, provide support for each other, and share experiences in order to help them come to terms with themselves. This is similar to the philosophy underlying such well-known programmes as Alcoholics Anonymous. The second is market research. Here, groups of paid consumers are assembled for a one-off session to discuss their reactions to new products or advertising materials and these reactions are then used to inform and to develop larger-scale surveys (Axelrod 1979;

Stewart and Shamdasani 1990; Templeton 1987). Focus group work is valuable to ethnographic and related qualitative research because it illustrates and explores the intersubjective dynamics of thought, speech and understanding. Within geography, it has received enormous stimulus through the work of Jacquie Burgess (1992b; with Harrison and Maiteny 1991: with Limb and Harrison 1988a, 1988b, with Bedford 2001). In 1996, the geography journal *Area* ran a special issue outlining how geographers had used focus groups in a wide variety of research: for example, on consumption (Holbrook and Jackson 1996), environmental damage (Zeigler, Brunn et al. 1996) and self-understandings of negotiating urban space while pregnant (Longhurst 1996). Elsewhere, and more recently, they have been used as a means to examine lesbian use of space (Taylor 2004) and to encourage immigrant workers to share experiences and discuss issues of employment (Pratt 2001).

SETTING UP

Before embarking on focus group work, it is important to ask what kind of, and how many, groups you might need to set up. So, first of all, will your project demand repeat sessions to enable rapport to develop between members and/or to cover multiple topics? If so, this will reduce the number of groups that can be coped with. And, second, will already-existing groups be useful? Most authors recommend avoiding this since, on the one hand, with members already knowing each other, there may be personal dynamics at work that the researcher will not be aware of which can have a significant bearing on what is said and who says it (Krueger 1988). On the other hand, though, finding an existing group does ease recruitment and can have advantages, particularly when groups are used not only to the topics discussed but also to the way that the group interacts (Stewart and Shamdasani 1990). In Mike's research with local history groups, he decided to tap into an already existing network in Bristol. Initially, he attempted to recruit in such a way as to mix up the members from different groups in order to avoid the above problems. Sitting in on meetings with a couple of existing groups, though, soon showed him that each involved fluid discussions of very local people and events. Yet, when these existing groups were disturbed by new members or inquiring researchers, for instance, their normally fluid banter (with its constant interjections, reminders of shared memories and so on) broke down and was replaced by longer stories which were listened to politely. Therefore, he concluded that creating new groups up would not only drastically alter the type of history spoken about, but also *how* it was spoken about.

There can be many advantages when working with already existing groups in the sense that they may give an impression about how issues are 'normally' talked about in familiar groups. However, if you wish to undertake research into issues which people may *not* normally talk about with others that they know, new groups can provide them with a forum for the kinds of conversations that they might have with strangers, like taxi drivers or people you meet on trains. As Kitzinger has argued, such groups 'can sometimes actively facilitate the discussion of otherwise "taboo" topics because the less inhibited members of the group "break the ice" for shyer participants or one person's revelation of "discrediting" information encourages others to disclose' (in Hollander 2004: 608). If all goes well, she continues, 'Not only do co-participants help each other to overcome embarrassment but they can also provide mutual support in expressing feelings which are common to their group but which they might consider deviant from mainstream culture (or the assumed culture of the researcher)' (Hollander 2004: 608). However, so much depends on the participants involved and the group dynamics that develop. Wellings et al. (2000), for example, point out that participants may just as likely find these groups inhibiting or intimidating.

Since any successful group will rely on interchange, banter and communication, it is vital that a relatively free exchange of ideas is promoted. However, there are a number of general problems inherent in group processes that may make this difficult. Most handbooks advocate a relatively homogeneous social group (Bellenger et al. 1979; Greenbaum 1988; Krueger and Casey 2000). Mike encountered problems with mixed gender groups because, while the men consistently spoke to a 'public' audience consisting of the group at large and the researcher in particular, the women often broke into one-on-one chats which were lost to the group as a whole, and were virtually impossible to record. At the same time, though, mixed groups can offer the chance to show up such gender relations, as they might not arise in single gender groups. Equally – depending on the topic – age, ethnic and other differences within a group can affect the openness of discussion (Morgan 1995). So, we would suggest that some heterogeneity is both inevitable and can add to the group process so long as members share relevant common experiences (Krueger 1988; Krueger and Casey 2000). Although theoretical sampling and time pressures may encourage the researcher to get together members from disparate or antagonistic backgrounds in a single group, many researchers have found that this hampers their inquiries (e.g. Swenson et al. 1992). Instead, we suggest that it may be better to convene a number of groups, each consisting of people with similar backgrounds, even if this may end up being more time-consuming.

The actual mechanics of approaching possible participants are much the same as suggested previously for interviews. And, as with other methods, it is necessary to bear in mind the practical effects of power relations in recruiting participants for group work. Busy professionals, for instance, will often not have the time to do repeat meetings and, even with one-off meetings, arranging a time which is convenient for all can be difficult (there can also be similar problems when convening other groups such as single mothers). Relatively disempowered groups, or those who have a practical interest in the success of the project, can often be easier to recruit for single or multiple sessions. It is also possible to use groups as an intervention in social processes, by bringing together people who experience similar situations but have not had a chance to share them. This can lead to rewarding sessions for participants who gain new ideas and perspectives, such as when Swenson et al. (1992) brought together 'community leaders' from rural Georgia who then discovered a wide range of previously unsuspected common interests that they were able to follow up afterwards (see also Hyams 2004). Therefore, groups can be used both where normal social processes are based on small groups as well as where they are noticeably absent. But, it has to be said, in both cases, that the researcher is constructing a discussion situation and must be aware that she/he is never simply a 'fly on the wall'.

When making decisions about how many groups to convene and whether to hold one-off meetings or a series, many of the same arguments apply as in interviews. In addition, it is useful to note that groups usually become more open as time wears on both in a single meeting and over a series of meetings. Here, then, it is important to consider how long it will take to cover the range of issues in which you are interested, and whether this will require single or multiple sessions. Either way, the suggested duration of a meeting varies, but Bellenger et al. (1979) recommend one and a half to two hours as reasonable. We would instead suggest that two hours is probably going to be very tiring for all concerned, unless it is perhaps broken up with some other activity like, for instance, a tea break or watching a TV programme to which you wish to get a response (e.g. Burgess et al. 1991). On the other hand, though, an hour is a little short unless you can guarantee a prompt start. Therefore, an hour and a half is probably about right. Always try to allow some slack time at the end, though, in case the discussion runs on. Normally a group is slow starting but then gets under way, and sometimes just won't stop. Mike had meetings that, although scheduled for an hour, varied from forty-five minutes (a bad day) to one and a half hours and, even after this, the issue had to be deferred to another time.

Next, you should consider how the size of each group might affect the range and depth of discussion. Most commentators suggest a group size of ten to twelve is large and that one of six to eight is small but lively. On the one hand, a large group may intimidate some people and restrict those who do speak in terms of how much time they have to say what they wish. On the other hand, a small group can mean a reduction in the number of experiences that can be drawn upon and may need continual support and encouragement to keep it going. In practice, Mike preferred smaller groups but also found that group size was difficult to control. With one oral history group, a normal attendance of twelve people rose to nineteen because word got out to people who attended only occasionally that something 'different' was happening. However, because the group became so large it fragmented into mini-groups, and he felt that the only practical option was to tolerate this and to work with one subgroup as best as possible. With a different group, inclement weather and car breakdowns reduced the numbers from seven to four and here the group found it difficult to build up any momentum in their discussions. Whatever size of group you decide on, we suggest over-recruitment by about 20%, which will allow a margin for non-attendance. Longhurst (1996) found that, for instance, one group dropped to only two people actually attending – which still allowed some useful material to be gleaned from a paired interview but was hardly the same as planned. With repeat groups, by providing a contract in which participants promise to attend and the researcher reciprocates by promising to provide summaries of meetings, researchers can be more confident about subsequent attendance (see Burgess et al. 1988a). Once again flexibility and adaptation are often the key words, and a sense that things can be salvaged from most circumstances.

One factor that can help to ensure attendance is offering money to participants. However, although market research companies can afford this, funds from university, department and research grant sources are less forthcoming. Paying informants raises a welter of further issues regarding the relative power of group members *vis-à-vis* the researcher, as well as who will accept money, the level of remuneration necessary and what impact this will have on the issues discussed – which may involve issues of ethical scrutiny about free consent (see chapter 3). But this issue doesn't arise if you haven't even got the money to pay participants their travel expenses, in which case it is essential to find a venue that is cheap and accessible for them while, at the same time, being quiet enough to hold a meeting which can be clearly recorded. In some areas, it may be necessary to give lifts to participants who are infirm or who are afraid of being assaulted or mugged (here, it may be possible to use a university or student union minibus). This was a regular problem for Mike in his group work, where community workers had to provide lifts for frightened members and all meetings had to finish before dark. The ideal arrangement here would have been to hold daytime meetings on a bus route in a low crime area, but beggars can rarely be choosers. However, in most places there are dozens of village halls, libraries and community centres that let out rooms cheaply, and some moderators even arrange meetings in the home of a group member. Together with the composition of the group, what is vital is that the setting helps members to feel able to talk about the matter in hand. This means thinking through the 'associational context' (Hollander 2004) of venues – whether they are associated with specific groups, types of interaction and power relations for respondents (Green and Hart 1999). A work venue may make respondents more inclined to follow roles and patterns of deference and dominance established in the work place, school settings might resonate differently with adults and children and so forth. Some people like to work in a setting that is homely – or indeed *is* a home – to put people at ease and/or to allow domestic topics to be broached. Others suggest that this relaxed set-up increases the pressure for consensus, and still others suggest that people feel better able to speak their minds in a more formal environment because they can feel confident in their anonymity (Krueger 1988; Templeton 1987). Finally, it is a good idea to arrange the facilities to provide cups of tea, coffee and/or other refreshments for group members. Again, tailor these to what the group might expect, and remember that everyone will be thirsty after an hour or so of talking.

GROUP DYNAMICS

Once set up, focus groups rely on the frank and fluent discussion of the topics in question and it is the job of one person, known as a moderator (who may or may not be the researcher), to facilitate a free exchange of ideas while keeping the group somehow 'on track' (Cameron 2001). One way of describing the ways in which ideas are put forward, shared, argued, and/or supported is in terms of the degree of liveliness or 'energy level' of such meetings, something which it is difficult to appreciate until you have gone through a meeting or two. Moderating can be a stressful yet exhilarating experience. Take the following quotation from one of Mike's group discussions:[1]

Jim: But who are we saving for? Tourists?
May: Well, who? Yes.
Jim: Children? The future.
Ruth: Well I'd like to think it was for our children yeah {grandchildren}.
Jim: Puts a different aspect on it.

This may look ordinary and uninteresting, yet what is important is that it was a group member (Jim) who asked the question – who are we saving [the past] for? – and thereby directed the conversation. In this kind of situation, comments made are usually reacted to and, as the discussion develops, group members often find that their memories are jolted or that their nerves become somehow touched by what the others have said. They may then butt in with support for a statement, an addition to it, or to disagree. So, as the group gets livelier, every statement that members make gets added to or interrupted for some reason or another and this is what we mean by a 'high energy' meeting. As David Morgan (1988) has outlined, in an ideal case:

> The group begins with relative uncertainty about the extent to which participants share a common set of perceptions on the discussion topic. As more members of the group present their experiences and perspectives on the topic, they typically find some common means for representing areas in which they both agree and disagree: they may ultimately come to some further realisations about the sources for their various levels of agreement and disagreement (1988: 27–28).

Therefore, one of the things a group session should most definitely *not* involve is the moderator going round the entire group asking each person the same question. Rather, she/he should try to get participants to react to what others are saying. Running a focus group, then, is usually a bit like riding on a roller coaster and hoping that, amid all the twists and turns and ups and downs, it doesn't go completely off the rails. Or, as Jane Templeton has described it, they 'are always something of a horse race, in the sense that you don't know what information you'll get out of them until you've gotten it' (1987: 11).

Given these sorts of dynamics, the researcher and/or moderator must be sensitive to the power relations which limit the scope of discussions and should encourage as many viewpoints as possible. A sensible start is to say at the beginning of the meeting that differing viewpoints are welcome, and that you are not looking for a final consensus. However, this is not always enough and other dynamics can still limit the discussion. One important example is so-called 'groupthink', where the group, or particularly a leading figure in the group, sets out an opinion early on which can become a mini-orthodoxy. Here other group members may be unwilling to disagree, and may essentially opt for the quiet life rather than face a possibly hostile reception to their views. This may be systemic on some issues, so Hollander's (2004) work on domestic violence found that although many people spoke about many things, later contacts revealed many participants also felt there was a lot they could not say in a mixed gender group where they might encounter people again. Even amongst a single sex male group, the men were less likely to admit fear of violence in such a public forum than in private. Alternatively, it might be that individual members rehearse stock arguments, particularly as a form of defence in disparate or hostile groups, rather than articulating and discussing how such ideas have been generated. It may also be the case that certain members try to dominate, particularly if they feel they are experts on the topic and they can rapidly become the fount of wisdom and no one else will risk appearing foolish by arguing with them. Finally, there can be friendship pairs who interact with in-jokes rather than engaging with the rest of the group. Most people suggest that these latter problems are most easily eliminated by screening potential participants in advance (Burgess et al. 1988a; Krueger 1988) and then separating friends, but this not possible with already-existing groups. What any prospective researcher has to appreciate, then, is that focus groups are subject to both 'problematic silences' and 'problematic speech' both in terms of moderating and making sense of them (Hollander 2004: 608; Hyams 2004).

Faced with these kinds of difficulties, the moderator can employ a number of tactics to try to aid the discussion. In the case of groupthink, she/he has the nerve-racking task of trying to force this apart, and will be concerned that an intervention in support of a different viewpoint might result in losing the cooperation of the entire group. In Mike's experience, one way around this has been to rephrase points using the third person ('some people would say that..' or 'didn't [so-and-so magazine] say something different..?' etc.) to broach issues and to hope that they will lead to renewed debate, while Skeggs et al. (2004) found their respondents talked through gay space in Manchester with reference to the TV series *Queer as Folk* (which was filmed there). A little preplanning can also ease such discussions. For instance, asking participants to write down what they think about certain matters before the discussion starts can encourage them to put together their ideas so that these may be more easily articulated later. The moderator would not then ask each person to read their answers out – this may cause humiliation or embarrassment and could lose the support of participants – but just thinking through and writing down their thoughts may help to give confidence to members who appear reluctant to speak. And, at the very least, they could be collected at the end of the meeting to get at the ideas and feelings of those who were not able to argue them out loud or to compare the initial written thoughts with what was later said (Greenbaum 1988; Templeton 1987).

Situations can also arise where one or more members of the group seem more reluctant to speak than are others. Sometimes, a less than full contribution can be a result of a lack of confidence, of participants feeling unable to get a word in edgeways and/or of their thoughts not being up to the speed of the conversation. But sometimes, they can result from participants being unhappy with what you are apparently trying to achieve through getting them together. Working with Latina girls, for example, Hyams (2004) interpreted numerous 'I don't know's' and changes in subject as their resistance to the idea that being given a voice would empower them. Whatever the reasons, the moderator can try specifically to include quieter members of the group by expressing an interest in their point of view. For instance, simply repeating the question or asking for a second opinion, using lines such as 'OK. [Turn to quieter member] Is that how you see it too?', can be effective. In contrast, when faced with a member who seems determined to dominate the conversation, it should be possible to get the support of the rest of the group who, you hope, would probably like to get a word in edgeways. Another tactic that can be used if the topic is very ordinary or very familiar is that of asking people to think about it in metaphoric terms that may help to de-familiarise it and to force questioning beyond routine terms (Branthwaite and Lunn 1985; Stewart and Shamdasani 1990). This may also help to get round awkwardness with some topics, or to bring abstract issues into a discussible format. We would, however, emphasise that none of these tactics is guaranteed to work. Occasionally they may backfire, both in terms of breaking up group discussion or, very occasionally, disrupting an entire meeting. As we have argued before, however, there is often much to learn from things apparently 'going wrong' like this. As Hollander (2004: 609) argues, maybe it is better to believe that 'conformity, groupthink, and social desirability pressures do not obscure the data. Rather, they are the data because they are important elements of everyday interaction.' Every moderator has problems with group dynamics, at some stage, and no 'bag of tricks' can be listed that offer readymade solutions.

Finally, we must emphasise that, in general, moderating gets easier with practice. Indeed, Mike found it better to have two people moderating, particularly with larger groups (cf. Burgess et al. 1988a; Krueger 1988). One moderator acts to keep the conversations moving while the other can try to pick out themes and keep the overall process on target. It may be possible to co-opt a community worker or another figure in the community into this sort of moderating role. Existing groups will normally have someone effectively running the group anyway. Although some texts would warn of 'bias' entering here (e.g. Krueger 1988), if you are studying group processes then the 'biases' of and towards a fellow moderator can – again – be very revealing. However, if dual moderation is not possible, solo moderation is eminently within the grasp of most of us, particularly when working with smaller groups.

MODERATOR ROLES

Given the inevitability of these group dynamics, it is important to regard meetings as interpersonal events where each member, including the moderator and/or researcher, constantly manages her/his self-presentation to the others. As with the other methods we have discussed, this colours what will and will not be said. Like interviewing, the first rule of moderating is to think through the meeting beforehand. Working from a topic guide is very helpful, whether it be a general one outlining issues to be covered in any order or a specific sequence or 'route' to steer the group through (Krueger 1988; Templeton 1987). A major consideration is also how prescriptive and detailed this topic guide should be. Most guides consist of six to twelve themes perhaps with some subpoints, and you may need all of them discussed or you may want to follow those in which the group is most interested on the day.

As with interviews, there is scope to move between directive and non-directive approaches. Therefore, the moderator(s) should decide how powerful a role they want/need to play, notably, in terms of deciding whether they want to hear the world views of participants rather than to simply find the reactions to the views of the researcher, and we would suggest that most ethnographies should incline to the less directive approaches (Stewart and Shamdasani 1990). To achieve this, a moderator can play the 'curious-but-uninformed' role on an issue to elicit information from members. Mike has found this to be particularly effective in getting round what members take for granted, since by being willing to appear ignorant and to get things wrong, more detailed explications can be prompted. It does mean you have to be willing to look a bit stupid, and you have to ensure you do not thus appear a fool who cannot be taken seriously – the aim is to appear naïve on the topic but attentive in running the group. The standard opening gambit is a 'grand tour' question such as 'How would you describe this area to a newcomer?', possibly a newcomer such as the researcher, and then move the question to another such as 'How do you feel about that?' (but not the direct 'Do you agree?'). As the description gets under way, she/he can cut in with 'I'm not sure I quite understood..?' so as to prompt a more detailed account. This kind of approach also positions the group members as experts, something which can increase their confidence in speaking. Yet, too much 'ignorance' on the part of the moderator can lead to members patronising or rejecting interventions. Without being insincere, it is helpful if this ignorance is a role and you do know (or wish to know) something about the issue – it is much easier to run a meeting on a topic that you have both a real interest in and questions about. Groups quickly catch on to a lack of interest or insincerity, while total ignorance means you cannot check or challenge what may be said.

Perhaps a robust discussion may need a more formal role for the moderator, who will be able to control the flow of conversation. This may vary with the size of the group and whether it is a repeated meeting or a one-off. This role-playing not only aids the running of a meeting but also helps the moderator to distance any conflict – and to avoid taking set-backs as personal. Less authoritative roles can lead to problems in running a meeting. Mike had some of his interventions brushed aside as elderly group members invoked the authority of experience over the 'whipper-snapper' in their midst, making asides like:

> Ray: As regards leisure nowadays, something I can remember as a boy and I expect all the *adults* can as well, was that they used to serve...[2]

Again this is not to say that these low-key moderating roles are some-how 'fly on the wall' because, by smiling and nodding, the moderator can still have a vast impact on what is said (Stewart and Shamdasani (1990) list several ways moderators can inadvertently alter discussion). By act-ing as a benevolently neutral arbiter of disputes, she/he can also come to be thought of as someone who is 'supposed to know', in the Freudian term (Lacan 1977), and who, returning to group therapy, can bring in issues of transference where participants can assume a variety of motives to the moderator and thus play out some of the unconscious parts of their personalities in the group (see for instance Hunt 1989). For example, if a group member treats the moderator as an 'airy fairy' academic, this can begin to suggest something about how they conceive of society, such as around poles of 'thinking' and 'doing'. Alternatively, in work such as Mike's involving self-appointed guardians of local history, the relatively silent academic researcher can be used as a welcome witness who vali-dates the accounts being given (Myerhoff 1982). However, adopting a low-key role can also reduce moderator effectiveness in the task of encouraging the group to develop interesting points. When such points are brought up, it is vital for the moderator(s) to ask for amplification as this can produce both material for the researcher and other members of the group to work on. She/he/they must also lead in topics and get them discussed. One way of steering conversations, then, is to pick up on issues that occurred earlier but weren't fully discussed, an approach which also provides the opportunity to bring in quieter group members.

Another problem with group work is that it can be terribly tempting to get wrapped up in the discussion and to take part as a participant, but this can lead to a loss of perceived impartiality, and thus of the ability to guide the discussion. If the moderator intervenes as a participant then group members may develop very clear ideas about what is wanted from them or may react and put the moderator down. Jane Templeton (1987) has advised that the moderator should establish her/himself as an expert on procedure, but leave the group to be the experts on the topic. This also avoids the moment when the moderator is told that she/he is wrong about an issue by a participant with first-hand experience. In this kind of situation it does not matter who is right, but the moderator must avoid making the group member look stupid since this would immediately prejudice all of the trust built up in the group. Moderators have to probe and to challenge, but must also be very careful not to accuse, aiming to promote critical self-reflection rather than immediate defensive assertions. However, to avoid the hierarchical structure that this role can impose (Oakley 1981), the moderator can draw on experiences or information and then add them to the discussion not to dictate a 'correct' view but to enable others to talk about them.

It is also possible to not be wrapped up enough in the group's conversation: to 'tune out', to become an observer, to become mesmerised by the discussion, to follow interesting debates or anecdotes wherever they might go, thus forgetting the purpose of the group. At this point, the moderator should try to stay alert to who is speaking and try to include people who appear to be being silenced. In a sentence, moderating is a balancing act of detachment and interest – the interest to follow up and probe and the detachment to keep the overall picture in mind. The whole operation should be kept on a friendly basis in order to foster the trust that may enable reticent members to speak openly. Unfortunately, the correct balance often only becomes apparent with hindsight. Few groups work perfectly, and there are nearly always people who don't say what they could and others who dominate. There are also always moments when the moderator overplays her/his hand and everything goes dead. In practice, out of a series of four meetings, Mike generally reckoned that at least one would be a disappointment.

These problems occur and have to be coped with. But, they are not death knells to the project. Reading some finished accounts, you would think that there were never any personality clashes or problems in getting issues discussed. We suggest that some thought be given to coping with the ups and downs – the moments when the group appears to have telepathically understood what the research is about, or where they reveal whole new dimensions to it, and moments where the group's purpose appears to be a mystery to them. It is worth thinking through some lead-in questions, perhaps a few illustrations if necessary, to get the concept across. Think how topics might be taken, and prepare to work on that and on how you can introduce topics so that they make sense within the flow of the meeting. With repeated meetings, it may be worthwhile giving out summaries of the last meeting as a matter of interest to members, to establish commitment and to help lay the ground for further discussion that picks up where it had got to and does not spend valuable time going back through the same issues. Although the topic may have been an all consuming interest for you, and transcribing may have consumed all your time (see the following section), the participants will probably not have been dwelling on the discussions and may well need reminding. Mike gave all members brief discussion outlines so that everyone knew what they were getting into and had some idea where things were (meant to be) going. This meant that some members would actually pause in the middle of a statement and ask if they were getting off the point, or would deliberately change tack to link up with the next topic. At other times, they had entirely different ideas as to how the meeting should go. But we should say that even the worst meetings can provide remarkable conversations about many topics, even ones that might appear 'private' or off-limits. As the group gets going, people are quite ready to talk about the most surprising topics, and the whole thing can be tremendous fun to do.

CONSTRUCTING INFORMATION

Many of the issues regarding the construction of information – or data – from focus group interviews are exactly the same as those for the single or serial interviews discussed earlier. If you haven't read that section already, we suggest that you do so now. The main difference between the data constructed in interviews and focus groups, however, is the simple fact that more people are involved in the latter. How, we need to ask, can researchers come away from a focus group discussion with 'the *best possible record*' of it? Again, this involves making appropriate combination of recordings, transcripts and field notes. But, we argue, group conversations add two new dimensions to data construction: first, there are the technical issues about the kinds of equipment you will need to adequately record them and, second, there are the practical issues about transcribing what's in those recordings and noting what's not.

All of the advice offered about recording individual interviews is relevant to focus groups, except for the microphones. In focus group discussions, participants are usually arranged in a circle, with the recording equipment place in the centre, often on a low table. Thus, to record what everyone says, it is necessary to have a 360 degree microphone. Although some recorders are supplied with two 180 degree microphones that will give stereo coverage, we have yet to see a satisfactory 360 degree microphone built into a recorder. So, if you choose to undertake focus groups, you will need to get hold of a plug-in 360 degree Boundary Effect or Pressure Zone Modulating microphone. These are usually the size of an over-thick credit card and rely on the surface on which they are placed to amplify sound. Models such as Sony's ECM-F8 and ECM-F01, Olympus' ME-7, Audio-Technica's ATR97, Crown/Realistic's PZM or Optimus' Omnidirectional Boundary Microphone cost between £12 and £30, will easily cover a six feet radius and are therefore adequate to record most focus groups. More expensive microphones, such as Audix's ADX-60 condenser boundary microphone (£160) or Audio Technic's unidirectional condenser boundary microphone (at around £220), will reduce the noise in the signal and extend the radius dramatically. You may be able to plug these directly into a laptop or digital audio recorder, but check before you buy and always familiarise yourself with the range and quality of the recordings that can be produced by doing a few dry runs before your first group meets. Finally, as we said earlier, even with all the right equipment, accidents can happen and recordings can and do go wrong. This is why data construction from focus groups must involve both transcription and noting.

Given what we have said about group dynamics and moderator roles in focus group research, it should not be a surprise that no one comes away with a definitive version of what happened in these meetings. It is too easy just to notice what assertive members were saying, or to remember a moment when it all came together or when there was a bruising conflict (Bers 1989). Mike found it useful (and fair) with serial groups to hear how members felt about his version of events in the summaries that he gave them. This is why high-quality recording and careful transcription are so important. Recording, noting and transcribing your groups (alone or with your co-moderator) will enable you to be able to compare your immediate impressions of, and feelings about, a meeting with the subsequent transcript. Notes taken after a meeting can attempt to describe these impressions and feelings, as well as any incidents which occurred off the record like participants' body language, who people sat next to where in the room, comments that were made before and/or after the taping and so on. Mike, for example, found that group members would often come up to him after a session to suggest what they would like to have said. And some confided that they knew he wasn't interested in what one member had said and, therefore, told him what they thought he really wanted to hear about. These kinds of comments can add new insight to what has just happened, and therefore need to be noted down. Then there is the process of transcription that, we have to warn readers, is an especially arduous task with focus group research. If you have reasonable typing skills, you should expect to devote up to sixteen hours transcription for each hour or so of meeting. Here, for example, it is likely that two or more people may be speaking at the same time, that more than one conversation may be taking place at some points, that it may sometimes be difficult to identify who is saying what, and that participants may regularly use the microphone table to rest their cups of tea. Finally we suggest, the fact that the researcher was present at and part of these conversations means that, more so than with individual interviews, she/he is the best person to transcribe the recordings. This adds some extra dimensions to the planning of such work.

7 Filmic Approaches

> The visualities deployed in the production of geographical knowledges are never neutral. They have their foci, their zooms, their highlights, their blinkers, and their blindnesses, for example, and these are central to both the subject of geography as a discipline and to its human subjects – those it studies and those who study it (Rose 2003: 213).

Traditionally, visual methods have had only a very small impact on ethnographic research, a situation that has led to the characterisation of most anthropology, for instance, as consisting of the visually illiterate seeking to study the verbally illiterate (Worth 1981). In contrast, we would seek to encourage researchers to look at the possibilities that such methods can open up. Most researchers confine themselves to the odd illustrative photo which is often assumed to be a factual record of the field (Ball and Smith 1992). Yet photographic theory has suggested that this is not so (e.g. Burgin 1987; Taylor 1994). In chapter two, we argued that people invest meanings and significance in the material objects around them. Photographs are taken purposively and displayed in contexts that can drastically alter their meanings. This is true of both art and news pictures, the subject's photos and the researcher's. And while, in this section, we concentrate on those photographs taken *by* the subjects of research, the arguments could equally be applied to researchers' photographs *of* their subjects.

Here, we will try to show that there are no singular or correct answers to the question 'what does a picture mean?'; but instead, we will discuss 'the production of empirically grounded responses to particular visual materials' (Rose 2001: 2). In the following subsections, we will:

- first, outline a few specific issues around the use of photography in ethnography,
- second, discuss what researchers can learn from people's already-existing photos and films,
- third, consider what can be learned by asking them to take new photos and films,
- and finally, question how data can usefully be constructed out of this process for formal analysis.

An excellent introduction to these kinds of approaches and the issues arising from them can be found in the work of Gillian Rose (2000, 2001). As she points out, any consideration of the visual has to consider not only the technical (as in type of media), compositional (as in choice of content) and social (as in institutional) aspects of producing images, but also how, for each image, these come together in different ways at moments of production, transmission/storage and for different audiences.

MAKING PICTURES IN AND OF THE FIELD

There is a long history of using photographs as ethnographic documents. In anthropology, modern ethnography and photography have gone hand in hand (Edwards 1992, 2001). And geography, whose history of ethnographic research is just as long, is often characterised as a profoundly visual discipline, where seeing (and showing) is close to knowing (Cloke et al. 2004; Rose 2003). Certainly the nineteenth and early twentieth-century ethnographies that aspired to a 'scientific objectivity' and impartiality saw photography as not only providing a useful medium to convey strange and exotic customs and artefacts, but also as a credible, realistic form of evidence (Rony 2003). The mechanical 'capturing' of reality in images, the direct and faithful depiction of 'the field', promised exactly the kind of 'truth' that, for many, ethnographies were about with a detached observer reporting what was 'out there' (see chapter 2). This goal of a transparent, apparently unmediated vision of other people's lives, customs, etc. has also framed approaches to 'writing up' fieldwork that will be discussed in our final chapter. Recent critical work has, however, highlighted three problematic issues regarding the 'reality' of photography, film, video and other visual media:

- First, photography can never show unmediated reality because the technology, its capabilities, and the social relations surrounding its use by photographers, the filmed and their audiences always make a difference.
- Second, still and moving pictures are often bound into existing discourses that mean they do not simply 'show', for instance, 'exotic peoples' in 'remote places' but help to *make* those people seem exotic and remote by foregrounding difference, hiding the photographer and so forth. It is important to note here that, in the nineteenth century, many ethnographers' photographs were recycled into popular culture in the form of postcards and magazine photos (Stephen 1995).
- Third, such photographs were also used to help 'reconstruct' visions of the 'primitive cultures' that they supposedly depicted in 'illustrative tableaux', including indigenous people imported to inhabit them,

made for the education and entertainment of the Western public at a series of 'great exhibitions' and 'world fairs' (Fusco 1994; Schwartz and Ryan 2003).

Photographs of 'Polynesia', for example, included stock pictures of semi-clad women, often a reclining nude amid foliage. Their composition drew on Western conventions of 'woodland nymphs'. So, in these allegedly 'realistic' and certainly 'factual' photographs:

The women [were] thus overtly transposed into a radically remote domain of fantasy, a fairyland that [was] distant not only from the metropolitan societies, but also from the ordinary circumstances of Polynesian life (Thomas 1995: 49).

The Edenic overtones of these images risked suggesting some noble or uncorrupted 'savages' in a domain untouched by white intrusion. But this was achieved by removing all signs of modernity, and by turning the individual, and real, people in the pictures, with their own ideals, biographies and dilemmas, into illustrations of cultural and social 'types', where they stood for and made visible abstract structures. We might say that colonial photography and film doubly objectified its objects, first turning people into pictures and, then framing the pictures more in terms of the characteristics of those filmed bodies than the contingent and subjective choices of the photographer (Rony 2003). And the point of this history is that it is by no means entirely confined to the past, as recent performance art reenacting 'primitive Amerindian tableaux' (Fusco 1994) and studies of the photographs used in publications like *National Geographic* have shown (Lutz and Collins 1993).

We wish to suggest in the following pages that although there are problematic inheritances with specific modes of visualisation, this does not mean we should ignore the potential of using visual methods in new ethnographic research. At its most basic, photographs taken 'in the field' – correctly filed and annotated – can usefully complement the writing of field notes. Here, pictures taken early in fieldwork can be revisited later, by the researcher or others. These may remind them of what was initially strange, but then became familiar, during the course of research or they may reveal things that escaped attention at the time (Hastrup 1992). But, just like the field notes they may complement, these photographs won't simply record facts from the field. Again, some scenes will be chosen in preference to others, the research's presence is likely to contribute to what is there to 'record' and so on. People invariably react to the presence of cameras by acting up to them (smiling, posing, rushing off to change clothes, asking that their photo be taken, etc.) and/or shying away from them (Howard 1994; Robson 1994). Taking more 'natural', 'candid' pictures is, therefore, often a case of catching people unawares. But this raises thorny ethical issues about consent, the preservation of anonymity and so on. Usually you should get consent to take pictures of the people owning a place and those being photographed in it. But if you later take a surprise picture you might need to recheck whether it is still OK with the people concerned or whether they may be embarrassed or hurt. But when, for instance, Mike was taking pictures of events with hundreds of people in the frame, there was no way of asking permission individually. Around him hundreds of others were taking pictures. Laws vary around the planet but a standard test is whether the people have a reasonable expectation that they might be photographed – say in a public place, or at a gathering. If they do, then requirements for permission may be more relaxed. Even if a researcher gets permission and thinks that, after a while, people may have 'forgotten their camera is there', it is likely that there will be limits about what, where, when or who they will permit researchers to photograph. Later on there may be issues about whether to display the pictures – for Mike, who anonymised a research site, it posed issues of identifying places in ways anonymised transcripts don't, or for that matter in Ian's case pictures identified the fruit.

As we said earlier, in many places carrying a camera can better allow a researcher to mingle in with the crowd, rather than stand out from it. For Mike, at heritage sites and reenactments, most of the audience were taking pictures – though clearly he could not use a camera when 'on stage' as a reenactor. It is also the case that a researcher carrying a camera can take on what, for many, is an acceptable and understandable role of the person who 'documents' things. This is what Karen Becker (2000: 101) did in her study of how multi-ethnic 'conflict and diversity' was negotiated by allotment gardeners in Sweden. She spent six years, on and off, undertaking interviews, doing walking tours and producing 900 colour prints and 30 black-and-white rolls of film. She found that these 'visual documents' helped her to better:

- 'describe' her visits to the allotments,
- record what people were talking about in interviews,
- see over time how the environment changed (for instance by tracking patterns of seed exchange and sharing) and
- establish rapport with the gardeners by offering pictures in exchange for their time.

Her approach worked, it seems, because allotments are in part *about* public display. But her role as the photographer didn't work equally well with everyone who gardened there. She found, for instance, that while photography allowed her access into the lives of the ethnically South East Asian gardeners, it also led to her being avoided by Islamic women. She also found that photographs taken for different audiences – for her and her future audiences in her field notes, or for those gardeners she took photos of – were framed differently. But, the act of taking these latter photos, and the discussions that this aroused, offered further insights into how different gardeners looked at the site and also into their kin and friendship networks as they passed these pictures around. When she organised an exhibition of pictures in the local community centre, her pictures proved both a source of discussion and controversy. And despite the fact that she felt she had found no evidence of inter-ethnic socialisation on the allotments, they were spliced together by a local newspaper to show 'A Botanical UN', to reinforce 'a popular view of what community gardening represents in Swedish society' (2000: 119). Here, images of a blooming backdrop along with, to her at least, clear signs of ethnic difference were said to show harmonious relations.

We do not then see pictures as just 'documenting' the 'field' and what goes on there, though that can be useful. Photographic researchers often think that it's necessary to take un-aesthetic, artless pictures for them to be taken as 'truthful' or 'objective'. This is, however, not necessarily the case. Just as there should be an 'art' to ethnographic description, for example, surely there should be room in academic work for the art of photography. Apparently 'descriptive pictures may accidentally produce aesthetic effects. For instance many documentary pictures of the 30s used a double reflex camera, held on the chest which the photographer looked down into – meaning that the camera was slightly tilted up at human subjects, often unintentionally imbuing them with a certain heroic quality' (Harper 2003: 254). Alternately the aesthetics may be intentional. Alan Sekula's (1995) richly illustrated book on global trade, *Fish Story*, is a case in point here. Sekula is a scholar and an accomplished photographer who deliberately shows the surreal and surprising conjunctions of forces in his work. Thus, by hanging around docksides where strange combinations of goods were being placed on ships crewed by people of diverse national origins, he was looking to frame photographs where 'for one moment the global supply network is comically localised' (1995: 32). In looking for the 'surreal' in the 'real', taking pictures which jar, Sekula has used photography to critique, rather than to reproduce, the medium's usually disembodied and despatialised knowledges and ways of seeing (Rogoff 2000). Powerful visual imagery can, in this way, help to unpack fantasies of stable places and pure cultures in a world of global flows, dis-location and proliferating hybridity. And you do not have to be a particularly accomplished photographer to do this. James Sidaway (2000a), for example, has used photography in an undergraduate field-class, asking students to take photos of the city they were visiting and then getting them to compare them to its official, public images. Here, the intention was not to identify images that were more or less 'true' to the city, but to show how they were all partial truths.

ALREADY-EXISTING PHOTOS

Another way of engaging with multiple truths, and literally and metaphorically multiple viewpoints, is to discuss the photos that people have already taken about the issue you want to study. It is possible that a wealth of photographs and/or film and video footage of the places or activities you might be interested in already exists. These may include, for example, the formal pictures commissioned by government or commercial bodies that appear in reports, brochures, adverts or postcards. Indeed, these may be a good place to start you research. You might, for example, be interested in looking at how a certain place (a country, region, or city, for example) has been commodified through tourism. Thus, looking at how brochures, postcards and other 'place promotion' materials frame this place could lead you to ask questions about how certain organisations try to depict place and how they build upon and create their audiences' expectations. So, for instance, Dann (1996) found out that local culture hardly figured in the tourist marketing of Cyprus, and Markwick (2001) found that the postcards available for tourists to show others the supposedly memorable places and activities of their holiday in Malta were very selective. Following on from this, we might also wish to go beyond these public representations and ask how they fit into other more private representations made by 'ordinary' people (Crang 1997b). Many people have access to cameras of varying sorts, and they may already be making their own records of events for their own purposes. These records are also people's own chosen representations unprompted by researchers. This is not, however, to say these can provide simple factual depictions free from 'researcher bias'. All acts of recording take place in social, economic and cultural contexts that invest the practice of photography, as well as its images, with meanings. Pictures are replete with people's ideas of what should (not) be recorded, how it should (not) be shown and so forth, and that is *precisely* what makes them useful, since they can provide insights into those social norms. Taking snapshots, for instance, is a voluntary 'nonessential' activity with no formal training that appears to take place more or less spontaneously in Western societies. Yet, what is fascinating about the photographs that are taken is that they appear remarkably standardised within cultures (Chalfen 1987). Indeed, as Pierre Bourdieu has written, 'there are few activities which are so stereotyped and less abandoned to the anarchy of individual intentions' (1990b: 19).

A compelling explanation for this standardisation is that, in everyday life, people take photos that they know will receive a favourable reception. Thus, it can be argued that photos provide an opening into a person's sense of what is expected and acceptable behaviour, and also into how they might wish to be remembered. Each photo is an act of (self-)presentation that involves the photographer, the photographed and the expected audience. Both the people taking the photographs and those who are in them are already aware of the social contexts that will determine the meaning of their actions (Jacobs 1981; Lesy 1980). Photos and the doing of photography therefore communicate social meanings and help people to express who they are, be it the 'camera buff', the student trying to be 'arty' or the tourist taking a snapshot (Bourdieu 1990b). Each year billions of photos are taken. If a person took some 3,000, each of which captures about 1/100 of a second of their life, only perhaps thirty seconds of a sixty- or seventy-year lifetime would be committed to film (Chalfen 1987). Such photography provides, therefore, an extremely selective and partial evidence of a person's life. However, as self-selected documents, they can provide insights into how people see themselves projected through past times and places (Becker Ohrn 1975; Holland 1991; Jacobs 1981). Photos are not to be divorced from their contexts and treated as a record, but rather should be treated as a means of revealing the processes of selection that are used in composing such a record. Richard Chalfen (1987) has argued that rather than giving immediate access to 'reality', photography shows how people try to invest meanings and reinterpret the world in what he has termed the 'Kodak culture' of the West. In analysing domestic snapshot collections he has noted that this:

> promotes the visual display of proper and expected behaviour, of participation in socially approved activities, according to culturally approved value schemes. People are shown in home made imagery 'doing it right', conforming to social norms, achieving status and enjoying themselves, in part as a result of a life well lived. In short people demonstrate a knowledge, capability, and competence to do things 'right'. In these ways, a sense of belonging and security is developed and maintained (1987: 139).

Photos can therefore provide more insights into the social milieu of actors than into the 'reality' they supposedly capture, and as a means for studying group 'cultures' they can also provide not only a useful 'way in', but may also already have a role in creating, sustaining, challenging and/or changing the 'culture' you want to study.

As we have argued throughout this section, the approaches we are outlining here are by no means separate. Filmic research is no exception to this rule. Michael Lesy (1980), for instance, has pointed out how photos can be used as a base for, and in combination with, interviews in a process that has been called 'photo-elicitation' (Harper 2002). Here, talking through an individual's or group's existing collections of photos can help to create a sense of their life histories, identities, world-views and everyday lives (Becker Ohrn 1975; Collier and Collier 1986; Harper 2003; Holland 1991; McCracken 1988a). Talking through photos involves the construction of stories that allow the researcher to be more sensitive to a person's and/or group's passage through time and space. This is because, not only do photo albums form a useful record in themselves (because of their selectivity which, itself, can be discussed), but they may also be a good way to prompt people to think back about their past(s) and to relate stories outside, or on the edge, of the photo frame (Becker Ohrn 1975; Lesy 1980; Reme 1993). This may then allow the researcher some vicarious access to the multiple times, places and experiences of the subject's life course (McCracken 1988a,b). Recently Kevin Markwell (1996, 2000, 2001) has used tourists' photographs to examine how people relate to their environments on a nature-based holiday in the jungles of Borneo. Here, their photography offered him a chance to examine:

- what they felt was memorable about the trip,
- any commonalities in what was depicted and how often and also
- how they used the photos to tell stories about their holiday to others when they returned home.

There is certainly much to commend an approach that follows photographs as they move through people's lives. Such research could start at the time and place a photo is taken, and follow it through its processing, first inspection and its subsequent selection, passed distribution, framing, disposal and/or storage. Photographs are, as we have said, not just 'images' but material objects that are taken into people's lives in various formats, being framed on mantle pieces, stuck in albums, tucked into wallets, attached to emails, sent as picture messages, made into collages, exchanged as presents and plenty more besides (Garlick 2002; Rose 2004, forthcoming).

AUTOPHOTOGRAPHY

It may be that the activities and events you are interested in are not covered in people's usual photographic collections. So another approach to using photography might be termed 'autophotography', where the researcher encourages or commissions participants to take pictures of parts of their environment or activities, in order to learn more about how they understand and interpret their world and themselves within it

(Dodman 2003; Kenney 1993; Ziller 1990). Thus Robert Ziller and Dale Smith (1977) have argued that researchers could attempt to learn about the photographer through her/his photography. Studies of this type have shown consistent patterns in the photographic records produced by different groups. For instance, disabled photographers recorded few instances of non-disabled people making eye contact with them, and thereby captured the avoidance strategies of those around them (Aitken and Wingate 1993; Ziller 1990). Many autophotographic studies have focused purely on the content depicted in such photographs, however, and have come dangerously close to being 'thin descriptions' of forms rather than thicker ones concerning the meanings invested in them by the subjects (Hastrup 1992). We would argue that the social meanings of photography allow the researcher to look at far more than how often things appear. As Sol Worth (1981) has put it, film (and photography) is not so much about what is 'out there' as what is 'in here'. As a non-verbal medium, photos may serve almost as projective stimuli that reveal routinised or unconscious responses that are scarcely thought about by the participants – for instance, in the way some images are accepted or constructed and in the tensions between how some absences are not noted or remedied in photographs but, at the same time, might still be spoken about. Robert Ziller (1990), for instance, has given an example where there appeared (to him) to be a conspicuous absence of black students in photos taken by white students around their 'mixed' college, while the latter would never say that there was racial 'segregation' on campus.

In terms of material requirements an autophotographic project can be quite cheap in that most people have access to a camera, while providing film is usually about £8 per subject, including processing. Alternatively, using digital cameras eliminates the processing costs (or at least reduces it to less than a pound if you are for instance going to burn a CD to either keep or return to participants). This has the added advantage of then being in a format ready for putting into some of the analysis software packages mentioned in the next chapter (though most universities offer scanning facilities that are almost as convenient). One thing worth thinking about, if the researcher provides a camera, is the level of anxiety that this may cause for the photographer, particularly if it is a sophisticated model. Our advice here would be to sacrifice some artistic potential and use a one-touch or even a throwaway camera. It may, however, be the case that some respondents could do this sort of project on their mobile phones and send in the pictures. Whatever the equipment, in autophotographic work, getting pictures is more important than getting 'fine art' – which is a point worth emphasising to participants to reduce the concerns which they might have about this. Alternatively, you may decide that drawings could work just as well to convey, for example, people's 'mental maps' of events and activities, like Young and Barrett (2001) did with street children in Kampala who they asked to draw their geographies of street life, places of safety and so forth.

FILM AND VIDEO

In the realm of the moving image, much of the advice about still photography also applies. The use of digital camcorders coupled with fairly cheap (occasionally free) editing software offers a useful observational tool at the least – if for instance you wish to record gestures and practices (for examples see Brown and Laurier 2004; Loehr and Harper 2003). With this continued technological drive towards simplicity and user control, video technology now proliferates. The camcorder is part of a global trade in funny clips and is the staple technology of programmes of 'eye-witness TV'. This has provided a new visual aesthetic of gritty realism, or 'cinema naiveté' as Richard Chalfen has termed it (1987: 49), a putatively sponta-neous capturing of the world 'as it happens'. Like cameras, camcorders are symbolic goods involved in status games, traditionally being mostly used by men (or their sons), still having class overtones in terms of ownership and being invested with ideologies about technology, novelty and being seen to be 'up-to-date'. The researcher hence has to be aware that this is in no respect a neutral medium. But this is not necessarily a negative feature, as we have endeavoured to show with other methods. Using video technology, Mike attempted to latch onto the momentum of the 'video diaries' series by the BBC's Community Programmes division, and to use an autophotographic approach. Thus, his research on the serious business of representations of the past has deliberately called upon a form of video that is aimed at fun and a staged spontaneity. This he hoped might get around people's retrospective accounting of their motives and behaviour – where in interviews they would tell him what they thought he thought they should have been interested in, rather than what they actually spent their time doing (see Box 7.1). Footage of bored parents ignoring historic sites, and kids using them as climbing frames suggested different ways of relat-ing to the past than critiques of what 'interpretation' the place suggested on display boards. It is worth noting that home video footage does not often follow a cinematic grammar, with carefully composed shots and so forth – we can tell this from the need felt by instructional magazines over the last thirty years to endlessly repeat exhortations to adopt a more cine-matic approach (Chalfen 1987). This repetition suggests that such calls are in vain and that most home movies are dominated by a discourse of fun, special events and staged spontaneity, and it is these sorts of criteria which will usually frame the movies that are made.

Box 7.1: Montaging Layers of Data and Interpretation

Mike found it hard to use video material in the footage, partly because technology in the mid-1990s meant he had to use a piece of software designed for picturing change in chemical crystals to produce stills, and partly because there was so much going on in each clip. Here are two still frames taken from one respondent.

Below each we set out columns or layers of interpretation: first the captions Mike gave to narrate the scene, second conversation recorded on the film and third, material from an interview with 'Rog' who shot the film. We will later come on to how Mike ended up trying to juxtapose these in his chapters to show multiple voices.

Reading books: disinterest in the past

Mike's summary

While Junior set off to 'explore' the castle – and Rog set off to record Junior's exploits – his wife preferred to stay behind and read a book. Rog chatted to Junior about moats and gatehouses. He filmed junior climbing and walking. His wife figured in only this shot and two staged shots where he asked her directly for her opinions. He later said she wouldn't have come had it not been for my 'project'. This was normally Rog's time with Junior – since he hardly saw him during the week – perhaps reflected in the 'buddy movie' they recorded as they set off round the castle.

Participant on tape

Junior: Wait here while I sneak up behind her and film mum.

Participant interviewed

Rog: '[She came along this time for you but my wife] doesn't have an historical sense at all, it's all a load of rocks to her. Actually she passes a comment "why haven't they knocked it all down and done something useful with it?" Sort of Mike: Playing it up? I mean deliberately play that up? Rog: No she's not into history at all. Not in the least bit interested in historic places. She doesn't mind something if it's spectacular. I mean you go somewhere like Dunster castle which is real, I mean you've got people living in it, she might be interested… What she would be interested in is the kitchens and furnishings. Once it's knocked down she doesn't have an interest in it. Unfortunately junior is completely uninterested [unless it is a ruin]'.

Box 7.1: continued

Junior walking

Mike's summary

Rog and 'junior' have just spent 20 minutes walking through the overgrown moat of a ruined castle. Though Rog did later cut short their trek through this outer defensive work of the castle – deciding he had seen enough and junior had been stung by enough nettles – throughout the video there were shots of junior jumping off things, sliding down them, leaping across rocks and hiding. Meanwhile there were shots taken by Rog as he fell down as he followed junior or as he pondered upon where junior might be and what he might be getting up to.

Participant on tape

' "Doctor Livingstone I presume?' [Rog's comment to junior as he shot this frame.]

Rog: Well it must make a circle from there where it goes on.

Jr.: Why?

Rog: Well otherwise the enemies would all walk in the gap . . . I think we can cut back along the road to your mother rather than do that next bit, though.

Rog: Hold on there I want to film this group of visitors cos I'll be interested to see if they do the same as us . . . [They repeat Rog's itinerary exactly] Hold on Junior you stand there because I don't want it to look like I'm filming them, while I film them.'

Participant interviewed

Rog: 'we normally take two or three pictures but then we do that anywhere we go. We were all at Thorpe Park yesterday, that was lovely got 4 or 5 shots. . . . But we don't TAKE photographs, not as you say like these guys with big cameras'.

Mike: 'instamatic type stuff?' . . .

Rog: 'Well kid's growing up really, yeah. Junior in front of castle one, castle two' [laughs].

Moreover, it is just these sorts of 'frames of expectation' that may be interesting in an ethnography because they may reveal the practices constituting the bounds of the normal, the spontaneous and the exceptional. Camera work can therefore be used to prompt transgressions or 'deliberate barbarisms' against expected behaviour. Participants may goof around for the benefit of the camera, and this may serve to highlight where and how normal routines are experienced (Bourdieu 1990b). But the costs of this sort of enterprise need some attention: with a camcorder costing around £500, and tapes around £8 each, you may break your research budget simply on hardware. Alternately digital memory camcorders are increasingly popular, where the costs of tape disappear – but you do then need to use a PC or laptop with considerable memory to store material, and probably a CD or DVD write function to make back-ups or move material if it is not your personal computer, and while there are cheap digital editing packages, that are good enough for most purposes (they may be even bundled onto your PC desktop as standard),[1] the sophisticated editing packages used to produce finished films, or to show multiple videos simultaneously (from Avid or Adobe), can cost up to £1,000.[2] And while it is certainly true that cameras are becoming more and more intuitive to use, you do need to be aware that the skills of using these cameras and the conventions for responding to them are by no means universal, even in Western societies, and that they may disrupt normal social interaction. Having said that, it may be possible to work with groups who already have access to video equipment, in which case your costs may be reduced and they will already be familiar with the technical and social aspects of their use.

If you intend to do something more like action research then filming (or photography) can again provide a useful tool (Aufderheider 1993; Dowmunt 1992). For instance, work has been done with young working-class kids to enable them to develop not only their own photographic representations of their world, but also the skills to critique other people's representations – and at the same time to acquire what may be a hobby or vocational skill (e.g. Dewdney and Lister 1988). This requires far more than existing 'snapshot' or home movie expertise as its intention is to alter the situation of the people involved by providing them with resources (equipment or skills) that were previously unavailable to them. As such, this approach may possibly call upon more resources (i.e. good quality photographic equipment), skilled instruction and time in which to develop a project. However, if a situation were to arise where you could become involved in such an already existing project, then this would be more feasible for most geographers. Perhaps you could try to provide the chance for a group or individuals to make a full film of aspects of their own lives – as in video diaries or films such as 'Through Navajo Eyes' (Worth and Adair 1972). In these circumstances, the researcher can seek to interpret not only what is portrayed in these films, but also what the form of portrayal might reveal about the group's world view. In 'Through Navajo Eyes', Sol Worth was struck by a sequence on smithying silver which began with a Navajo mining metal when, to his knowledge, Navajos had never mined metal but had always traded for it. When he questioned the accuracy of this part of the film, it was explained to him that stories had to have both a beginning and an end so the filmmakers reconstructed a beginning to make the film fit their rules of storytelling (Worth 1981; Worth and Adair 1972). Meanwhile, in Western cultures subtle changes in the use of film can also be found. Thus, Sol Worth has also reported how black urban youths have filmed themselves in many activities and have been very eager to appear on film while white, male, middle-class youths have preferred to remain behind the camera in control of the images eventually screened. This has led him to support theories of the way a 'gaze' forms part of a nexus of knowledge, power and pleasure (Worth 1981; cf. Pinney 1992).

Alternatively, you could try to make a film of and with the people studied. There is a considerable literature on the restrictions and possible benefits of this (e.g. Crawford and Turton 1992; Ginsburg 1991, 1993; Kindon 2003; Ruby 1991; Turner 1991). The most pressing problem for the geography student setting out to make an ethnographic film which will be both the finished product and the research material, concerns the skills and resources needed to do this. The cheapest introductory course on editing costs around £90, and you will need some practice after that, and semi-professional classes are more like ten times that figure. However, if you have the time and the money to learn how to make a full-blown film, then movies such as Michael Moore's (1989) *Roger and Me* (a useful example of a filmed ethnography of a town destroyed by deindustrialisation: cf. Jones and Natter 1993), or Nick Broomfield's (1991) *The Leader, The Driver and the Driver's Wife* (a useful illustration of the doing, as well as the subject, of an ethnographic film) would be well worth watching as both filmmakers have relied on and shown the inter-subjective processes in their work rather than claiming to construct cinema verité or 'fly on the wall' documentaries (for a recent comparison of their approaches, see Richardson 2004). There is a lot that can be done that stops short of making your own films though. We would certainly draw attention to the possibilities of using films as inspiration and contextual material in many projects, as mentioned in the sections on interviewing and focus group work. Films may also serve as materials through which people understand places, informing the actions through which they reproduce and engage with places – places which, in turn, have been produced by other people reproducing and engaging with their representations of areas (cf. Burgess and Gold 1985).

Using visual methods as part of ethnographic research creates both new avenues and new dangers around the issues of incorporation, representation and empowerment. First, while it is often commented that geography is a visual discipline, there has been little attempt to move from text-based productions in dissertations, theses and even methods books. There is an entire genre of 'visual anthropology' to which researchers might look which explore ways of using visual material not just as 'data' but also as part of the final product: for example, a photo essay (like Sekula 1995) or film. Making such films offers possibilities to get beyond some of the stereotypes of the gaze objectifying people. Thus classic films were cinema verité: that is long uncut shots, typically in the middle distance, where the researcher is off screen and there is a disembodied third-party narration which echoes textual forms of producing sense of objectivity and the detachment of the observer from a pristine social world. Russell (1999) and Grimshaw (2001), however, explore the variations in avant garde aesthetics that have unpacked the truth claims of such scopic regimes from within. Rony (2003), for example, looks at how Marlon Fuentes' film *Bontoc Eulogy* (1995) uses apparently found archive footage, in flickering black and white, to recount an ethnography of his grandfather, who was brought to the USA as a member of the Igorot 'tribe' from the Philippines to be exhibited in a 'native village' at the St. Louis world fair for popular visual consumption. So instead of seeing him as an 'untouched' example of premodern life, his grandfather is shown enmeshed in circuits of power and knowledge that produce him as an 'exhibit' – and the film deliberately undercuts the normal ethnographic gaze. The film however has a further sting in the tale, since at the very end it puts up a disclaimer that all events and people portrayed are fictional – it thus asks the audience why they might trust such archive footage and about their need to believe in the authority of ethnographic film. This is not to say the film is untruthful but rather that it might encourage audiences to think about the events portrayed and how they come to (dis)believe in stories about them. It reminds us that all ethnographies are fictions, as in created textual worlds, and that, to rework the literary theorist Frank Kermode, 'fictions are for finding things out' to which we might add 'they are also for being found out' (Kamberelis 2003: 693).

Second, a multiplying field of visual techniques is being deployed by people that may well allow the researcher to make a wider impact than just on her/his own degree result. Around the world, various groups have been producing videos for schools and/or to counteract the effects of global media corporations. During his research in the city, Mike encountered four community photography projects ongoing or exhibiting in Bristol alone. Equally, groups all around the world have been attempting to represent themselves on broadcast video. As the cost of video equipment has fallen, such counter-hegemonic organisations have grown in number, making a diversity of programmes whose contents have ranged from Australian aboriginal myths through to Innuit language soap operas (Dowmunt 1992; Ginsburg 1993; Thede and Ambrosi 1991; White 2003). These groups have been trying to move from being images in the culture of hegemonic groups to producing their own images of themselves on TV. If you can get access to these sorts of groups, then you may be able to gain access to various processes whereby numerous communities are attempting to redefine themselves in the modern world. For instance, large projects like Arab Women Speak Out have involved many women making documentaries about their lives that then serve as the focus of meetings with women in other places that have involved more than 60,000 participants in total. The aim is to empower those often seen as objects of a colonial gaze or at best powerless victims to portray their own active agency by featuring 'the stories of women who are actors in their own right, rather than objects of other people's decisions or of other's representations' in what is often called participatory video (Kindon 2003; Underwood and Jabre 2003: 237). In the spirit of engaging with people's own understandings of their worlds, Holliday (2000) adopted a video diary approach with participants – to enable their self-representation, and engage with issues of reflexivity and autobiography (see also Lomax and Casey 1998). Her work is explicitly framed to avoid the disembodied, detached, thus supposedly objective but certainly objectifying observer of the documentary tradition echoing in some ways the aims of more avant garde anthropological aesthetics (Pink 2001b). We can certainly now trace a range of different 'ethnographic gazes' and approaches in film that might serve as templates for geographical work (Banks 2001; Pink 2001a; Russell 1999; Taylor 1994). These also raise questions of how we might set about interpreting filmic materials, and how specific these might be to visual ethnographies (Collier 2000).

CONSTRUCTING INFORMATION

There is perhaps one key question to consider when thinking about constructing filmic information or data: to what extent, if at all, would your photos and footage need to be textualised to be systematically analysed? The way that you might answer this question would depend on your research aims, whether you created your own (audio)visual data and/or are working with others', and the form you wish your final 'writing' to take. In many finished accounts of research, pictures form little more than an occasional illustration that conveys sometimes nothing other than a sense of immediacy, and the authoritative claim that 'I was there' or 'it happened'. More often, perhaps, pictures are used to show some object or place that would be hard to describe vividly or concisely in words alone. Visual materials often form a significant part of most people's field work. So, it is worth thinking a little more about how these materials can be, and are, constructed. Alongside the kinds of audio recordings, transcripts and field notes described earlier, you may well end up with hours of video footage and/or dozens, hundreds or more photographs. This may not even be your intention as these materials often get collected and/or made along the way as opportunities arise. Ian, for example, collected lusciously and sometimes bizarrely illustrated exotic fruit brochures from the supermarket buyers that he visited (as well as being sent copies by anyone he knew who found them in store), took photos on the papaya farm and a neighbouring sugar estate, was in the right place at the right time to watch the making of, and appear, in a Jamaican TV programme about papaya farming for export, and managed to get a video of this and an older Jamaican TV programme about the success of Jim's farm. In the next chapter, we discuss how various forms of primarily textual data (field notes and transcripts) can be brought together and systematically analysed. Filmic data can be translated into textual form and analysed in the same way. But, is it really necessary to do this? What might be lost in that translation? How might you want to use your (audio)visual data *in relation to* data constructed via those other methods? And/or are you setting out to make, or might you end up making, them a large part of your final research product (e.g. can you, and do you want to, submit a video documentary as part or all of your dissertation or thesis)? Depending on your answers to these questions, the construction and treatment of your filmic data will vary.

You may have strong ideas, or little or no idea, here. Either way, we need to start off by thinking through the practicalities of the still and moving pictures that we're talking about. For a start, we need to ask, are they (likely to be) analogue (e.g. paper photos, negatives, cine film, or video tape) and/or digital? What equipment do you have access to and can you (or could you learn to) use to help make, edit and/or analyse these materials? If we're talking about computer-based editing and/or analysis – arguably the most affordable, user-friendly and accessible option for the novice – (how) will you be able to digitise analogue media? Do you have the expertise and access to the hardware and software to do this? How long will it take just to convert that data? And what's the capacity of your computer's hard drive? A single high definition colour photograph, for example, can take up to five megabytes of disk space (which can be a problem if, like Mike, you're working with an archive containing 4,000 images!). Then there's digital video, an hour of which can take up to 20 gigabytes of disk space! As far as the digital storage of your filmic data is concerned, then, the limits of your hard disk capacity will mean that you will have to come to some compromise between its quality and quantity. If you store more at a lower resolution, will it be sufficient to see (and hear) what's going on in enough detail to properly analyse it? And what quality would be necessary for anything that might end up in your 'final product'? So far, we've only been talking about what's needed to *store* the 'data' derived from filmic research. If you want to use software that will play back and help you to edit and/or analyse your video footage, especially, you will need even more disk space. It is worth noting that professional media processing computers often have two hard drives, one for running the computer's software and one for storing large video and other files. So, if you don't have access to such equipment, the question is whether it is worth converting analogue into digital at all? Might it be better to 'convert' filmic materials into a primarily textual format? Before answering any of these questions, it's often a good idea to ask an expert, if you aren't already one yourself, and/or take an appropriate course.

The 'conversion' (or translation) of one kind of data into another is central to both participant observation (experience into field notes) and interviewing (tape recordings into transcripts) research. And, in a general sense, turning still and moving pictures into text involves the kinds of detailed descriptions of settings, interactions, etc. associated with the former (for stills) and the verbatim transcription of speech associated with the latter (for film and video). However, as we argued earlier, researchers who use filmic approaches are not only concerned with the content of their own and others' work. They are also keen to know what goes on behind the lens to set up the settings, interactions, speech, etc. that get recorded. This means that it's important to get down on paper how compositions (apparently) try to convey specific impressions and construct specific sorts of truths. If you are doing your own photography or filming, or working with others while (they are) taking photos or making a film, this may simply involve writing appropriate participant observation-style notes and/or arranging interviews with participants about what you saw them doing, transcribing the recording of those interviews and then – in either or both cases – linking this textual data to specific pictures or clips via appropriate cross-referencing. Here, this textualised data could be the subject of your formal analysis and you might only go back to the original (audio)visual materials when you need to check things or produce your final report. However, it's important to note that filmic researchers pay a great deal of attention to questions of shot framing, focus, distance, angle and point of view (for still and moving images) as well as shot duration, tracking, cutting and continuity between shots (for moving images only) (see Rose 2001: 49–52). These extra considerations will therefore need to be outlined on the kinds of field-noting and interviewing checklists described earlier, and can also be used to structure tables that you could fill out for each photo or scene in a film (see below).

Below, we want to outline four different ways in which researchers have attempted to translate their raw filmic data onto paper in order to more or less conventionally analyse it. First, Robert Ziller (whose work we referred to earlier) has developed an approach which involves making systematic notes about the content of images, defining in general their items or styles, and then counting these in order to produce numerical summaries of what is depicted and by whom (e.g. Ball and Smith 1992; Collier and Collier 1986; Kenney 1993; Ziller 1990). The interpretative work thus comes in two phases:

(i) drawing up lists of contents (which requires a lot of work to decide what is 'worth' noting for your research), and then
(ii) analysing their frequency and patterns (to work out, for example, which groups of people take pictures with what sort of contents most often).

We have already expressed our reservations about how this process reduces the importance of visual images as communicative events embedded in social life. However, particularly with large numbers of photographs, it can reveal general patterns and backgrounds. These can serve as 'thin descriptions' and can be fleshed out via other means.

Second, there are a number of researchers who draw on a broad tradition that has treated visual representations as a form of language so that images can be interpreted according to the codes of representation that they appear to embody. This kind of interpretation can also be applied to ethnographic material, in terms of identifying key symbols and their relations (Leeuwen 2000; Rose 2001 chapters 4 and 5). Here you might ask why certain groups are often displayed in certain poses or against certain backgrounds, or why advertisements consistently code some activities as masculine/feminine, high/low class or associated with specific racialised identities (Goffman 1977; Hirsch 1981; Kenney 1993; Lutz and Collins 1993). This is not the place to outline how to do such analyses (see Ball and Smith 1992; Emmison and Smith 2000; Leeuwen and Jewitt 2000; Rose 2001 for a summary), but it is worth noting that this approach can help to analyse data produced through a variety of research methods. An attention to symbols and relations among symbols (and with associated discourses) might, for example, suggest tacit assumptions about what is 'natural' in a given social milieu or provide ideas about symbolic connections. Ian's admittedly rough analysis of the guides produced by British supermarkets, for instance, suggested that – through recurring images of bowls of tropical fruits set beneath palm trees on deserted beaches – consumers were being given the impression that it was the fecund 'nature' of the tropics that produced papayas rather than farmers, farm workers, tractors, irrigation equipment, pesticides and so on which he knew more about, and that this was a key element of the fetishising of these commodities. However, in terms of the place of such analyses in larger ethnographies, we would warn that this kind of approach can very easily allow the researcher to discuss higher orders of archetype and symbolic structure that can seem abstracted from the 'rustle of daily life' that ethnographers are supposed to be primarily interested in (see Lesy 1980).

A third way of producing data from photographic/video media which is perhaps closest in spirit to the approach advocated in this book is that associated with Richard Chalfen (1987; cf. Musello 1980). His approach involves combining the identification of patterns and regularities within and between images as above with a sensitivity to the practice of filming and to the ways in which taking photographs and making films are communication events. As a heuristic guide, we suggest that researchers think of two axes roughly corresponding to image and practice. Along the first are headings for questions like the following about content and composition:

(i) *Participants:*
   - Who were the participants?
   - Was everyone always included, or were certain people were left out on certain occasions?
   - Did you notice any differences between who was part of the group (or who was depicted as part of the group) in different kinds of representations?
(ii) *Topics*:
   - What events and topics did the photographer/filmmaker try to communicate?
   - Were these holiday photos or films?
   - Was the photographer/filmmaker trying to show spontaneity and domestic life, or to record members of the family and/or their activities?
(iii) *Settings:*
   - What settings occurred as contexts for what topics and what participants?
   - Was the photo/film taken in a public or private area?
   - Did the photo/film show people in the kinds of places they might expect to be seen (e.g. mothers in kitchens)?
   - Was the photo/film apparently intended to document that the participants were in a certain place at a certain time?
(iv) *Form of the finished image:*
   - Was it made to be circulated by hand?
   - Was it made to be placed within a family album?
   - Was it made to be framed and displayed in a particular place?
   - Was it made to be shown as a slide for communal display?
   - Was it made digital to be attached to emails or put on the web?

(v) *Stylistic devices*:
- What, if any, genre did it apparently draw upon?
- Was it a formal portrait, a landscape study, a snapshot, or a 'candid camera'-type shot?

Not all of these questions will apply to every type of picture. Rose (2001: 188–90) for instance, offers a different set of more general questions to ask about the production, composition and audience of images. They fitted Mike's work with tourists taking photos at historic sites, but he modified them for working on archival pictures. Moreover, when he used these headings, he did not apply them mechanically in a matrix helping him to identify frequencies of cross-occurrence. Rather they were used in a checklist, much like those he prepared for his interviews that enabled him to interrogate these different pictures (paralleling the treatment of textual material in the next chapter). In other words, categorisation and annotation helped him to turn paradoxically eloquent yet dumb bits of celluloid into useful textual information.

The above comprise just one axis of Chalfen's data construction. The second axis addresses how these pictures came to be produced, and involves using headings and questions like those below:

(i) *Planning:*
- Were these images staged or candid, or staged as candid?
- Were the people in them aware of the photographer?
(ii) *Filming events:*
- What events were depicted and what others (often necessary for the image to have been produced) were not?
- Where was the picture/film taken from?
- How was it set up?
- How was it decided who should take it and who should be in it?
(iii) *Editing processes:*
- How and why were certain images selected to (not) be shown to the researcher?
- How are they cropped, blown up or otherwise altered?
- How and where are they stored and/or displayed?
- With digital photographs which are printed out, which are burned onto disk and which discarded?
(iv) *Display:*
- For whom were these images usually displayed?
- When, where, for how long and how often?
- Were they intended to be viewed by the general public, the photographer's family and/or just the photographer her/himself?

To these, we might add one more issue and related questions. Going back to what we said earlier about the struggles of various groups to represent themselves rather than to be represented by others, we suggest that researchers should also think through the power relations involved in constructing information around, about and with visual imagery. And these are the power relations that are apparent both between the research participants, and between participants and the researcher. Thus:

(v) *Power relations:*
  - Who controls and edits a picture/film?
  - Who learns what skills (if any) from this process?
  - Are people(s) just reduced to images simply for the viewing pleasure of others?
  - Who decides who these groups/people(s) are anyway?
  - How can/should/do researchers make use of their/our power to invade people's private spaces to render them public (Berko 1992)?
  - Are researchers actually encouraging research participants to reveal themselves when researchers them/ourselves would not?

Again, as with the other approaches outlined in this book, there are no straightforward answers to these questions, and all that we would advise is that you try to address them as best as you can within the political, ethical, moral and interpersonal contexts of your own project. After working with children in Colombia to produce videos of their own areas and histories, for instance, Gómez (2003) argued that the film outcome and the skills in media production that participants gained were less important than how the children's interviews with local informants served to reconnect them and enhance their sense of collective belonging. All of these contextual questions are important in working out the meanings of particular photos/films to different people in different situations as they move between the places where they are taken and the spaces where they are displayed. Catherine Lutz and Jane Collins (1993), for instance, used Chalfen's approach to try to unpack the multiple contexts of photographs taken and selected for reproduction – institutional, political and technical – by variously interested actors for *National Geographic*. Alternatively, recent work on tourism has focused on how specific types of performance are associated with particular places, and how we can see behaviour scripted according to social norms exemplified in, and reinforced through, the practices of family photography (Bærenholdt et al. 2004). Along this second axis, then, it is important to emphasise that the pictures are a way of *getting at* information rather than being the information themselves.

Going through issues of filmic content and context together means that it's possible to go back and ask research participants questions about the patterns you identify in their photos or films. Moreover, adopting filmic, interviewing and participant observation methods can enable the researcher to understand more dimensions both of how images are used and what they can mean to the people who possess and/or produce them (Lesy 1980; Reme 1993). An explicitly multi-method approach to constructing filmic information therefore, and not perhaps surprisingly, comprises our fourth and final approach. And here we would direct readers to, for example, Waitt and Head's (2002) research in which they showed postcards of the Kimberley national park in Australia to tourists to look at and studied how they responded to them and how these responses shaped their expectations; and to Marc Neumann's (1999) ethnography of tourism at the Grand Canyon, which compared contemporary and historic official pictures, tourist pictures, commercial advertising materials, art works and his own pictures, with interviews and participant observation to get at how people 'saw' the Canyon. As we argued at the start of this section, each of the methods we have outlined here is appropriate for producing certain kinds of data, but none are appropriate for all. Indeed, we have had trouble separating them out.

SUMMARY

It seems apt to pause and tease out some threads from the different ways of constructing ethnographic information that we have presented in this section of the book. It should be clear that we both chose the methods we used because we thought they would work for particular issues or projects. We are not proposing these methods as 'mandatory' for every project. Not every issue needs a focus group, not every dissertation has to include a semi-structured interview, and we have outlined how some methods may be impossible or inappropriate at times. We have not then tried to produce a template of what projects should include. It should be obvious that both of us tend to the eclectic, and mixed and matched according to our questions but also according to the opportunities that came up in the field. Equally, there are other methods that we have not used here (or ever) that could be useful for you. Work with participant diaries, participatory methods, drawings or media sources or archival work may well form part of the mix in other projects. So our selection is in no way meant to be exhaustive. However, the diversity of methods here is meant to respond to both practical and theoretical issues.

Practically, having a range of approaches in your head can help deal with situations where new issues emerge or where your planned method does not work. Thus interviews may prove possible when you cannot get physical access for participant observation, participant photographs might help when you cannot get written diaries and so on. While no method simply replaces another, flexibility and adaptability between them help deal with the ups and downs of the research process. We tend to see methods here evolving in the 'to-ing' and 'fro-ing' between field and theory – so rather than choosing a method to be applied regardless, in a read-*then*-do pattern, we suggest that as we learn more about the field we may rethink and possibly try doing things another way.

Theoretically, we have tried to show that different methods do not simply offer different ways to understand a social phenomena. Yes, they each offer partial insights but that is because they each construct different understandings about those phenomena. While it is common-sensical that using several approaches may offer a more rounded account, we do not think that it is the case that if only you had enough different methods you would come up with a complete and exhaustive account. One common way researchers talk about this is by analogy with 'triangulation', where one method is used to confirm the insights from another, just as in navigation bearings are taken from several points to fix your location. This notion is something with which we have sympathy, but we would not want to imply that you have to use multiple methods, that may spread your limited time and resources too thinly and it may be better to get more depth on fewer approaches. Nor do we believe that if you do use multiple methods they always reveal the same thing, and produce convergent accounts. It may be that different approaches develop divergent insights about a phenomena – and that can be a good thing too.

Section 3

Pulling it Together

8 Analysing Field Materials

Every time I have been in the field and become truly involved I have had to struggle with an impulse to stay longer than I should have stayed. By this I mean that I felt an almost irresistible urge to gather more data rather than face the grim task of organising and reporting on the data I had. But in every case, the longer I stayed, the less time I had to write, and the poorer became my final report. Indeed most of the data gathered at the expense of the time I had allowed for writing is still languishing in my files. It's a horrid but inescapable fact that it takes more time to organise, write and present material well than it does to gather it.... The sensible researcher will allow as much free time to write his [sic.] report as he spent in the field. If he is really astute and can get away with it, he will allow more time (Wax 1983: 193–94)

INTRODUCTION

In the literature on qualitative methods, 'data coding' or 'transcript analysis' has tended to be conspicuous by its absence, forming only some 10% of all major accounts, and often just a line or two in journal papers, despite taking up at least as much time as fieldwork (Miles and Huberman 1984). This is remarkable as it leaves the impression that all the 'experiential richness' of the methods we have been outlining are effortlessly transferred into finished reports. 'Findings', it seems, are just found and included in snippets, and readers are asked to take it on trust that they represent field materials and respondents' views (Baxter and Eyles 1997). It may be that these snippets, and the arguments that surround them, have come to the fore via the systematic analysis of systematically constructed data. But it may also be the case that they have arisen from looser analysis of more loosely constructed data. Earlier, we argued that the latter was the kind of approach that gave plenty of ammunition to those who would describe qualitative research as woolly or subjective. Being systematic, we argued, was a way of countering such accusations and of being able to make more concrete and convincing arguments. Yet, ethnographic research necessarily involves following up leads, adapting to contingencies, and (re)designing research 'on the hoof'. It involves disparate bits of 'data' made through odd conversations, first-hand experiences, fact-finding, referrals, collected bits of paper, sketching and photography, web-searching, reading and so on. Much of it might be in multiple forms of transcripts, statistics, textual and visual materials, research diary notes and so on. And the 'analysis' of this informally constructed 'data' is likely to be via an informal process of piecing things together, figuring things out, gaining focus and direction as the research unfolds. There needs to be a sense then of balance of creative and structured processes, checks on our interpretations yet also room to develop ideas. Thus, what we advocate is a process in which both less *and* more systematic data construction and analysis are necessary for good research. A project will therefore involve less *and* more systematic phases, producing less *and* more systematic data, which demands less *and* more systematic data analysis.[1] In the following pages, then, we concentrate on the 'more systematic' side of the process, and outline some basic but important ways in which to make formal sense of the primarily textual(ised) data produced via the participant observation, interviewing, focus group and filmic methods outlined in the previous chapters. In doing so, we want to neither set out an exhaustive account nor a mandatory process, but to provide enough of a framework to aid a first-time researcher without stifling her/his creativity.

Like everything else we have discussed so far, analysis is a creative, active, making process that can be done more or less carefully and thoroughly, and with more or less accountability and transparency (Bailey et al. 1999; Crang 2001; Rennie 1998). It often starts off with a too often fleeting sense of satisfaction, after you have gathered all of your data together, on your desk perhaps. All being well, you will be faced with a mass of what you think is pretty good stuff. After the twists and turns of fieldwork, it is an achievement to have produced such original, detailed data, but how are you going to turn it into a cogent, hopefully illuminating and maybe even impressive 'analysis'? That's the cornerstone of any dissertation or thesis based on this kind of 'fieldwork'. Everything hinges on it. But, just as you laboriously constructed that data, you now have to laboriously analyse it, make sense of it, and produce some order out of it. The research process is far from over. But it's not as if you'll be trying to create order out of chaos. The way that the data has been constructed means that it is far from 'raw'. It has already been partly analysed, made sense of, ordered in the research process, for example, through the:

- focusing and refocusing of research aims and questions,
- formal phasing of your research to address specific issues with specific people,
- methods used and the kinds of data they help you to construct,

- individuals and groups you chose to try to involve in your research,
- issues you jotted down on your interview checklists,
- ways your participants and others took photos, wrote accounts, and told stories and
- ways you tried to make sense of research experiences in your research diary notes.

What this formal stage of analysis is supposed to do, then, is to reconfigure this data, to look at it much more carefully and critically, and to perhaps de- and recontextualise different parts so as to be able to see new themes and patterns in it.

The analysis that we're talking about here is, therefore, another stage in an ongoing critical and creative research process that takes place in another part of the project's 'expanded field'. It's not that separate a stage that takes place in a detached space. It's a connected and connective process. For example, it is not separate from the initial formulation of research questions because it can point you towards those that were answered without you asking them. The themes that become such an important part of formal analysis usually start their lives in the data as it's constructed, then get scribbled on the margins of the data, and on separate pieces of paper, as it's formally analysed and can eventually appear in the headings and subheadings of any analysis chapter(s). Similarly, while the formal analysis we're going to discuss may bring important themes to light (with pages of illustrations to back them up), they still have to be ordered so that a convincing analytical narrative can be woven through them. Throughout the research process, writing and analysis are inseparable. Themes or issues may also come to light that suggest some more fieldwork or data is needed – projects can thus develop in an iterative way between doing, ordering, interpreting and writing. But, what we outline below is a specific form of 'analysis' which involves formally identifying themes, deciding upon their relationships to each other, and selecting important ones that lead to theoretical ideas. It is a process that involves doing nitty-gritty things with paper, pens, scissors, computers and software. It's about chopping up, (re)ordering, (re)contextualising and (re)assembling the data we have so diligently constructed. It's about translating a messy process into a neat product. And the materiality and actuality of how we go about this affects the conclusions we draw (Kittler 1999). For example, identifying themes in qualitative data may seem like a straightforward thing, but different approaches have been suggested for researchers working through different philosophies and agendas (Ryan and Bernard 2003 identify 12 of these!). Below we outline probably the most common approach, using ideas of 'grounded theory'.

PRELIMINARY WORK

Let us take a common situation where, after a period of work using a variety of methods, you find yourself with a stack of transcripts, field notes and so forth. For the sake of brevity, we'll call all of these 'primary materials'. At this stage you will no doubt be able to remember lots of juicy morsels and not a few embarrassing slip-ups, but such memories are far from rigorous analysis. This is where researchers must face the task of turning what often seems like more or less inchoate experience into a fixed and somehow ordered rendering of reality (Throop 2003). Thus, in the early stages of your analysis you should begin by going back and rereading all of these primary materials. In doing this, you will be able to remind yourself of the contexts in which these were constructed as your research progressed and what your thoughts were on this at various times. At the same time it is highly likely that you will feel that a (large) proportion of what you have compiled is somewhat irrelevant, naive and/or gauche. This is normal. Having gone back through these materials once, though, you should

- have some ideas about interesting happenings at the time, and
- have refreshed your memory on your working ideas of how to interpret these events, and on how these ideas directed the construction of further materials (Bogdan and Taylor 1984).

Having done this, you should then prepare for a more in-depth study. It is a good idea to start by getting word-processed copies of your primary materials formatted, say with a wide right margin, so that you have plenty of room to annotate them. Next, you should make sure that every page has the source of the material on it (say in a running heading), and that each speaker, event, setting, sketch, photo etc. is labelled so that any page or excerpt can be placed in the wider body of the materials (for the same reasons, lengthy sections of text should be numbered by page and, probably, by line[2]). If you have access to appropriate computer hardware and software, it is worth noting that some programmes provide built-in facilities for formatting different kinds of primary materials for analysis together (see Box 8.1). On top of this, whatever you do, it is also advisable to make one copy of everything and put it in a safe place since this will serve as your backup should everything go horribly wrong.

After having done all of this, you should then take your main copy and begin to work on it. Most researchers recommend starting an analysis by reading these documents one line or sentence at a time, and trying to concentrate on what was going on step by step and to reconstruct the events to which each part refers (McCracken 1988b; Strauss 1987).

Box 8.1: Software Packages for Qualitative Data Analysis

There are now specialist packages (there are more than a dozen widely available, and many more besides if you hunt around) to help you handle qualitative data. When you are doing a project you may then be faced with the issue of whether to use one. If one or more of the software packages is available, it may be that you will be offered, or have to take, classes training you to use them. Alternatively, you may have to teach yourself. In both cases, you may end up asking yourself 'is it worth it?' The answer is 'it depends'. There are several factors to weigh up here. First, how good are you with Information Technology generally – how fast are you likely to learn to use the system? This is a time cost. However, most people will say that the systems, once learnt and once the data is there, do greatly 'speed up' the mechanical processes of analysis – a time saving. So the second question is how much data do you have? Will this gain outweigh the cost of learning the software and inputting material? This too depends on how comfortable you are working on screen or if you prefer to work on hard copy. In Mike's experience, the pay-off begins at around twenty to thirty interviews (if they are say one hour semi-structured ones). But you might also want to think, third, even if the software will not pay off now for the project at hand, is it a useful skill I may use in the next project or something I want on my CV?

If you decide to use a package the next question is 'which one?'. There are several reviews (Crang et al. 1997; Fielding and lee 1998; Hinchliffe et al. 1997; Lewins and Silver 2005; Weitzman and Miles 1995) but software programmes continue to evolve and/or disappear, and new ones appear. Your choice may be limited by the software site licences that your institution has, since the packages normally cost around £250–£400 to buy for yourself. So we are not going to give a guide to using specific packages nor offer an extensive 'compare and contrast' list of functions and features. We do, however, think that there are five issues that can usefully be thought through here.

First, each programme is written by someone who has their own way of doing analysis. One programme designer, Lyn Richards who works on NUD*IST and NVivo, once commented in a training session that 'grounded theory is the bumper sticker we all wear'. And that is true of those two programmes and The Ethnograph and is also claimed by Atlas/ti. But to illustrate differences in emphasis, John Seidel (1991) who wrote the Ethnograph criticised people who thought computers meant they could use bigger 'data sets', as a sort of quantitative envy. Rather he designed the Ethnograph to enable more intense work on small ones. NUD*IST enables team work and shared inputting, reflecting its background by contrast in collaborative project teams, rather than the lone researcher. We would advise you to think through not just what features the package offers but what you will use – thus NUD*IST has probably the best search functions (allowing you to search for words in the text, overlapping codes you

Box 8.1: continued

have created, sequences of codes and even nearness between codes and terms) but these are not functions Mike, for instance, has ever used. HyperResearch offers some very simple, easy to learn mechanisms, which suffice for many smaller projects, and a 'Hypothesis testing' function, that no one in Mike's department has ever used.

Second, the corollary from this variety of functions is to look at some demo versions and see if they 'fit' with how you think about your materials and what you want to do with them. Mike always found that the Ethnograph chimed with his approach, while he had real trouble getting a handle on the terminology and structure of perhaps the most popular, and thus 'successful' programme, of the 1990s – NUD*IST. He now works on Atlas/ti which again fits how he thinks. Others disagree, and to fit with collaborators he has used NUD*IST and NVivo on different projects.

Third, do look at some specific functions if they appear to help – for instance some packages are very good at analysing the text, by say searching for 'concordances' of terms (that is specific patterns of speech or language) while others enable you to connect analysis to a statistical package if you wish to, say, relate what your informants say more easily to their social background.

Fourth, think about the formats in which you have collected your data. Thus Atlas/ti allows you to have pictures as well as text, it allows importation of Excel tables or even Powerpoint if that matters to you (it never has to Mike). NVivo offers connections to video software, the (super-)HyperQual programme (originally for Macs, now with a windows version) has settings which allow the inclusion of materials from sketches, pictures and literature reviews alongside those from diaries and interviews. Moreover, other programmes may be more geared to specific sources or allow specific combinations (see Fielding and Lee 1991; Tesch 1990 on the origins of different programmes). It is important here to think through what might help you, but also not to get too seduced by an impressive array of possibilities that you will not use. Some researchers have argued that using something as simple as Microsoft Word's table function, with text in one column and other columns for numbered codes can allow for chunks of text to be categorised pretty efficiently (La Pelle 2004).

Fifth, and finally, we have so far been assuming that you, like us, tend to be a sole researcher working with your own computer. If you are part of a team you might like features in some programmes (e.g. NUD*IST, Atlas/ti, NVivo) that allow different people on a research team to share files and to label and date what they have done and how they have changed things. A recently developed programme 'Ethnonotes' (Lieber et al. 2003) specialises in cataloguing the multiple types of data and entries that comprise field notes and making them accessible among a team of multiple researchers in multiple sites, whose output can be exported into some other types of analysis software. You may even have to think that some

Box 8.1: continued

programmes straddle MacOS and Windows, and that say Ethnonotes or Atlas/ti, by using XML format exports, offer some interoperability between the two within a project. If you want to look at some of these, we would suggest you read the academic reviews to see what kind of programme might help you; most have online demos, and a number of web sites offer useful descriptions and links. Good starting points might be

http://www.textanalysis.info/qualitative.htm

http://dmoz.org/Science/Social_Sciences/Methodology/Qualitative/Tools/

In doing this, it may also be advisable to play back your tapes or audio files again and to look through your research diary (which you may want to type up and include as part of, rather than supplementary to, your primary materials) in order to recapture some of the emotional flavour and the interpersonal situations that produced the material (Portelli 1981). This kind of approach may help you to avoid producing a cold, over-rationalised account that does not do justice to the intersubjective richness of the research encounters that it has drawn on (Hunt 1989). Such a close study of tapes, notes and so forth invariably reveals a welter of things that researchers had not noticed at the time when they/we were trying to manage these encounters. The emphasis here should therefore be on thinking about what was being said and what the meaning and intent of each statement (your own as well as other people's) might have been, and as you go through your materials you should write these down in your wide right margin alongside the text. Anselm Strauss (1987) has termed this process 'open coding' (see Box 8.2), and has stressed that in this initial stage of analysis there is no need to look for significant themes or relations because this may lead to a prejudgement of events later on in the materials (but, in contrast, see Ingersoll and Ingersoll 1987). In practice, though, because of the ways in which you will have constructed your materials, and particularly because they will have been inspired at various stages by specific ideas about what was important at the time, no researcher can confront such a text quite so 'innocently'.

Additionally, either as you go along or going back over the materials after having completed an entire 'cycle', you might then 'code' your annotations. Very simply, here similar events or themes or actions or parts of events or sentiments should be given similar labels. The form that these labels can take will vary depending on your preference and/or the scale of your study. In doing this, some researchers use different coloured pens to highlight codes which refer to different phenomena, others

Box 8.2: An Example of Open Coding

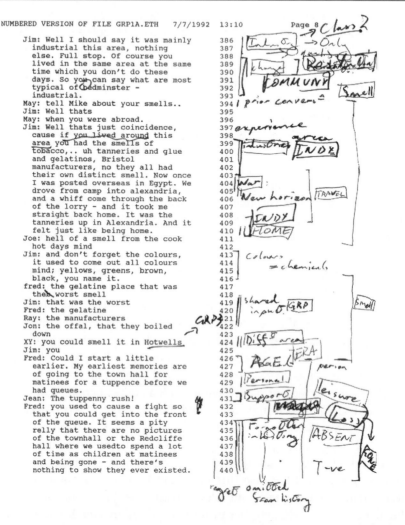

NUMBERED VERSION OF FILE GRP1A.ETH   7/7/1992   13:10   Page 8

```
Jim: Well I should say it was mainly      386
  industrial this area, nothing           387
  else. Full stop. Of course you          388
  lived in the same area at the same      389
  time which you don't do these           390
  days. So you can say what are most      391
  typical of Bedminster -                 392
  industrial.                             393
May: tell Mike about your smells..        394
Jim: Well thats                           395
May: when you were abroad.                396
Jim: Well thats just coincidence,         397
  cause if you lived around this          398
  area you had the smells of              399
  tobacco,.. uh tanneries and glue        400
  and gelatinos, Bristol                  401
  manufacturers, no they all had          402
  their own distinct smell. Now once      403
  I was posted overseas in Egypt. We      404
  drove from camp into alexandria,        405
  and a whiff come through the back       406
  of the lorry - and it took me           407
  straight back home. It was the          408
  tanneries up in Alexandria. And it      409
  felt just like being home.              410
Joe: hell of a smell from the cook        411
  hot days mind                           412
Jim: and don't forget the colours,        413
  it used to come out all colours         414
  mind; yellows, greens, brown,           415
  black, you name it.                      416
fred: the gelatine place that was         417
  the worst smell                         418
Jim: that was the worst                   419
Fred: the gelatine                        420
Ray: the manufacturers                    421
Jon: the offal, that they boiled          422
  down                                    423
XY: you could smell it in Hotwells.       424
Jim: you                                  425
Fred: Could I start a little              426
  earlier. My earliest memories are      427
  of going to the town hall for           428
  matinees for a tuppence before we       429
  had queues.                             430
Jean: The tuppenny rush!                  431
Fred: you used to cause a fight so        432
  that you could get into the front       433
  of the queue. It seems a pity           434
  relly that there are no pictures        435
  of the townhall or the Redcliffe        436
  hall where we usedto spend a lot        437
  of time as children at matinees         438
  and being gone - and there's            439
  nothing to show they ever existed.      440
```

It is worth noting here how code categories which survived or were transferred into later sections had been boxed, others over-written or altered. For example. 'AGE' (lines 426–27) initially referred to the date of participants' memories and their longevity but was changed to 'ERA' to fit in with other groups and to include the periods from which memories tended to cluster. The initial note made at the bottom of the page – 'regret omitted from history' (lines 439–40) – was later coded as 'ABSENT' (lines 434–40) with the addition of a '-ve' marker to show that this absence was apparently regretted. Moreover, while many categories were emic (e.g. 'Smell' – lines 394–411), a note that the group dynamic was one of 'Shared input' (lines 418–23) was later coded as 'GRP' to indicate group dynamics.

underline, highlight or mark sections with abbreviations. Whatever is most comfortable for you, though, will probably be best. These codes may cover a single word, line, feeling or a whole chunk of text. There may also be multiple codes applicable to any given segment of text. It may also be worthwhile to develop codes that allow you to analyse or to note the context of remarks or observations – whether they were sarcastic, defensive or said with insistence and, in group work especially, the pattern of dialogue i.e. whether a coded theme was a feeler put out by a group member to test the water, was said by several members or repeated by one, involved someone summarising another person's ideas (Krueger 1988), was triggered by something said earlier, was a response to a question or was simply unsolicited.

After initially going through your materials, it will probably be time to begin rereading them to firm up your codes. As you go through the materials again, you should try to note down all of the categories you have invented on a separate piece of paper. This can have several uses, in that it will allow you to see how many categories you have, whether there are any very similar categories that might be usefully amalgamated and what categories you have already found/invented. This last point is by no means as flippant as it might seem: we have all had times when we have failed to use an appropriate code because we had temporarily forgotten about it. Moreover, we would suggest that the researcher needs to be sensitive to how much prior categories can determine what s/he subsequently looks for and to what extent such categories may be said to be 'found' in the material. This last problem is largely the reason for suggesting an 'open coding' procedure as the first step, so as to avoid imposing some outside set of categories, and this requires a sensitivity to what have been called 'emic' and 'etic' categories in analysis. As Michael Agar has written:

> In many ... anthropological discussions, emic and etic are used to characterise a .. distinction roughly translated as the 'insider's' versus the 'outsider's' point of view. The problem here is that it is difficult to imagine any ethnographic statement that is not a blend of these (1980: 191).

Roughly speaking, emic (or 'in viva') categories are those that have been used by the people studied to describe their own worlds. Given that ethnographers usually have a clear interest in how people interpret the world to themselves, particular care should be taken to note these kinds of categories as you pore through your materials (cf. Patton 1980). However, as we have already argued, it is virtually impossible for the researcher to banish all of her/his prior thoughts from the analysis, since her/his research will have been based around a theory-driven selection of participants, and because even noticing an 'emic' code will have required interpretation. Like Agar, then, we would certainly not argue for a clear distinction to be made between these two categories since we have ample experience of how difficult it can be to interpret an allegedly 'emic' categorisation when, for instance, we have suspected that it was being used ironically or was the result of how the respondents tried to present themselves to us in ways they thought matched our interests. Thus, instead of adopting a strict emic/etic binary, in the following pages we will suggest an approach which involves a general drift from emic to etic coding (in which we still consider it useful to ask questions such as 'to what extent is this a participant's world view or some composite of my representation of her/his world view?'), but which is also subject to the provisos mentioned above. Thus, the move from one to the other is not taken here as being a simple or straightforward process.

DEVELOPING CODES

While working through your materials you are likely to see vital connections and/or glimmerings of new ideas. It can be a good idea to take another sheet of paper to note down these sorts of insights and hunches, or indeed to create what might be termed your 'must remember to check' notes. Anselm Strauss (1987) has termed these theoretical notes, and has suggested that they should be reviewed regularly to guide and to develop more ideas. These notes and those from the field can begin to form cumulative chains relating (to) certain ideas, and they should help you in making sense of your materials and in developing new ideas about how your codes relate to each other. Moreover, on yet another sheet of paper/notebook it is important to try to write down in full what you mean by the codes you are generating and how you think they are working. This is useful both because it should help you to think through what went on, and what patterns you are seeing, but also because it is all too easy to forget what an abbreviated note meant or why you made it in the first place. Hopefully, this 'paper trail' of working notes should help you to remember and to trace those connections that you have thought of while going through the materials.

After this has been done, and in order to gather your materials into a manageable form, these connections and relations between statements need to be sorted through. There are again several ways of doing this depending on the amount of materials, the time you have to sort through it and your inclination. It is possible to enter the materials and codes onto a computer using qualitative data analysis packages (see Box 8.1 for a brief outline of issues to consider about these packages). It is equally possible to do this sorting manually by cutting up chunks of notes and transcripts and placing them in coded piles on your floor (this is what Ian did for his MA research) and/or by making an index card for each code and recording on it the location of each occurrence in the materials. What should then begin to happen is that the focus of analysis shifts from the individual statements to the ways in which they relate to each other (see Box 8.3). To make sense of how your materials fit together (and to find relevant bits), many researchers end up establishing some sort of cross-referencing system to

---

Box 8.3: Relating Themes Using Qualitative Data Analysis Software: an Example

This section was retrieved using The Ethnograph software, as a search for the overlap of two categories from Mike's groupwork material. At the top of the page, the source of the material (GRP1A May) and the categories which were searched for (SC: COAL REP MEM) has been printed, while the text in which these overlap has been indicated down the right hand side by the symbols $ (for COAL) and % (for REP MEM). Other categories also punctuate the text and are bracketed down its right hand side (e.g. the code SOURCE by the symbol *, or the code LOCN by the symbol @). Within this there are various sizes of coded chunks and different types of codes. For instance, COAL was a broadly emic category covering those parts of the transcript where group members talked about topics relating to coal mining in Bristol, while the REP MEM (standing for REPORTED MEMORY) code which it was paired with was a broadly etic code covering those parts where Mike realised that they were recounting events which they had not personally experienced. The brevity of the codes used here again indicates the necessity of writing down somewhere what each means in full.

```
GRP1A    May

E: #-INDY

SC: +COAL +REP MEM

$-COAL        %-REP MEM    *-SOURCE
        : May: How much do you actually       298  |  -$ -% -*
        :    remember of the coalmines?       299  |   $  %  |
        : Sid: Well, no nothing much (..) our 300  |   $  %  |
        :    parents had worked there our     301  |   $  %  |
        :    fathers had worked down there.And 302 |   $  % -*
        :    you, you                         303  |   $  %  %
  *-SOURCE
        : May: But were the buildings still   304  |   $  % -*
        :    there that you'd remember?       305  |   $  %  |
  @-LOCN
        : Sid: No there's a few miners        306  |   $  %  |  -@
        :    cottages still down there in     307  |   $  %  |   |
        :    Marsham st                       308  |   $  % -*   |
        : XY: Ashton Rd.                      309  |   $  %      |
        : Ray: the Brickyard                  310  |   $  %     -@
  *-REMAIN    --SOURCE
        : Sid: and you've got the um there was 311 |   $  % -*
        :    a hole still left of the um mines 312 |   $  %  |
  @-LOCN      ^-REMAIN
        :    of years ago. Thats down the end 313  |   $  %  | -@ -^
        :    of um Silbear Rd outinto the     314  |   $  %  |  |  |
        :    fields there and its still there 315  |   $  %  | -@  |
        :    the hole. Protected..            316  |   $  % -*     -^
        : Grace: Did they have one out the .. 317  |   $  %
        : XX: They did.(yes)                  318  |   $  %
  *-ECONC     ^-GONE
        : Jim: Oh there was quite a few in    319  |   $  % -*    -^
        :    around Bristol weren't there?    320  |   $  %  |     |
        :    Coalmines                        321  |   $  % -*     |
  *-SOURCE    @-REMAIN
        : May: Dean Lane was already a park   322  |   $  % -* -@  |
        :    when you were                    323  |   $  %  |  |  |
```

render a complex series of notes comprehensible by connecting relevant sections with other similar cases (see Jackson 2001). However you do this, it is important to realise that the categories and similarities on which your system will end up being based will not have been decided in advance but will develop as you make connections through the (re)reading, (re)coding and (re)ordering of your research materials.

SIFTING, SORTING AND MAKING SENSE OF IT ALL

As you sort your materials and connect your codes, it is likely that there will be some things that don't appear to fit together or which contradict each other within your codes. This is where the idea of an iterative process is useful. When faced with these misfits and contradictions, you should go back to see why these occurred:

- Was a particular case due to a 'clerical error' in filing?
- Was it a genuine difference between sources? or
- Was it because, through your coding system, you had erroneously grouped together differing phenomena?

As a result of asking such questions you may then:

- be prompted to clarify interpretations between two conflicting sources (something which may necessitate further fieldwork),
- decide that this contradiction is part of normal human inconsistency or
- think that it is a crucial part of your understanding of a particular theme.

Most likely, though, you will have to go back and reclassify the other occasions on which that code was used. However, it is only through this continual going back and forth from source to categories to source and so on that your codes will begin to become more consistent as you develop them to cover all of the incidents and differences in your materials. As this process goes on, though, you should find that there are fewer and fewer misfits and contradictions in your coding system.

By this stage, you should have some ready indicators of what the important themes/events or categories in your materials might be. You can then place your primary materials to one side and begin to work on your coded sections. Here the idea is to sort these sections into 'piles' by topics if you are literally cutting and pasting (they are called 'stacks' in Hypersoft, 'code segments' in The Ethnograph, 'families' in NUD*IST or Atlas/ti, but the principle is the same as 'piles of paper' on your floor) and then to move these around as you begin to think them through. Look at the relations within and between these piles, and reread them in order to trace out more carefully the similarities and differences you identified in the previous stage of analysis. The idea is to consider how categories (i.e. 'piles') relate or overlap with each other – are they 'sub-codes' of a major idea, are they mutually exclusive with another or do they consistently overlap in one way with another code? These patterns among the categories bring us to looking at the connections among the materials.

These 'piles' will come to be the dimensions of your analysis. Each one may relate to some key issue, and Anselm Strauss has suggested (1987) that researchers should explicitly tease out the different properties of each pile/category. For instance, with reference to Mike's groupwork transcripts, he began coding statements that suggested different kinds of 'loss'. However, this category grew to contain an enormous number of segments that he then sorted into a continuum. Through this process, the category could no longer be labelled simply 'loss', but became a progression of categories – 'gone', 'disappearing', 'derelict', 'unused' and 'remaining'. Thus, beginning with a general code identified at the primary stage of analysis, a whole axis of codes was subsequently developed.

Another way to assist in your attempt to understand the material is to keep thinking through the theoretical notes that you made as you went along concerning what appeared to be leading where and so on. You could also draw diagrams of how your categories appear to relate to each other, or you could even physically/electronically move the groups of coded chunks around. Going back to noting these categories on a separate sheet of paper, Mike has tended to sketch out possible patterns and linkages between these by placing them in little boxes on an A4 sheet, drawing lines/arrows between them and thereby constructing a 'code map' (cf. Jones 1985; Miles and Huberman 1984; Strauss 1987; see Box 8.4). Moreover, the subtleties of connection can also be drawn out by annotating these lines to indicate antagonisms, similarities or causalities. We are not suggesting a need to draw neat conceptual boxes here. Instead, we want to stress the usefulness of drawing and redrawing such diagrams to think through and plot the key themes and relationships in your materials. This process can also help to identify glaring gaps for instance when a 'flow diagram' stops or when all of the interrelations point at an issue that you have not yet raised. As an example of using diagrams to visualise patterns and to look for breakdowns and relationships, some researchers have constructed matrices (e.g. Agar 1986). For instance, we mentioned earlier how Richard Chalfen (1987) took the practices of photography and juxtaposed them with the images produced. Again, the idea here would not be actually to produce a matrix as the final output from the research, but to use it as means to think through and to plot key ideas and relationships. So, again, you could ask yourself what boxes were empty or overfull, and why?

Box 8.4: An Example of a 'Code Map'

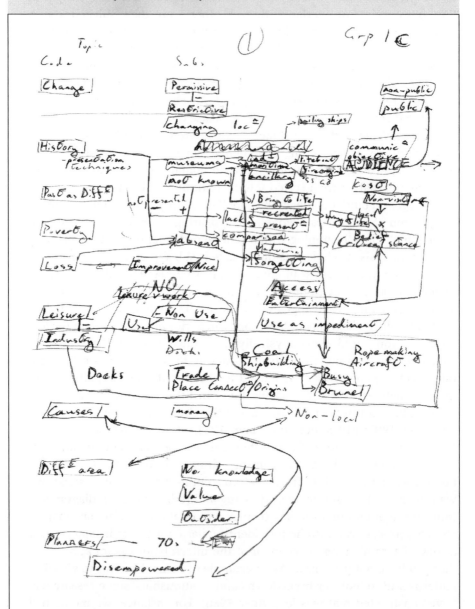

This sketch was used by Mike to keep track of the codes and subcodes referring to one group meeting about the presentation of a local area's history by official bodies. As can be seen, this is not like a finished 'matrix' but is more like a 'map' of the interrelationships between the issues which were covered in the meeting.

Box 8.4: continued

Broadly, these were traced from the general codes on the left where, among other things, the group referred to change occurring ('Change'), to the presentation of history ('History'), to how different the past was ('Past as Difft'), to the industries then present ('Industry'), to the causes of change ('Causes'), to the relationships with different areas ('Difft area') and to the alleged role of town planning ('Planners'). Generally the words are mnemonics for categories, those closer together are related and, as can be seen, this 'map' shows a dense development around some of these issues and not around others. Much of this will be fairly illegible to most readers, but it is important to state how this mapping worked as an aid to thinking, how it changed and how new relationships were drawn into it. Its messiness and sudden long connecting lines show how ideas can change, evolve and shift as new ideas come to light. Moreover, it may be worth noting that some computer packages (e.g. Atlas/ti, Hypersoft and Hyperqual) have facilities for incorporating and/or producing such 'code maps', albeit in a limited fashion.

Having said all of this, it is not wise to become too sold on the elegance of your 'code map' at this stage. For, as you progress through sorting your materials, it is highly likely that there will be more breakdowns in your schema. Suddenly, what had appeared to be a logical distinction or relation may no longer work. You may have to break up or subdivide a category or remodel the relationship between two or more categories. As mentioned above, you are likely to develop a schema until it breaks down, at which point you will have to go back through all the cases which were bound up in it in order to develop an alternative one. Each breakdown can thus force a rethink and a backtrack in order to reorganise your thoughts. This is one reason why Michael Agar has termed such analysis as 'maddeningly recursive' (1986: 29) and why others have referred to it as 'a messy, ambiguous, time-consuming, [and, we must emphasise] creative, fascinating process' (Marshall and Rossman 1989: 112)!

Any idea that analysis is some process of mysterious cogitation should be dispelled by now. Every researcher faces a task that is nearer 99% perspiration and 1% inspiration. These statistics have three important implications for doing ethnographies:

- First and foremost, the successful analysis of ethnographic materials is very far from a mystical process of intuition that only the chosen few are able to perform.
- Second, it is important, as we emphasised earlier, to allow plenty of time to interpret these materials.

- Finally, the 'paper trail' of notes and revisions which is central to such analysis is evidence of its 'reliability' because the reasons for your interpretations are explicit, and you can show that your analysis is much more than just 'quarrying out the good bits' or using field material to lend an eye-witness authority to your account (Atkinson 1990). Some software now provides an electronic 'audit trail' of what was done, by whom in teams, at what stages, what was abandoned and changed, but it remains rare for the detailed practice of the analysis to be written up a finished product (Bringer et al. 2004: 253–54).

However, as with the ways in which we have set out the various fieldwork 'methods' in this book, it is also important to note that this process is intended as a means rather than as an end to analysis. It is meant to aid the interpretation of your ethnographic materials rather than to dominate it.

CONCLUSIONS: VALIDITY AND RELIABILITY

To finish this chapter, it is perhaps worthwhile to think through how this process of analysis may tie in with the theories and practices of fieldwork that we have discussed throughout the booklet. How do we say the interpretation produced relates to 'the field'? How do we say it is 'truthful', 'valid' or 'reliable'? Baxter and Eyles (1997) suggest adapting ideas from Lincoln and Guba so that we assess the:

- *credibility* of the account (i.e. authenticated representation of what actually occurred),
- *transferability* of the material (i.e. making what occurred intelligible to the audience),
- *dependability* of the interpretation (i.e. that it is not illogical, or how partisan it is) and
- *confirmability* of the study (i.e. the ability to audit the process that made it through personal reflection, audit processes or opportunities for informants to reply).

At the start of this book, we argued that one of the ways to validate the truth claims of ethnographic research was in terms of its theoretical adequacy, i.e. how your research relates, theoretically and empirically, to other studies. Thus rather than saying that it is 'replicable', like a science experiment, you may start by saying it speaks to a unique group of people at a specific moment in time. From there you can suggest your approach has been logically consistent – that paper trail of working notes lets anyone else see how you arrived at your conclusions. Readers may ask whether someone else would arrive at the same conclusions. The answer is 'probably not', since you brought your own interests, issues, positionality and, let us not forget, talents to bear in doing the project. But they should be able to understand how you worked through the issues. That's a matter for what's usually called 'writing up' (see chapter 9) though it may now be possible to let supervisors or colleagues see your analysis work online using shared software, not so much to see if it is right but to supplement, challenge and reassure you about your ideas (Bringer et al. 2004). This leaves the issue of how your conclusions relate to the world you studied.

The analytical processes sketched out above follow what has been termed a 'rules and units' approach in which the researcher breaks up her/his field materials into conceptual units (Taylor and Cameron 1987). After this, she/he tries to find the 'maps of meaning' within which these units are organised and related in a 'world view', a 'culture', and/or a 'life world'. Much care is needed in discerning how these units and rules relate to the ordering encountered in the field – as in the earlier discussion of 'etic' or 'emic' categories. If the categories developed are broadly 'emic', then the interpretation is much more direct in terms of its relation to fieldwork experience. However, this is a tautological process, since it uses the researched's own categories and how they see them working to define the relations of the researcher's analytic categories and how these work. It does not require a huge leap in imagination to see cases where this can be wildly divorced from what might be termed the 'objective relations', or the academic account of relations, between either things or categories. To take an example of this as it has cropped up in the literature, Pierre Bourdieu, in his study of the social significance of 'taste' (1984), has suggested that while interviewees would assert that their tastes were unaffected by class, the practice of those tastes was highly class bound. For this reason he has gone so far as to suggest that searches for statements of motivations expressed by actors may sometimes be a blind alley, since believing the explicitly stated reasons may obscure the very constructed nature of those reasons (Bourdieu 1990b).

One way to follow up on how the rules and relations that you have constructed relate to those of the people participating in your study may be to think in terms of what 'rules' you are searching for, and how you theoretically see the 'maps of meaning' you are trying to reconstruct from the materials. A division could be made here between 'rules' conceived as those of a 'cultural grammar' and those of 'socially sanctioned norms'. The former may be said to operate whether or not people are aware of their functioning, while the latter suggest the possibility of deviation and amendment, although this may incur social sanctions (see Taylor and Cameron 1987). Equally, the work of Pierre Bourdieu (1984) and Anthony Giddens (1984), which we used earlier, suggests that many of these rules exist immanently in people's thoughts and actions, often in the context of the routinised practices of 'practical consciousness'. To account for these situations you may need to derive an 'etic' schema, but this can never be straightforwardly imputed to your participants. Their/our actions may respond in accordance with such rational rules, but these rules remain (y)our (academic) constructs and not the cause(s) of their (practical) actions (Bourdieu 1990a). Likewise, all these categories that we painfully construct may make it appear as if the world comes prepackaged in neat sound bites. It doesn't. There is a danger of reifying categories until they become what the exercise is about. The fracturing of the field experience for interpretation constructs categories, it does not 'reveal truths'. A real danger here is that these constructions can become divorced from the experiences that they try to encompass, particularly with 'etic' categories or rules, whereas the strength of ethnography is in trying to grasp how people understand their own worlds. In balancing these two sides of privileging our own or our subjects' ideas, then, we would agree with Michael Patton who has argued that:

> It is the ongoing challenge, paradox and dilemma of qualitative analysis that we must be constantly moving back and forth between the phenomena… and our abstractions of that…, between the descriptions of what has occurred and our analysis of those descriptions, between the complexity of reality and our simplifications of those complexities, between the circularities and interdependencies of human activity and our need for linear, ordered statements of cause-effect (1980: 325).

One 'solution' suggested to some of these dilemmas of validation are so-called 'member checks'. That is where the researchers feeds back their conclusions to their respondents to see if they agree with the conclusions drawn. This can be an important part of say a participatory approach to research and is often one of the measures an ethical review board likes to see. An issue here is that validity is often entangled with ethical concerns about giving our respondents a voice and agency in the research. However, it is perfectly possible that respondents, if they can be persuaded to read it, will not like your interpretation. There is a risk, often encountered in ethnographic work, of assuming that respondents are truth telling and pleasant people with good motives (Fine 1993). You may be critical of what they do, or what they believe, and you may have good reason. Take the example of work studying a large multi-national corporation. Let us suppose then that they disagree with a critical report into some aspect of their activities; do you give them the right of reply? Or what do you do if you have given them the right to veto your interpretation (Bradshaw 2001, see also chapter 3)? Thus, the caution we would urge applies to both your own accounts of the world and those encountered in the field.

We argued in the opening section that researchers have never had an omniscient view and that the temptation to set up your analysis as such must be resisted by constantly cross-referring between your abstractions and the contexts that gave rise to them. Equally, we would not wish to over-romanticise the accounts from the 'field' since people there also have partial perspectives; there are no pure subjects or perfectly knowledgeable informants. As James Ferguson puts it with regard to his work in the urban Zambian copper belt:

> Here there is much to be understood, but none of the participants in the scene can claim to understand it all or even take it all in. Everyone is a little confused (some more than others, to be sure), and everyone finds some things that seem clear and others that are unintelligible or only partially intelligible... Anthropological understanding must take on a different character when to understand things like the natives is to miss most of what is going on' (cited in Hannerz 2003: 210).

Even when we research powerful elites and managers, we should remember that they do not have perfect knowledge of how everything happens – even if they like to suggest that they do (Oinas 1999: 358). Moreover, there are unlikely to be singular accounts of singular cultures but multiple competing versions, and it is by shuttling between these different versions that ethnographers can begin to perceive the way in which people produce and reproduce the world throughout their/our lives. For instance, what we are told in interviews or during participant observation may be more akin to gossip, more or less well informed, more or less well intentioned, than 'objective truth' – indeed you may have been the subject of gossip in the field as people tried to work out what your 'angle' was, or your respondents may have been the subject of gossip in the academy. This does not mean that any of this is worthless; in fact it may enable you to look at a range of social interactions and positions, because all these statements are partial truths from specifically positioned actors and are ways these actors make sense of the world (see for instance van Vleet 2003). It might be that you look to create a 'transgressive validity' that problematises or crystallises the issues of reliability and truthfulness rather than confirming one view or another (Guba and Lincoln 2005; Richardson 2000a). The process of analysis is not a matter of developing a definitive account, but of trying to find a means to understand the inter-relations of multiple versions of reality – including not least that of the academy – so that it serves to stress the interconnectivities that we outlined in the first section. These different forms of validity and knowledge production will then relate to different ways of writing and making sense of your work.

9 Writing through Materials

...modern versions of knowledge presentation are systematic, which makes it possible to follow their logic. However, they are often boring. Whether and why that is, is subject to debate. My opinion is that modernist work stomps out the life energy within the 'data'. Stories read as if they had been processed, summarised, and dumped into the article, like an industrial hamburger patty. Half the time I can't even get through these types of articles (Blumenthal 1999: 377).

INTRODUCTION

However much writing has been done during the research process – in the form of field notes, transcripts, letters and emails, chapter outlines, draft chapters, and so on – there is usually a definitive text – a dissertation or thesis – that needs to be submitted for assessment by some (un)known people. We generally know what kinds of expectations they might have of such work. These texts should probably:

- start off with key aims or questions that our research will address,
- begin to do so by working through relevant academic literatures,
- develop coherent and appropriate methodologies that bring together aims/questions and those literatures,
- produce and carefully analyse a sufficient depth and breadth of research data,
- come to some conclusions that return to those starting aims/questions,
- be well structured, well argued, and well written throughout and
- show that something original and meaningful has been learned in the process.

Some readers may have read this book to help out with their research 'methodology' and the dissertation or thesis proposal and/or chapter they have to write about this. Some may also have read it to gain some ideas about how to analyse and 'write up' the findings of that research. Most of the chapters in this book do, after all, show how to justify, plan, undertake, analyse and write through the results of certain (combinations of) qualitative methods. It might therefore be reasonable to assume that this concluding chapter will discuss ways to write through the methodology and analysis chapters in what, for many, is the standard dissertation/thesis structure outlined above. But that's not quite what's going to happen, here. We have, right from the start of this book, been advocating a deliberate entanglement of reading, doing and writing, and arguing that research takes place in an expanded field. So, we're not going to end up suggesting that writing is a matter of disentangling and separating things out in a final text. All of the expectations outlined above need to be met in most people's theses and dissertations, but we're convinced that there's more than one way of doing this, and doing it well. There are many ways to 'write ethnography which is both scientific – in the sense of being true to the world known through the empirical senses – and literary – in the sense of expressing what one has learned through evocative writing techniques and form' (Richardson 2000b: 253). Here, we'll be talking through just a few.

There now exists an awful lot of writing about ethnographic writing. There's far more than there was when we did our PhDs, and there's far more than we can write about here. This means that we can't provide a compendium of writing options from which you can choose. Rather, we will illustrate certain ways of writing to which we were drawn because they were appropriate, interesting and doable for us in specific circumstances on specific topics. We did not pick these from a list but sometimes we would try something different, find that it worked (for us and others) and subsequently look for a full body of literature to justify, refine and perhaps name what we had done. So, in the following pages, we want to:

- first, outline some general issues that are important to consider in writing any kind of final ethnographic text;
- second, show how our choices to write in certain ways emerged from what we were taught and came across by chance in the expanded fields of our research and
- third, discuss the kinds of criteria that are now being advocated to help readers judge the quality of such (un)conventional writing.

In section two of this chapter, we outline three main writing styles that we have adopted to present our dissertation and thesis work to its audiences: 'code-writing', 'autoethnographic writing' and 'montage writing'. The first is the kind of writing that logically follows on from the coding process that we outlined in the previous chapter. The second is a style of writing that tries to evoke more personal relationships in a text between researcher/writers, their research participants and their readers. And the third is a style of writing that makes, takes and places in juxtaposition various bits of more or less processed 'data' to illustrate and think through the fact that the various parts of a topic that we have studied don't necessarily cohere. In section three, we briefly discuss the kinds of assessment criteria that advocates of the latter, more experimental, writing styles have (somewhat reluctantly) begun to put forward to help writers and readers to judge the quality of such work. However, before getting into these styles and criteria, it's necessary to first talk through some general points about writing as research practice.

WRITING AS RESEARCH PRACTICE

Let us start by saying something both about the process of writing and the reason why it is such an important and controversial issue. Imagine yourself at that stage when you begin putting notes and material together into drafts by, say, taking lots of participants' quotes on a topic and some bits of literature and developing an argument. If you are like us, you will have a go at this for the first time, look at the results, conclude that it's pretty crappy, and then start to move things around and alter or begin to build new arguments in the hope that you can make that writing better (Richardson 2000a). Reworking, re-reworking, and re-re-re... working drafts is quite normal. A key issue that we raised in the previous chapter was the difficulty in separating what counts as 'analysis' and what counts as 'writing'. Indeed, this is a point that we often raise with students who say they plan to finish their 'analysis' before they 'write up'. After all, we do not stop interpreting in order to write. Interpretation starts in the field as we choose, say, what to write up in our field notes as significant, what questions we ask, what follow-up questions we ask based on the answers we get and so forth. Katy Bennett's (2000) account of participant observation among farming households offers a version of interviews where the anticipated audience, the reader, was implicated in her fieldwork. Far from writing coming later, thoughts of what she would write, and how that would make her look, kept intruding into the fieldwork as she struggled with relating the imperfectly performing 'me' to muddled and always partial senses of a true 'self', let alone understanding 'them' – the participants. Thus, rather than stages we might see the whole ethnographic process as involving 'many levels of textualization set off by experience [and t]o disentangle interpretative [or analytical] procedures at work as one moves across levels is problematic to say the least' (van Maanen 1988, cited in Wolfinger 2002: 86). Producing a finished chapter, report, dissertation, thesis or journal paper is just one of many levels of textualization through which we make sense from our materials, and is one where the discipline of piecing materials together into a textual account often reveals the flaws and contradictions buried in our materials, forcing us to look again and rethink our ideas.

There is then a fuzzy boundary between our notes and reflections in analysis and our draft texts destined for the wider world. And the advent of word-processors has meant there is now even more direct blurring of working notes into finished works as they are cut and pasted, imported and reedited. As Jacques Derrida noted, this has enabled a new rhythm to working through materials:

> With the computer, everything is so quick and easy, one is led to believe that revision could go on indefinitely. An interminable revision, an infinite analysis is already signalled, held in reserve as it were...Before crossings out and superimposed corrections left something like a scar on the paper or a visible image in the memory. There was a resistance of time, a thickness in the duration of the crossing out (1999: 8).

There is now an immediacy of qualitative data software and word processors, a de-distancing that brings the text closer to us and makes it more malleable, less sacrosanct yet makes it somehow thus 'weightless'. It seems we can play with meanings almost endlessly – composing and recomposing our material. This state of boundless play is in one sense exhilarating, yet also scary and debilitating in equal measure, since amid all these proliferating versions and permutations we must eventually send one out into the world. We have eventually to decide how to shape it all, to decide what version in what format and style will be sent out to whichever audience we hope will read it.

Before asking what textual style, though, we need to say briefly why the issue of style has become important. At the start of this book, we critiqued accounts that seem to present the world as an objective fact depicted by a detached observer. Ethnographically, this style of 'realist' account tends to try to represent the world to us as though we were there. It tends to try to offer a glimpse of the world 'as it is'. Or, to put it another way, it tends to claim to hold a mirror up to reality, so we can see it without obtrusive framing. The text is therefore 'self-effacing', and we may not notice that, or how, it is framed (Fine 2003: 42). Such an approach is seductive, but it has come under heavy and sustained criticism because:

- just because the textual, rhetorical and scholarly techniques used to convey knowledge about a place fade from view does not mean that they, or their effects, are absent: it is just that we have stopped paying attention to them,
- the notion of 'transparency' as a goal in prose tends to rely on a series of visual metaphors and assumptions that knowledge involves perfect omniscient sight: yet we have spent most of this book suggesting none of us, researchers, students, teachers or participants, can claim to have such a viewpoint and

- if field experiences are constructed from many entangled, contingent and unstable relationships, we cannot suggest that the representations based on these experiences can somehow be stable and self-evident.

Ethnographies are especially susceptible to the lure of trying to 'tell it as it is' since one of their strongest appeals is precisely that contact with the rustle and hum of everyday life. One of their claims to authority, for saying they are truthful, is precisely the sense that the researcher was there, a witness and/or participant. The point is not that clarity is bad, but that it is just as much a textual contrivance as any other approach. It may reach out to some readers, and this may be important, but it may do so by occluding some of the processes and power relations of fieldwork. Critics of experimental or unconventional writing often suggest its complexities obscure issues and that it becomes an academic game of textual complexity for its own sake (Murphy 2002: 251). Our point is rather that such complexity is necessary to deal with complicated realities. As Jacques Derrida put it:

> One shouldn't complicate things for the pleasure of complicating, but one should also never simplify or pretend to be sure of such simplicity where there is none. If things were simple, word would have gotten around (1988: 118, cited in Doel and Hubbard 2002: 352).

However we structure our accounts, once we sit down to write about and portray our experiences, we are making representations. We are creating and making stories. So it is important that we think through what that entails, how we can do this appropriately and how we can do this well. Now this can be a liberating moment as it then opens out the question of what sorts of stories we want to tell, in what ways and with what (imagined) effects upon whom, where and when (see Ellis and Bochner 2000). It also places a burden of responsibility upon us because there is no 'natural' or given way of accounting for our work so, instead, we have to think through and justify what we do. We do not stop our critical examination of the relationships of researcher and researched just because we are writing. The texts we create are not above or absolved from the issues of positionality and partial knowledge we have detailed in fieldwork. As Heidi Nast (1994: 64) has put it: 'a written text is merely a point amidst a continuous fabric of other texts that includes all communicative forms through which researcher, researched, and institutional frameworks are relationally defined'. So, it is not surprising that many researchers end up feeling torn between, on the one hand, being extremely careful about exactly who and what they write about for ethical and other reasons and, on the other, being able to write the kind of vivid, in-depth, account of their field experiences which good ethnographies are supposed to contain (Stacey 1988). Taussig vividly conveys the dilemma:

> But just as we might garner courage to reinvent a new world and live new fictions...so a devouring force comes at us from another direction, seducing us by playing on our yearning for a true real. Would that it would, would that it could, come clean this true real. I so badly want that wink of recognition, that complicity with the nature of nature. But the more I want it the more I realize it's not for me. Not for you either...which leaves us this silly and often desperate place wanting the impossible so badly that while we believe it is our rightful destiny and so act as accomplices of the real, we also know in our heart of hearts that the way we picture the world and talk is bound to a dense set of representational gimmicks which, to coin a phrase, have but an arbitrary relation to a slippery referent easing its way out of graspable sight (Taussig 1993: xvii).

Acknowledging this tension has led to whole raft of 'textually aware' ethnographies that attend carefully to their representational techniques and tropes. Chapters about 'writing culture' in books such as Clifford and Marcus (1986), Marcus and Fischer (1986) and Rosaldo (1989), along with monographs like Malcolm Ashmore's (1989) *Reflexive Thesis* and Michael Taussig's (1987) *Shamanism, Colonialism and the Wild Man*, certainly affected the way we did our research and how we thought about writing as part of this process. We felt that we needed to understand how the way we wrote could shape the worlds represented through (our) ethnographies. We needed to think about what we were doing and what effects this could have. We needed, therefore, to be reflexive. A great many authors have followed a similar path of reasoning. But this has not gone down very well with some of our/their colleagues, especially when reflexive writing is seen to go 'too far'. Critics argue that using up too many words writing about *our* field experiences is 'facile', 'falsely radical', 'narcissistic', 'arrogant' and/or 'solipsistic', and diverts ethnographies away from their prime purpose: making sense of *other people's* realities (Bourdieu 2003; Cintron 1993; Murphy 2002; Pile and Thrift 1995). But, it is important to note, this attention to field experience is only *part* of the debate. Broadly speaking, the purpose of reflexive writing is to 'link the micro-level activities of the lone ethnographer with macro-level processes' (Herbert 2000: 562). Thus, properly reflexive writing should also involve the consideration of:

- how academic institutions, disciplines, theoretical/empirical traditions and 'ways of seeing' that individual research fit into and come out of affect the 'conditions and modes of organising knowledge about other cultures' (Bourdieu 1990a, 2003; Callaway 1992: 32) and
- the structural preconditions that shape the activities of, and relationships between, (those who can be the) researchers and researched, such as the way that world historical events have 'asymmetrically organised contact between the world's people' (Dwyer 1977: 148).

Throughout this book, this more rounded account of reflexivity is something that we have always tried to keep in mind, and we will think this through in more detail later in this chapter. We would argue that it is precisely because such positionings tend to be obscured and hidden in our 'normal' academic language and modes of writing that we need to think how to 'make visible our own critical positioning within the structure of power' (McDowell 1992a: 413). However, here, we want to offer some caution before self-reflexivity is seen as a panacea to these problems by thinking through, in a little more detail, the interpersonal element of reflexivity. We think that it's important to ask what we can know and say about the role of the self in the self–other relationships of our research. Even if we decide that it is important to make sense of this relationship, we have to ask how aware we can become about the subconscious and structural factors affecting our research. Gillian Rose (1997), for example, has pointed out that theoretically the dream of self-knowledge is one that has eluded even psychoanalysts, let alone ethnographers. If we ask ourselves why we did something, occasionally (often?) we have to admit that we're not entirely sure. Expecting our research participants to give sure answers, or providing sure explanations ourselves for their actions, can therefore seem suspiciously certain. Rose's (1997) discomfort about writing reflexively came through her research experience. As she explains this:

> The event that brought my difficulty home to me was a joke made by one of my interviewees. We were sitting in the café of an arts centre talking about his work, with my tape recorder sitting on the table between us. He's Scottish and working class. As a friend of his, another worker at the centre, walked past us, he laughed and said, 'look, I'm being interviewed for Radio 4'. She laughed and so did I, and the interview – a long and very helpful one for me – continued. But that joke has bothered me ever since; or, rather, my uncertainty about what it meant has bothered me. Was it just a reference to the tape recorder? Was it to do with his self-consciousness at being interviewed? But Radio 4 is a national station of the British Broadcasting Corporation, which means in effect it's English, so was his joke a reference to the middle-class Englishness of my accent? If so, was the joke a sign of our different 'positions'? But does he like Radio 4's Englishness? And how do any of these possibilities relate to how the interview went? I don't know the answer to these questions, and this, I felt, was my failure. Indeed, now I think about it, I can't even be sure he said 'Radio 4' and not 'Radio Forth', which is a regional commercial station, which would raise some but not all the same questions, and some more besides. Or not. I don't know what the joke indicates about our position, let alone how to write it into my research (Rose 1997: 306, see also Delph-Janiurek 2001).

This difficulty of interpretation, she suggests, is a much wider and more fundamental problem about how researchers can ever truly understand others', and even their own, motivations.[1] For some, these problems of reflexivity may be so intractable that the only option seems to be a (perhaps) reluctant return to 'distance' and 'objectivity'. But, we argue, this would throw out the baby with the bath water. Falconer Al-Hindi and Kawabata (2002) point out that there is an inevitable problem of difference in research where 'people wish to learn from and about others because the latter are different from the former, but the fact of difference itself may distance them from one another, making such understanding difficult' (2002: 106). So, they suggest that rather than striving for transparency of the self (and the other) through introspection, a transformative, dialogic reflexivity might be developed in which both parties reflect back their mutual (mis)understandings and use these as resources for interpreting their different views on the world.

Clearly we do not accept the most dismissive of critiques of reflexivity in ethnographic research. While we have both been haunted by and have wrestled with many of these critiques, our experience of incorporating academic debates about reflexivity into our research processes isn't one in which they have led to our research going astray. Sometimes these debates have even helped us to rescue research that seemed to be going astray for other reasons. There are, it seems to us, ways of writing through these issues of positionality and politics in practical and useful ways (see also Berg and Mansvelt 2000).

WRITING STYLES

In this section, we discuss the ways that we have taken these issues on board through three main styles of writing which we have used in various pieces of work (theses, mainly, but also book chapters and journal papers) which came out of Ian's MA and both of our PhD research projects. Each, at least in part, reflects key issues that we have highlighted as inevitably part of any ethnographic research process. The first – 'Writing through codes' – highlights the ways in which such research is always dialogic, i.e. co-constructed by researchers and their research participants. The second, – 'Writing autoethnography' – highlights the ways in which such research is always personal and iterative, i.e. it is rooted in what matters to researchers, and changes its shape as it proceeds as her/his expectations are (not) met and new opportunities, ideas and challenges present themselves. And the third – 'Writing montage' – highlights the ways in which such research rarely achieves closure: i.e. places and processes under study are rarely stable or fully understood by anyone (researchers included), so writing has to be based on fragmentary understandings.

Writing Through Codes

Perhaps the most straightforward approach to writing is to build directly out of the formal analysis of research materials as discussed in the previous chapter. As we suggested above, there may not be that distinct a shift between 'analysing' the materials and writing – both we suggest involve configuring materials and weaving them into a new whole. If you have thus been developing categories and the relationships between them, it may be that these form the structure for your writing. This might certainly be the case if you are attempting to provide a more inductive or a thick descriptive account, but could also be true if your writing is being more thematically driven. This approach would see you effectively taking the 'piles' of material about a topic, or all the bits on a specific theme retrieved through your computer, and using them as the starting point for sections of writing. This was very much how Mike began to write through his oral history PhD materials and how Ian wrote through the serial interview materials from his MA research. So, imagine having done some systematic (probably) interview-based research, talking to a number of (groups of) people about the same things and having done the kind of formal analysis outlined in the last chapter (perhaps including your participant observation notes and other 'codable' materials). Imagine those piles of paper on the floor, and the code map in your hand that you have put together to indicate how all of those categories and sub-categories fit together. All you have to do is turn that map into a linear argument with the classic academic section-and-subsection structure (see Box 9.1). Writing is just a matter of going through the code piles in the right order, summarising 'theoretically saturated' arguments, putting them in a logical order, quoting appropriate passages, and doing so over and over, pile by pile, until they 'work' as arguments: individually and as a whole.

If your codes have relationships of opposition or causal connection then this may be an effective way of writing to allow these connections and antagonisms to structure the text. Thus opposing categories might show contrasting reactions of different people, or the chain of causality may mean you talk about the material in one code followed by another that describes its consequences. For instance, you had a coding scheme that used something like a flow chart – this might then organise the narrative structure of your text. One issue to bear in mind when doing this is that your analysis may well have pursued routes and avenues that do not fit say the particular chapter you are writing, or maybe you discover some detailed elements are not required for what you are writing. Moreover, with the speed and ease of assembling text using software it

Box 9.1: The Classic Section-and-subsection [and Sub-subsection] Structure

Below, we outline chapters from Ian's MA and Mike's PhD whose section and subsection headings were based on the codes and sub-codes emerging from the kind of data analysis outlined in the previous chapter. Excerpts from underlined subsections below are quoted in Box 9.2.

(a) Chapter six: 'Richard' from Ian's MA thesis (Cook 1992)

Introduction

(A) Contingencies and interpretation
(i) storytelling; (ii) family life; (iii) pointers

(B) Major life themes
Introduction; (i) serving his country; (ii) working with people; (iii) Christian beliefs

(C) Diagnosis and rehabilitation
Introduction; (i) going blind and dealing with it; (ii) rehabilitation

(D) Day to day life
Introduction; (i) home (his room; the remainder of the house and yard); (ii) social contact (friends; acquaintances; strangers); (iii) travel patterns (pedestrian travels [sensory experience; devices; travel infrastructure; destinations]; vehicular travels [bus, 'wheels' (a dial-and-ride service); rides])

(b) Chapter seven: 'Gone but not forgotten: community and memory' from Mike's PhD thesis (Crang 1995)

Introduction

Group praxis and shared experiences
(i) seeking the subaltern, (ii) chattering classes? Group work and historiography.

Counter-hegemony and critique
(i) hidden histories and lost voices, (ii) speaking and recognition, (iii) producing popular and official history and (iv) reminiscence in landscapes of erasure.

Constructing communities of the past in the present
(i) a hermeneutic understanding of the past, (ii) imagined communities of the past, and (iii) mutualities of the oppressed.

The end of community
(i) communal values, (ii) abstract space and the destruction of mutuality, (iii) rootless modernity, (iv) retrospective harmonies and (v) alterity as critique.

Remembering the past: linking places and times
(i) remembering as emplotting, (ii) authoring lives and (iii) placing memories.

is very easy to get carried away. Mike found that the ability to call up examples from participants and export them into a word processor was a real boon. However, in thus pulling out materials about the major themes he also realised, to his shock, and that of his supervisor, that very quickly he had produced a chapter that contained some 60,000 words – and not many of those were his. When we start adding theoretical ideas or material from readings to build up an argument and say why things are significant, and when we start situating and discussing examples, the word length can run away from us.

This then exposes some tensions that may be inevitable in any ethnography. The first is simply that using quotations and descriptions is wordy – and most of the time we are writing to a word limit. So suddenly writing can cease to be choosing examples from your studies to develop an idea and turn into a more discriminating search for either the best example, or the example that says the most in the fewest words. It may be that in order to keep to your word limit, you decide that rather than thinning every category, you should scrap some sections or topics to give you room to focus on those that matter most and treat them with the depth that will do them justice. There are often hard choices to be made in successive goes at editing down material. It is important to remember that while, for you, the fieldwork you report may have been all-consuming, you still have to win the interest and retain the attention of the reader. Within the sections that you decide to keep, achieving the right balance between summarising and quoting from your research materials is crucial (see Box 9.2). When working through a pile of materials cut up and placed under a code, it's important to

- read and reread every piece of paper,
- check back to the original source to make sense of loose ends,
- start to note persistent arguments or framings of the issue and
- pick out the quotes that you might use in your account.

You could then start to write out the argument you want to make in that section, constantly tacking back and forth, in the process, between your evolving chapter draft and the bits of material to make sure that what you're saying is faithful to the data. And this is a difficult task because what it involves is the final stage of wrenching this data out of the contexts in which it was generated (in those interactions between those people, there and then), and inserting it into an entirely new context in which it will be judged (in that piece of writing, in relation to those other quotations, ideas, theoretical points, literature, etc, by those examiners).

So, when we're going through those piles for the umpteenth time, how can we be sure that we're doing that data justice while writing in a way that

Box 9.2: Summarising and Quoting

(a) An excerpt from Ian's 'Richard' chapter (Cook 199: 202–03)
This issue requires illustration to give a sufficiently rich flavour of the content of, and balance between, the summaries and quotes from those piles of coded transcript bits that ended up in our theses. The excerpt below is based on Ian's interview series data constructed with Richard, where the intention was to appreciate and convey his experience of visual impairment and blindness in considerable depth and detail. One chapter of Ian's thesis was devoted to each participant's experiences and, therefore, all of the quotations and summaries were based on the separate coding of each participant's transcripts. This part of Richard's chapter attempted to illustrate the effects of his sight loss on his day-to-day life, and is the second part of the subsection on its effects on his home life (see Box 9.1). Richard's chapter followed JD's, and therefore contrasts and similarities between their experiences were noted where significant.

––––––

The remainder of the house and yard:
As a house owner, Richard spent a certain amount of time maintaining his investment. Even though his poor vision may have made simple household jobs more difficult to do, he could often get round this quite simply:

> 'I have to fumble around a lot of times. I do a lot of repairs around the house now. . . . That globe light – now I've rewired that one. . . . It's kinda touchy 'cause it's electrical, but I cut the plugs and disconnect the fuse plugs at the box and then I wire stuff, and I go screw it back in and wait to hear if anything's going to explode (laughs)! But, you know, I try anything mainly because, see, I did so much before I lost my sight that I still have a sense of feel.'

During his recorded activity week, and throughout that summer, much of this maintenance work had revolved around the small above-ground swimming pool in the backyard. Richard had built this himself *after* becoming blind:

> Richard: The average guy with sight, with maybe help from another guy, uh, could probably put it together in at least two days. It took me a month.
> Ian: Why didn't you get somebody else to help you?
> Richard: Because I didn't want to. I'm brickheaded sometimes. I want to try to do things. This is the only way that you can learn to do things and get along.

This was therefore *his* creation, and a testament to his competence as a blind person. He gave the impression that he could perform any routine maintenance

Box 9.2: continued

task around the house yet, unlike before his blindness, they took longer. When I put this to him, he replied:

'That's right. That's the whole gist of when people say that, "Well, you can't do anything any more." *Bull*, you can still *do* things if you put your mind to it but, like you say, it takes longer.'

His poor vision could not, however, always be compensated for by simply spending more time on things. Take the following situation, for instance:

'I keep hollering about glasses in the sink, or something clear sitting in the sink, or, like a glass bottle or something....I go to sit something in there and – *SMASH!* – I sit something on top of something and I'm liable to break it, you know, and I'm always afraid I'll break a jar or glass and then end up cutting my hand or something.... It's just an instant fright, you know, you've done something that, all of a sudden, it's like getting shot.'

Thus, although, like J.D., Richard had lived in his this house for quite some time and had, to a large degree, internalized its dimensions and rhythms, he still had to be cautious in certain places and at certain times. The structure of the pool pump was constant and, therefore, predictable. Yet that of the kitchen sink was not, being constantly filled with, and emptied of, washing up – some of which he could see with his residual vision and some of which he could not.

will be acceptable to our examiners? How should we think about that relationship between summarising and quoting from that data? Is it a matter of using 'evidence' (e.g. quotations) to back up our arguments (summaries)? In part, this surely must be the case. But it also sounds like the kind of writing that critics of qualitative research could rightly have problems with, i.e. those strong authorial arguments with juicy quotes apparently chucked in to illustrate them. Katz (2001, 2002) suggests that passages of field description or interview should be used to achieve seven effects:

1. when they set up a problem for explanation because they set up with enigma, paradox or apparent absurdity,
2. when they are strategic either in that they implicitly negate a major alternative one, say by comparison, or they show significant turning points in subjects' lives or the flow of events,
3. if they are rich and varied so they rule out some approaches and anticipated answers,
4. if they are revealing forces shaping social life that are routinely overlooked, purposively hidden or ontologically invisible,
5. if they show why certain choices or actions are contingent or situated,

6. when they show especially colourful, or vivid aspects of cultures that convey a sense of what life is like for respondents and not just as adding rhetorical flourish, credibility or 'local colour' but to show for instance respondents's 'crafty, idiosyncratic ways of finessing persistent problems' (2002: 74) and

7. when poignant moments capture transcending concerns that structure persistent patterns in respondent's lives.

What we want to advocate here is a combination of summary and quotation that talks through the data to create 'vulnerable texts' (Behar 1996) that draw attention to the limits of their analyses, rather than trying to be 'authoritative'. So at moments in his thesis, Mike wanted to show that the process of knowledge creation came through participation and contact with what were a despised group in some academic circles (including the ones in which he worked). So he wanted to insert his presence into the account to make himself vulnerable to the same charge. This meant, for a start, writing in the first person, and then showing his working practice. That first step disrupts many classic conventions – as he found when he tried to publish the material and found that, whereas normally there are only typographical and grammatical changes between sending a paper to the publisher and receiving the proofs, his entire paper had been rewritten by the editor into the third person and only by dint of fraught negotiation could any first person positionality be salvaged (Crang 1996b). The second step of showing the process he followed in the thesis was by embedding excerpts of field notes which he called 'Postcards from the Field'. Although these were field notes, they were also meant to parody and play with academic authority by reducing academic field notes to a similar format as touristic postcards sent while on holiday, while also stressing that for participants this was a vacation and reminding the reader of the detachment felt by the researcher in the field. The headings and moment depicted deliberately spoke to the classic structure of ethnography of separation in the field, gaining access and acceptance and so forth. Thus from Mike's notes he put in excerpts pretty much unedited into his final text:

Box 9.3: Mike's Tudor Moments (Crang 1995: 308–11)

The following excerpts are fairly 'raw' parts of usually taped field notes given titles and arranged rather like a montage of moments – again pulling on Benjamin's ideas (see later). These were put into a section of the chapter that was otherwise written as a polished reflection in the past tense, to try and disrupt the ethnographic present and show the fleeting and specific nature of encounters, especially

Box 9.3: continued

the way Mike's knowledge developed over time just as reenactor's own knowledges did.

_____

Recruitment – the returning participants all very much in the know and greeting each other, chatting about lord knows what. It feels really exclusive –.... I don't know anyone, so the three mid-twenty year olds huddle together while lots of teenagers give us the 'seen it done, worn the' err 'smock' I suppose. The twenty-somethings are all broke and looking for a cheap holiday – though we all ask each other 'why are we doing this?'. None of us can provide an answer – except my weird one, which neither they nor I find wholly convincing. Returnees are in costume – eeks that means making one – while others are wearing 'White Company' sweatshirts. This is my entrée into this exclusive community – I can trade stories about cannons from [another reenactment group]

Out of place – Surreal, totally bizarre. Was in the centre of Bradford tootling along to a gig by a band that would be playing in the beer tent later, oh the organiser asked a group to go to raise the profile of the event. So I drove into town with a car load, only got lost a couple of times, but we were walking along and suddenly shouts of 'Hello ducky' and 'howdy partner' (strange). Forgot we were in costume. Got to the hotel late and the bouncer just said 'they went that away' as Stu said 'how did you know who we were looking for?' Mirth all round. Felt somewhat strange in a room with a hundreds of 'normal' people they all wanted to borrow hats and so on and giggle – wished our gear was a bit more upper-class, had more panache than the drab rain stained stuff we were in.

Tudorese – Everyone down the pub is in costume and trying to not speak Tudorese – and failing. Horribly contagious and hanging out with Jasper is bad news – he is one of the worst offenders, I can't imagine him actually holding a conversation in plain English. Kate describes it as coming down with a touch of the verily merrilies. Apparently there is a forfeit for the first person each year to sound like they are off Blackadder.

These excerpts have barely been polished, let alone turned into an analysis of various social interactions. They also are in places embarrassingly written, going through Mike's feelings at times of stress during fieldwork. Other illustrations covered how people reacted to him, and the roles into which he felt he was forced or fell – and that did not make him feel entirely comfortable. But in the ones above the main theme is of becoming a part of the group – picking up 'Tudorese', just as others were doing, finding some previous contacts to enable him to develop a 'sub-cultural' capital among members, forgetting about being in a costume until being shouted at in the centre of Bradford and so forth. There are also notes of anxiety about thus being brought into the group where as soon as he turns on the tape all he could think to say was how 'surreal' the evening had been. And the starting excerpt parodies the 'arrival scene' which is often the only personal point in classic ethnographies, where Mike was recruited at an interview, alongside many others who knew as little as he did, or even less, about the community – inverting the standard narrative of arriving somewhere remote, entering a functioning community and recruiting informants. It was only (much) later Mike realised he was setting up a 'becoming a . . .' type of story, equally generic in sociological ethnographies of the second Chicago school of the mid-twentieth century studying groups where the rhythm of the study echoes that of regular recruitment and induction in organisations (Katz 2001: 457).

Within the bounds of this systematic, building block approach to writing, these texts could draw readers through enough of the lives and stories of our research participants to appreciate how our ideas about them developed. Creating vulnerable texts means admitting that the strength of ethnographic research and writing includes its affective capacity to move us and to evoke an emotional response (Ellis and Bochner 2000). It certainly means letting our participants' personalities come through more, and trying to give them as much respect and room to talk to each other and to us in the text as we did in the field. Earlier, we mentioned rights to reply (Willis 1977) and member checks (Bradshaw 2001) as ways of allowing participants to comment on our work. But we would also include simple practices such as including the full range of opinions from a person. As we argued in previous chapters, many participants apparently change their minds and/or express contradictory views on the same subject during researcher's work with them. It can often be the case, for example, that later in an interview someone backtracks on an extreme statement they had made earlier. And participant observation research can cause us to question differences between what people say they do and what they are seen to do. So, if we design research that allows us (as we suggested) to think this through, to consider when, where, why and with whom different opinions and versions of events get offered, we need to think how to represent that contradictory and ambiguous reality. However, if our coding systems just look for topics and take people's words out of context, we may be removing some of that dimension from our account. One quote lifted from an interview – maybe the most extreme statement – can therefore end up being misrepresented as apparently straightforward evidence.

Thus, if we are trying to be faithful to our participants, to give a fuller appreciation of what they said in our conversations with them, then it is probably necessary to show that they were complicated and conflicted people. On a basic level, this means that we should probably quote our questions as well as (parts of) their answers to show how our data was *dialogic*, i.e. it was made up of what they said in response to things that we (and others) said rather than being their unmediated beliefs (Pratt 1986). As we discussed earlier when talking about transcription, we may also need to think about how to get across a more multifaceted sense of the conversation (to show say the emotions or non-verbal gestures associated with a remark) and the participant (e.g. to show dialect). Having done this, we may then have to think about how to describe our own emotions and non-verbal gestures in all of this, and how any transcription of our participant's dialect might contrast with our academic prose, making them appear parochial or 'authentic', perhaps. Finally, we may also have to pay attention to the connotations of any pseudonyms we use. Mike, for example, gave his seventy-plus-year-old, working-class oral history participants names like 'Bert Tanner', 'Ruby' or 'Flo' not Tarquin, Kevin, Siobhan or Kylie. But it may also be the case that participants want the full report and want to be identified in it by their real names. This was Mike's experience with his oral history participants who wanted to be seen to be contributing to (his) writing the history of their area. So, in his thesis they were given pseudonyms, partly because this was standard research practice and they had all signed agreements to this effect, and partly because Mike didn't want any of them to get caught up in any potential controversies arising from his interpretation of their comments. But, in the report that he wrote for the Avon Oral History Network, he replaced their pseudonyms (which were used throughout the analysis) with their real names.

All of these considerations make a difference to the colour, life and emotional complexity that we retain in (and/or give to) the texts of our research. At the time we were writing our PhD theses, calls were being made for ethnographic researchers to decentre their voices and allow participants' voices to be heard more in so-called 'polyphonic' accounts (P. Crang 1992; McDowell 1994). This meant using extensive quotations, not just snippets, to try to show that (and how) participants' views and agendas shaped researchers' understandings and research trajectories. And we liked this, despite the lingering worry that we – as authors – remained very much in charge of what bits of whose voices were quoted where in our texts. The answer to these worries seemed to lie in the way that research data was used in the construction of an argument. According to Gary Fine (2003: 45, 47), this is a matter of 'the extent to which a rich and detailed account of the world being observed is presented, as opposed to the inclusion of a few instances of data to bolster one's analytical points – in other words data build a case, rather than simply illuminate it'. Following this advice seems to imply sacrificing a breadth of coverage to provide background details about the individuals and events concerned, (hopefully) allowing the reader to sense the depth of their personalities.

This was certainly what Ian was trying to do in his MA research. His aim was to use in-depth qualitative research to appreciate the heterogeneity of individuals lumped together, and treated by many researchers, policy-makers and members of the public, as an homogeneous group: 'blind people' who, together, lacked this, needed that, etc. This project was derivative of his supervisor's PhD, which had been based on in-depth ethnographic research with five elderly people, each of whom had a chapter devoted to (his interactions with) them (see Rowles 1978a) which had been a highlight of Ian's degree. Mike's group work had been inspired by a social history agenda to hear voices of those people normally silenced in official histories. He therefore felt that he had to give voice to what mattered to them. As Katy Bennett (2000) notes, not only are we trying to be reflexive in the field, we must decide how to present ourselves as narrative agents in the text – a knowledge which can also intrude into our field practices; so far from just reflecting what we did in what we write, our desired persona for the final text can carry back into our fieldwork.

Writing Autoethnography

This recognition of the often tangled and awkward relationships between researchers, their audiences and research participants, brings us neatly to our second writing style: 'autoethnography'. At its most basic this refers to self-centred ethnographic writing, in which the central narrative threads are the selves of researchers and/or researched. If these threads are those of the researched, then this writing is about 'instances in which members of colonised groups strive to represent themselves to their colonisers in ways that engage with colonisers' terms while also remaining faithful to their own self-understandings' (Butz and Besio 2004: 350; see also Butz 2001; Pratt 1986). However, writing whose central thread is the researcher's self is what we will discuss here, primarily because this is the kind of autoethnography that Ian ended up writing in his PhD. To some critics, as you may imagine, this kind of writing really does take too far the arguments about reflexivity that we discussed earlier. Introducing their edited *Mapping the subject* book, for instance, Steve Pile and Nigel Thrift (1995) compared the tricky business of writing about subjectivity with a game of 'snakes and ladders'. When intellectuals did things properly, they could scale the ladders but, when they didn't, they risked sliding down the snakes. So, they argued:

One more ladder. The intellectual needs to be reflexive and, in particular, reflexivity is a crucial tradition of modern work on the subject. These maxims are crucial to the practice of modern ethnography, up to and including the vogue for auto-ethnography. The snake is that, too often, the results of a writer's attempts to use reflexivity to interrogate the self/other relationship come perilously close to narcissism and solipsism. Every early childhood slip, every parental flaw, every departmental tiff, every conference slight, becomes grist to a 'falsely radical' mill. We end up with something remarkably like the confessional, romantic hero of yore that the writer has just spent blocks of print criticising, but now reconsecrated by the act of self-criticism. The result is that the writer's subject becomes the writer's object and the writer's object slides gently away (1995: 16).

Ouch! But is this necessarily what autoethnographers are trying to do? Is this how their work necessarily works? In many ways autoethnographic writing doesn't require research that's particularly different from that which we've outlined in this book (see Ellis and Bochner 2000). What it does involve, however, is more personal attention being paid to a) why a research topic is chosen in the first place, b) how it gains and takes shape through the research process and c) how researchers, researched and readers can all become involved in the process of interpreting its findings. Ian's thesis took this as a model for its structure (Box 9.4).

Box 9.4: Ian's PhD Thesis

Below is the table of contents of Ian's thesis. Part one was an autoethnographic examination of (his) disciplinary research practices, and was partly inspired by Malcolm Ashmore's (1989) *The reflexive thesis*: a sociological study of the sociology of science that was so close to home that its participants said it was 'like looking up your own anus' and meant that he was 'bound to make an enemy of everyone' (1988: 20, 22). Part two was a critical autobiographical reflection on constructions of Ian's white English male self. Finally, to finish things off, part three outlined an undergraduate course that Ian subsequently taught where students were encouraged to take UK–Caribbean connections personally through writing first-person journals (see Cook 2000). Only chapter four, you will notice, was based on his 'proper thesis' – the papya ethnography described in this book (see chapter 8, footnote 1 and later).

A GRUMPY THESIS: GEOGRAPHY, AUTOBIOGRAPHY, PEDAGOGY

Introduction	2
1) The individual	9
2) Extroverted senses of the self	16
3) Pulling together then pulling apart	27

Box 9.4: continued

The fact that our choices of research topic are often (always?) personal is perhaps best illustrated in Carolyn Ellis' (1999; Ellis and Bochner 2000) account of her meetings with 'Sylvia', a psychology PhD student studying breast cancer who wanted Ellis to be on her dissertation committee.[2] Sylvia came to Ellis's office to ask if this would be OK, and began to outline what she wanted to do: interview maybe thirty survivors to see how they have adjusted to life after cancer; combine quantitative and qualitative approaches, include a diverse group of participants so she can generalise; and so on. Ellis, however, interrupted to ask how Sylvia had become interested in the subject. Sylvia said that she herself was a breast cancer survivor and her experience had raised all kinds of questions that she wanted her PhD to answer. As Ellis recalls it, Sylvia said ' "I'm interested in other women's experience", . . . adding hesitantly, "you know, how it compares to mine. That's not something I've admitted before, the personal part, I mean" ' (Ellis and Bochner 2000: 737).[3] So, the question that needs to be asked here, is why shouldn't we admit such things in our writing? While it is becoming acceptable to write about messy serendipities of fieldwork, it is still less common to address the framing and development of research. If at all, such personal beginnings are only reported in introductions or prefaces. This includes the kinds of discussions taking place, and readings passed around, in one important part of researchers' expanded fields: departmental spaces such as tea rooms, seminar rooms and offices. This is where and why Malcolm Ashmore's (1989) *Reflexive Thesis*, for example, had such an influence on both Mike and Ian's writing. Mike had ordered it on interlibrary loan, liked it a lot and told some of us that we really should read it. But, why situate what we do in the rarefied atmosphere of abstract literature reviews identifying holes in literatures for us to fill? Things don't always make the best sense when argued this way. For instance, Ian vividly recalls an informal postgraduate meeting during the first year of his PhD in which he tried to situate his research in such holes. What came across, however, was academic gibberish. So one asked, 'Yeah, but why do you really want to do this?' Ian then found himself talking about how he'd had trouble encouraging undergraduate students he taught while doing his MA to see why learning about other people and places was anything to do with them. Taking something that they could buy in a local store and showing how it connected their lives to those of 'others' was one way of combating this sense of disconnectedness. Ian had never explained his topic choice this way before. But, it was *exactly* why he had wanted to do this research. 'Ah, I see', one said, 'so, why didn't you say that before?'

The fact that ethnographic research invariably changes as it proceeds, and therefore that researchers need to be prepared to be flexible, is something that we have been talking about throughout this book. None of us can be entirely sure where we will end up when we start a piece of research. Writing a thesis or dissertation in which the often systematic but shifting, tangent-ridden, circuitous and continually reorganised nature of research is translated into a neat, linear, orderly, chunked up and certain argument is a deceit that's often necessary for us to be seen to be good researchers. But, suppose your topic emerged from quite personal experiences. Suppose it changed as a result of funding priorities, supervisory advice/instruction, selective gatekeeper assistance and other power relations. Suppose it changed a lot as you tried to do it. Suppose you couldn't do it at all, or a central part of it remained unfinished or proved impossible to do. How could you write your dissertation or thesis in that 'good researcher' style, as if you had set out from the start to do what you did and find what you found? What questions would you have to invent after the fact? What literature would you have to read back through to justify them? What retrospective methodological fictions would you have to invent to bring together those questions and literatures? How much jiggery-pokery would this involve? Could you pull it off? Or, would you be better off writing an autoethnographic account of your research: a piece of writing that asks the reader to follow you through the research process, to appreciate why you did what you did, what influenced that process, how you tried to make sense of this and where you ended up?

Asked to comment on what she was looking for when reviewing auteothenographic work, Carolyn Ellis wrote:

Optimally, I want to feel and think with the story... I want to be immersed in the flow of the story, lost in time and space, not wanting to come to the end (as in a good novel), and afterwards unable to stop thinking about or feeling what I've experienced.... (2000: 273)

Many of us can only dream about our writing having such an effect. But autoethnographic accounts often evoke surprisingly positive responses from their readers. Take the correspondence that Leigh Berger (2001) received after writing about her relationship with her deaf sister and her father's mental illness. Here, she says, 'Individuals have shared with me their own experiences with disability and mental illness, allowing us to feel connected by mutual experience. On another level, those who have not been personally affected by either disability or mental illness have communicated with me about the various ways my stories connect to their own lives and experiences, allowing them to access new perceptions and worldviews' (Berger 2001: 509; see also Behar 1996: 14; Cook et al. 1998: 27–29). But who can write such work, and what do you need to be able to do to write it well? Now may be a good time to read an extract from Ian's work in this area (Box 9.5).

Box 9.5: Writing Autoethnography

The autoethnographic part of Ian's PhD was intended to detail why he could not get his 'proper' PhD written on time and – in combination with the rest of his thesis – why his examiners should award him a PhD nonetheless. In this part, he drew on his research diary, written work, written comments on this work, vivid memories and other evidence to construct a story of trying to get his PhD research done in academic and other spaces not normally discussed in such work. Laurel Richardson (2000a) has called this subset of autoethnography 'writing-stories', and this box contains material from a book chapter that he was asked to write about his PhD while he was waiting to hear the final verdict on its second submission. At the time, he had been struggling to write more conventional research papers. He decided to structure this one, however, through the kind of conversation he'd have in his head about this on his drive to work. The first two words of that chapter were, therefore, a request to 'Situate yourself'. Answering this, and the questions that followed, allowed Ian to develop a voice that he felt was 'his', that he was used to thinking in, and that he wanted to write in, rather than struggling to translate things into that anonymous, homogenised academic voice that is part of many academic writers' 'professional socialisation, rewards, and punishments' (Richardson 2000a: 925). Ian found that, once he started writing in this voice, the floodgates opened. This voice had a lot to say. The first draft of this chapter ran to almost 19,000 words (the 'director's cut' – Cook et al. 1998), which was cut down to 9,000 words for the published chapter from which the following extract has been taken.

––––––

Extract from ' "You want to be careful you don't end up like Ian, he's all over the place": autobiography in/of an expanded field' (Cook 2001: 108–12)
So, we need to be careful we don't end up like you, then..?
In many senses, yes. But, in others, maybe not. See what you think. I've used this warning once before in the title of a talk I gave in the Easter break of 1994, six months before my 4 year submission deadline. And I think it's apt here, too....

Imagine yourself in a small banked lecture theatre in a manor house owned by a large university in the South of England and run as its rather plush conference center. You are a first year human geography PhD student and are in an audience of perhaps 30 people. Most of them are also at the same point in their research careers, but some are lecturers in the departments which make up the consortium that has organised the conference. One might be your supervisor. You are about to be told about 'things going wrong' by the three speakers who are sat behind a table at the front. They've all just about finished their PhDs. You would like to be in that position one day (in less than four years' time, of course). Attending this conference is part of your research 'training'. One of the speakers is a tall, white, scruffy-looking 28 year old English male. He is the last one to speak, and does so from a script where what he says is apparently written word for word. He won't stand up, or even sit on the table. He is really nervous. He'd had a rough ride with his last conference presentation. He is reluctant to look up from his script as he speaks. He grins a lot, but not because he thinks what he is saying is particularly funny. Or at least that's how he remembers it four years later, as he's writing a book chapter like this one...

He begins with an anecdote from his time as a postgraduate in Bristol. In his third year there, a story had come his way of a fellow postgraduate who had been warned by a member of staff 'You want to be careful you don't end up like Ian. He's all over the place'. He says that he's going to use this rather flippant point to address the issue of 'things going wrong' with PhD research. He tries to situate his arguments in 'the literature' within and beyond geography where the politics and ethics of ethnographic research have been discussed. He suggests that, while you have probably been encouraged to research and write about, through and against the 'dodgy politics' of the world around you in your work, you probably haven't been encouraged to research and write about these politics closer to home, in your department and/or university for instance. He is about to do just this, though. He doesn't believe in that 'ivory tower'/'real world' divide (and you probably don't believe in it either). He has plenty of experience of academia as – in its own way – an exploitative and cut-throat business....

He mentions how the transition from being a postgraduate at the University of Kentucky to being one at the University of Bristol was difficult; how things went wrong 'in the translation' (so to speak) between two very different academic locales; how, in the process, he became a rather bitter and angry student who was a pain in the bum to supervise; and how things got worse during his third year due to a lack of funds and a disturbing reaction to 'that' conference paper. But he tries to make sense of this process not by reference to theories addressing the contemporary politics of education, but to a short passage taken from Michael Taussig's (1987) book *Shamanism, Colonialism and the Wild Man*. Here, he says, Taussig tried to make sense of the 'cultures of colonialism' and the dynamics of their (trans)formation by South American people and the Europeans who colonized their territories at the end of the 19th century. And he quotes Taussig's argument that, there and then, there 'were, in effect, new rituals, rites of conquest and colony formation, mystiques of race and power, little dramas of civilization and savagery which did not mix or homogenize ingredients from the two sides of the colonial divide but instead bound Indian understandings of white understandings of Indians to white understandings of Indian understandings of whites' (109). He (Cook, not Taussig) then makes the point that, if you remove the physical violence and communication problems, and then substitute 'cultures of cleverness' for those of 'colonialism', you might have a useful way of thinking about the politics of postgraduate life in your department. It worked for him. Sort of. To make the

Box 9.5: continued

point as clearly as he can, he paraphrases Taussig's argument by arguing himself that, on entering departments, first year postgrads are initiated into 'cultures of cleverness' which bind staff understandings of postgrad understandings of staff to postgrad understandings of staff understandings of postgrads. The way that he has written his paper will illustrate this point, if you don't quite get it yet. He had to think about it for a long time before it clicked.

He then goes on to say that he takes the staff/postgrad binary with a pinch of salt, that these aren't the only people whose understandings of each other's understandings help to create, sustain and transform these 'cultures', and that these relationships have to be seen as situated within the wider cultural politics and political economies of higher education. There are, for instance, still far too many white middle-class men like him, and perhaps like you too, teaching and researching in geography departments. This is certainly the case in the UK. He also knows exactly what feminist geographers like Linda McDowell mean when they criticize these academic 'cultures' as being invariably 'masculinist'. He quotes one of the quotations that she uses to make her point. This describes postgraduates' initiation into such 'cultures' as learning the:

'process of one-upmanship by which we learn to be critical thinkers. In graduate school we are taught that the measure of our intelligence is the extent to which we can show others to be wrong. Thus the best students are those who can offer the most masterful critique, pointing to the methodological flaws, finding gaps in the argument, and using the most sophisticated language. One consequence is an enormous loss of self-confidence and self-esteem, so that it is the unusual student who emerges from a graduate program as a confident scholar who feels good about herself or himself' (Anderson in McDowell 1992a: 402).

This neatly encapsulates his experience of being a PhD student, and it's nice to know it's not just a Bristol thing (it's all over the place) and he's not an unusual student. When he first read this passage it was, at once, a depressing and fantastic thing to be told. He thinks that this passage may have a similar effect on you. He can't possibly know, though. . . .

He then tries to up the tempo. In one of his characteristically long sentences, he says that, through writing about postgraduate research as embedded within the kinds of tensions, contradictions and inconsistencies which constitute these structures of power/knowledge – through ambivalent complexes of accommodation and resistance, through contextual performances of identity, and so on – he believes and/or hopes that you (or at least he) can capture, think about and, at least partially, deal with what goes wrong with such work *in* such work. The point he's making is that, when you think that things are going 'wrong' with your research, they might be going 'right' if you think about them differently – as something that you can learn from and perhaps follow up. And he would like you to learn from his 'mistakes' in this respect, if you can and want to do so. He argues that reading about the 'expanded field' is useful training for these mental gymnastics, and recommends that you read Katz's (1992) work in particular. By design and by accident, he believes that there's much to learn if you tackle head on the 'fact' that your research is almost inevitably going to go, and going to be, 'all over the place'. He seems to want to turn this criticism into an observation, or perhaps even into a compliment.

To a very large extent, the way that autoethnography 'works' depends on the readers and how they can engage with this style of writing in general, and in the story told in particular. It is certainly not everyone's cup of tea, to read, write or supervise (Ellis and Bochner 2000). But, if you are interested in having a go at this, there are two main issues that are worth noting. First, writing autoethnographically could allow you to make a more faithful sense of what you learned on your journey through the expanded field of your research, however much it stayed on or went off the rails (Richardson 2000a). And you don't need much of an outline to work from, except perhaps for a title and rough chronology of the main events and issues that this journey might and/or did connect (Ellis and Bochner 2000). Rather, what's important is to start such writing *before* you know exactly what you want to say. As Laurel Richardson (2000a: 924) has explained, 'I write because I want to find something out. I write in order to learn something that I did not know before I wrote it' (see also Lie 1988). Organising your writing this way, you create the structure of your narrative *as you write*, edit and rewrite it over and over again until it's done (Bennett and Shurmer-Smith 2001).

Second, autoethnographic writing is supposed to discourage readers from being passive recipients of your 'results' by repositioning them as active participants in your research journey (Behar 1996; Ellis and Bochner 2000; Heyman 2000). To do this, among other things, it's necessary to:

- write as an 'I' and address your readers as 'you' to talk about a subject community that is an 'us' (Ellis and Bochner 2000);
- write in jargon-free ways that try to be more or less equally accessible to academic and non-academic audiences (Agger 2002 Richardson 2002);[4] When you're sitting down to write and trying to imagine your audience, one tactic is to think what you would say to, or want to hear if you were part of, a general audience in a lecture;
- write 'vulnerably' – i.e. not as the objective master of all you purvey, but as someone in the thick of things, experiencing clarity, confusion,

joy, boredom, pain and more – so that your readers can *respond* vulnerably (Behar 1996; Berger 2001; Ellis and Bochner 2000);[5]

- write an academically rigorous text that is also open to interpretation, that gives your readers plenty to think *with* rather than about, and that offers them 'multiple places to stand in the story, multiple levels of emotionality and experience to which they can connect... [so that d]uring this process, readers interact with the characters in the text, becoming ethnographers themselves and coming to their own conclusions about what it all means' (Agger 2002; Heyman 2000);

- write *stories* that are 'truthful fictions' in the sense that not only are all ethnographic writings 'fictions...in the sense that they are "something made", "something fashioned"...not that they are false, unfactual, or merely "as if" thought experiments' (Geertz 1973: 15) but also they can be more 'truthfully' constructed through 'fictional writing techniques such as dramatic recall, strong imagery, fleshed out characters, unusual phrasings, puns, subtexts, allusions, flashbacks and flashforwards, tone shifts, synecdoche, dialogue, and interior monologue' (Richardson 2000a: 931);

- aim to write a (partly) autoethnographic dissertation/thesis in which your self doesn't overshadow those of the people whose lives you are studying: as Carolyn Ellis advised Sylvia, 'You might start the dissertation with a short personal story, to position yourself for the reader, or tell a longer story as a chapter. Or you might integrate parts of your experience into each participant's story, each of which could form separate chapters. Or write your story in comparison to one of the participants who is similar to you' (Ellis and Bochner 2000: 757);[6]

- improve your style by reading autoethnographies and novels, getting lots of feedback on drafts from critical but supportive readers (Ellis and Bochner 2000) and, finally

- 'Try to write so that you would want to read your own writing!' (Agger 2002: 457; Cook 2001).

Having provided these pointers, there are a couple of questions that we should now ask to finish off this section. The first is the extent to which you think that the writing in Box 9.5 has some or all of these characteristics, and if they work for you in the way that they're supposed to? Contrary to the impression that these extracts may give, this style of writing isn't only appropriate for 'salvage ethnographies' like Ian's (although it might well be worth filing 'autoethnography' under 'last resorts' should your research project also end up going too far off the rails).[7] But what difference would that make to the design and conduct of your research? How would you fit your theoretical, substantive and methodological reading into this as important elements of a developing research process? When would you start writing this? To get an impression about what research that's autoethnographic from the start may look like, you could take a look at some examples of research as process. One might be by the artist Shelley Sacks (nd; see also

Sacks and Cook 2000), where she narrates the story of her social sculpture project *Exchange Values: Images of Invisible Lives*, stretching from her childhood fascination with banana skins in South Africa, via art school in Germany, to her encounters with the Caribbean banana producers whose skins and stories were the core materials of the project, and to banana consumers' engagements with the sculpture after its UK debut. An example of personal postgraduate motivation might be by Rachel Saltmarsh (2001; see also Cloke et al. 2004: 366–67) doing her PhD on the changing working class cultures of the former pit villages in the North of England where she had grown up but was moving away from through her higher education (or see Gold (2002) on her religious motivation).

Second, and finally, it's worth asking whether a lot of the advice offered here is *only* relevant to autoethnographic writing. The writing tactics suggested by Carolyn Ellis, for instance, could easily incorporate the code-writing that we discussed earlier, the montage writing we're going to talk about next and plenty more besides. The advice on how academic writers could make their writing more evocative and engaging could be taken on board by anyone. Being inspired by, and borrowing and adapting styles of (re)presentation from non-academic sources is certainly something that we both found worthwhile for other bits of our writing.

Writing Montage

Film-makers, photographers, artists, novelists, academics, musicians and others have been using the technique of montage since at least the 1920s.[8] Dictionary definitions cast montage as a process of creating one text/ photograph/film/artwork/etc. from apparently unrelated or disparate fragments of others. Whatever their medium, montage-makers do their work through overlaying, overlapping, superimposing, cutting and/or juxtaposing these fragments with the overall aim of setting up new meanings that don't come from within the fragments but, instead, from the way that they work with and/or against one another. And it's important to point out that there are two kinds of montage: *mundane*, which involves 'Montaging items together in accordance with established norms of representation so that an audience has an impression of a set of ideas or story being smoothly communicated', and *intellectual*, which involves 'Montaging items...together in a disruptive and surprising way to try and make people stop and think about something in a new way' (Spaul nd: np; Marcus 1994).

In this chapter, we will be concentrating on the second type of montage, versions of which were used by Mike and Ian to write through (parts of) their PhD research materials. In particular, we will be talking through, and illustrating, *Mike's Textual Montages* (which were inspired by the between-the-wars writing of Walter Benjamin), and *Ian's Cinematic*

Montage (which was inspired by (analyses of) Amos Gitai's 1983 *Ananas (Pineapple)* documentary). In neither case were these fanciful choices. For both of us, the topics and methodologies that we had chosen meant that montage writing helped us to make a better and/or more faithful sense of what we found. Our choices to write in bits are probably related to our choices to research in bits: both of our PhDs involved multi-site ethnographies, Mike's being comparative and Ian's being connective (Marcus 1995). But it is worth making three general points here about why at least parts of most ethnographic research could be written through montage. First, there is the argument that we have been making right from the start of this book that isolated, 'pure cultures' no longer exist (if they ever did) for researchers to study 'out there' and bring 'back home'. Culture, George Marcus (1994: 50) has argued, 'is increasingly deterritorialised, and is the product of parallel diverse and simultaneous worlds operating consciously and blindly with relation to each other'. Thus, ourselves and the people and places we study are almost bound to be 'made up' of bits and bobs from here, there and maybe everywhere, and/or to have senses of belonging with more than one 'people' or place as members of travelling or diasporic cultures (Clifford 1992, 1997).

Second, all (academic) accounts are in some sense already montages because they are based upon, and bring together, disparate sources. 'Texts' stretch beyond their bindings as citations and intertextual links bring in other texts (Derrida 1999). As we have shown in this book, dissertations, theses and other work can only ever be partial readings of other people's work. This work will also inevitably have been based upon these authors' partial readings of the work by yet more others, ad infinitum. With qualitative research, this is further complicated because it relies so much on conversations and other interactions between the 'author' and her/his research participants with answers to what they thought the questions were, and so on. Finally, authorship also involves relationships between those who do, advise, supervise, judge, referee and/or edit such work as it is transformed from first draft to final-final version (Agger 2002; Hughes and Reimer 2005; Shokeid 1997). All research, and thinking through and making sense of materials generated in the process, means leaning very heavily on other sources. Hundreds, maybe more. But, for dissertations and theses at least, we have to take on the identity of the 'sole author' who has created this singular piece of work. Both of us, for example, had to sign a standard 'author's declaration' to insert in the first few pages of our PhDs. This read:

> This thesis is the original work of the candidate except where acknowledgement is given and has not been submitted previously for a higher degree in this or any other University. The views expressed here are those of the author and not of the University.

Proper citation, referencing and quotation from our sources also helps 'sole (and other) authors' to position their writing as academically credible and convincing. We usually have to appeal to the authority of the 'great and good', and mobilise other texts as established 'facts', in order to support the approaches we have taken and the findings we have come up with, and to rule others out of court (Curry 1996: 195). This, in turn, can help to make them appear transcendent and context free. However, like autoethnography's 'writing stories', what this fragmentation/montage approach can do is to make these hidden connections, collaborations, power relations and entanglements *part of the argument* about theories, analyses, whatever.[9] It can allow us to illustrate how we fashioned our material through a bricolage of knowledge – being embedded in social milieux, and taking what we found, sometimes serendipitously, to *make* something from this process.

Finally, as we have also tried to show throughout this book, formal ethnographic data construction and analysis is a process of producing and working with chunks and fragments of interview transcripts, diary notes, tallies, photos, codings, etc. which are often supplemented by informal collections of brochures, photos, postcards, letters, newspaper clippings, maps and more besides. We may have considerable trouble pulling these together in a straightforward or authoritative way. And they may have been constructed and collected in an expanded field where what we saw and did often felt more chaotic than orderly, confused rather than coherent, contradictory rather than consistent. So, how could we present a nice neat account of these worlds? Could we present things more as we understood them, through arranging our fragmentary understandings in some kind of montage? And would we use this way of writing to structure (parts of) our empirical or other chapters, or our whole dissertation or thesis? Like autoethnography, montage writing can be attractive for those who cannot, or do not want to, explain their research through the standard dissertation/thesis outline set out at the start of this chapter.

Mike's textual montage

Mike's turn to montage writing was affected by all of the factors discussed above. About halfway through his PhD, when he had done the bulk of his research, a sense of dread began to grow as he struggled to work out how to write his thesis. The various parts of his research had involved using five different methodologies to address five different heritage practices, with three different groups of people, in between four and eight locations.[10] This was not a conventional ethnography of a people (singular) and their life in a place (singular) – though he sometimes now began to wish it had been. The standard thesis writing model of theory, context, methods, empirical material and conclusion, however attractive in its neatness, seemed woefully unsuited to the task. How would anyone be able to recall that the issue set up theoretically in chapter 2 subsection 5 was applicable, via the methodology in chapter 4 subsection 3 to chapter 5 data but not chapter 6 or anywhere else? It seemed absurd to write, let alone to try to read, anything like this. Eventually he decided the problem was that he was still looking for a (singular) style. Having effectively studied five different sorts of heritage practice, surely it made sense to use different styles for each one? Rather than having theory, context and methodology chapters for the whole thesis, individual chapters could have their own theoretical, contextual, methodological and empirical content. The literature arguing for the use of each method and the integration of field/theory seemed strong. And he knew he could use it since one thing he was writing alongside the thesis was the first version of this book! Box 9.6 shows the end result of this thesis-structuring deliberation.

Box 9.6: Mike's PhD Thesis

Below is the table of contents of Mike's PhD thesis (Crang 1995). This is clearly very different from Ian's (in Box 9.4). Mike was trying to get away from a tendency in the literature that he read to suggest one 'correct' way of experiencing the past, or one kind of audience for accounts of these experiences. His main aim in structuring the thesis was, therefore, to show that different forms of heritage involved different social practices, were experienced in different ways and tended to reach different audiences. The thesis began quite conventionally, with an introduction (chapter 1), and an outline of important academic and policy debates (chapter 2).[a] The next two chapters comprised reviews of existing work that argued how the past is used in terms of taste and social status (chapter 3);[b] and is shaped and made useful by a variety of institutions (chapter 4). These were followed by two conceptual chapters: one that explored the role of places and space in framing notions of time (chapter 5), and one that introduced theories of consumption as an active process (chapter 6). And then came the more empirical chapters: on Mike's oral history research in four Bristol neighbourhoods (chapter 7); the circulation and publishing of archival photographs of Bristol (chapter 8); the research in which he'd followed tourists from one town to eight historic sites (chapter 9); and the research he'd done with two groups of living history reenactors (chapter 10). A concluding chapter (11) attempted to tie all of this together and finish off the thesis. NB the underlined sections below are those from which the excerpts in boxes 9.3, 9.7 and 9.8 are taken.

----

[a] Another introductory chapter was written and included here, but had to be cut from the final version because of the word limit.
[b] Another chapter on landscape and history was written and included here, but had to be cut from the final version because of the word limit.

THE PRODUCTION OF SPACES FOR THE PAST: A CULTURAL GEOGRAPHY OF THE HERITAGE INDUSTRY IN ENGLAND

Contents.

Box 9.6: continued

Box 9.6: continued

Mike's montage writing in his thesis worked at two different levels. First, at one level the whole thesis was a montage of different forms, audiences and practices of heritage consumption between which the reader was supposed to see differences, and make connections. And, second, there were the montage approaches used within some of the chapters. This latter approach was in large part inspired by the writing of the theorist Walter Benjamin, who was working in Paris in the 1930s and 1940s. Benjamin was a voracious reader of theory, journalism, and historical documents – indeed almost anything – for his project on reconceptualising urbanism. His working method was to file items from a vast variety of sources in different registers. Each corresponded not to a 'source type' but rather to a theme of analysis – likening his work to that of a collector, he suggested. Here different materials butted up against one another as they were reconfigured from their original contexts and recontextualised in new, and intriguing, relationships. So, far from trying to represent the field 'as it was' Benjamin suggested that 'The true method of making things present is to represent them in our space (not represent ourselves in their space)' (Benjamin 1999: H2, 3). It was the connections between apparently contrasting pieces of information that Benjamin wanted to show through the juxtaposition of elements that were not normally found together, which thereby produced new irruptive truths. As he explained:

Method of this project: literary montage. I needn't say anything. Merely show. I shall purloin no valuables, appropriate no ingenious formulations. But the rags, the refuse – these I will not inventory but allow, in the only way possible, to come into their own: by making use of them (Benjamin 1999: 460, N2, 1).

In Benjamin's work this was linked to the then emergent aesthetic practice of surrealism and collage. Here, fragments of one material, from one context, are taken and reused in another, with the whole creating a new meaning through what Benjamin termed 'dialectical images'.

Benjamin developed this textual style to *perform* the fragmented and disjunctured nature of life as he saw it. It did not involve theoretical approaches standing over, and reflecting upon, the world but rather had ideas emerge from among and through the materials. As an approach to writing through research materials, it has attracted increasing attention (see Becker 2001; Denzin and Lincoln 2000; Kamberelis 2003; Pred 1995, 2000). It is now more acceptable to write texts that disrupt contrived and inscribed boundaries of what might normally be seen as culturally distinct and bounded practices and spaces (see for example Pluciennik and Drew 2000; Pred 1995, 2000). This writing needs to be a process neither of logical deduction from pregiven theoretical ideas, nor of induction from patterns in the data. It needs, rather, to be a process of 'abduction': a process where researchers/writers pick up ideas from the world and develop them not so much to prove them right or wrong but to see where they can lead and what they can do.

Mike became especially interested by the way Benjamin had picked through discarded ephemera and pulled together diverse materials (especially because Mike had accumulated drawerfuls of such ephemera – pamphlets, brochures, newspaper adverts, illustrated guides and so forth – during his PhD research). Mike therefore felt that drawing on Benjamin, both as an inspiration and as an authoritative source, meant he could, for example, inset statements from marketing brochures into 'academic' accounts, with the aim not only of exemplifying the arguments but also of disrupting them (see Box 9.7 – from chapter II of the thesis). Or amid the serious commentaries about ontology in chapter IV of his thesis, he inserted humorous adverts, suggesting that this was not always taken seriously and indeed that the heritage business did not take itself as seriously as he – as an academic researcher – felt he was supposed to. Juxtaposing different ways things were textualised revealed these tensions of expectation. This was not the only form of montage writing Mike used in his thesis. As mentioned in an earlier chapter, perhaps the most surprising element of Mike's research experience was that many of the people he worked with were expert researchers themselves, and often drew on the same popular and academic literatures that Mike was looking at in his PhD. This made it extremely difficult to write from the superior viewpoint of the 'outside expert' because it was often extremely

Box 9.7: Mike's Writing Fragments

This section of Mike's thesis was making an argument about 'recreated environments', such as the living history sites in which he did his participant observation. Here he is mixing the academic commentary alongside excerpts from brochures and leaflets promoting these establishments. He could have tried a more formal semiotic or discourse analysis. Maybe he should have but he thought inserting little fragments also showed how these claims were stumbled over by people – not as coherent body but in little dribs and drabs. But the strategy was less innocent than that. Writing in this way what he was trying to imply was that, yes the commentators were reflecting the rhetorical claims sites made, but also that they were doing little more than that – whereas he had tried a more ethnographic engagement. Therefore this textual style was meant to allude to the way these ideas were indeed prevalent in both academic commentary and the 'real world' but also to make his work look good for being more than just about marketing hype. The material below is thus a snapshot of a page from Mike's thesis to show how this looked on the page:

"They are all places out of time - anyway, out of *this* time. They are visits to times past. They allow us to play, for a time, in another time. In order to do this, some of them, rather worryingly to some of us, begin to play with *time*. death and decay are, it seems, denied. Strangely and paradoxically in the context of institutions nominally preoccupied with the passage of time, these phenomena are not allowed to occur. This denial of the realities of time, this artificial omission of any interval between then and now leads to the ready assumption, indeed the implication, that then and now are very similar, and that *we* and *they* are, except for a few superficial differences, similar also."

Sorensen (1989:65).

Delaney (1992:141) parallels such forms of temporal manipulation to Foucault's idea of heterotopia (1986:16), where the permeation of forms of space is also a process of heterochronism which, while celebrating a diversity of times also works at the abolition of different times.

With painstaking attention to detail, the colliery buildings are alive once more with the familiar sights, sounds and smells of a now past era. Journey back in time with us, and experience the unique character and culture of the Rhondda, as seen through the eyes of three generations of one 'typical' mining family.

The example Foucault uses is, revealingly, that of tourism to enter another culture entirely 'to get away from' our own time and experience another

Stepping back through the gates of ... is like stepping back nearly 100 years in Australian History.

time in totality which simultaneously mixes different times and abolishes them into a liminal now (Cohen 1989a; Shields 1989). Now let us be clear that regardless of these implications this is a major step beyond the absence of the popular or ordinary found in so many 'traditional' museums in a field where up until recently the 'pristine technology' of industry and the logic of the technostructure was all that could be shown (Alfrey & Putnam 1992; Buchanan 1989), relegating ways of working and conditions of use to the sidelines. Meanwhile to show the home at all is a major innovation although still so much is shown in terms of domestic products rather than tools for a feminised and unpaid labour-force (Porter 1988).

Open the Door to the Dark Ages .. A Living Village

So we can access a version of the people's past but one premised on a different to disentangle in what ways what Mike learned in the library was different from what knowledge he gained in the field.

Let's take two examples to flesh this out and point back to the way in which he could write about this. First, Mike had to deal with the fact that he was constantly bumping into his 'literature review' during his 'fieldwork'. For example, there was the evening when he mentioned a book he had read to the participants in one of his reenactment groups, only to find that one had read it and another later produced a book review from the group's newsletter. Mike would clearly have to be one of those social analysts who now had to 'grapple with the realization that [their] objects of analysis are also analysing subjects who critically interrogate ethnography – their writings, their ethics, their politics' (Rosaldo 1989: 21). Then there was the way that Mike found that the Bristol archivists already arranged their pictures in books almost like Benjamin's 'dialectical images',[11] or that museum curators cropped up as reenactors, or commissioned surveys on what he was working upon, the head spinning list goes on! Thus, he felt he had to think of a way to portray 'them' in a way that was faithful to their performative knowledges and input to his research. So he took sources that academic authors are supposed to take as authoritative – i.e. academic books – and turned them in to equally subjective, unreliable field guides. He wanted to illustrate how as Trinh Minh-ha (1989: 68) put it, ethnography is 'scientific gossip' where, like gossipers, academics 'act in solidarity, leaning on and referring to each other for more credibility'. He wanted to show how academic judgments on historical reenactment, for example, emerged out of a field of opinions and social positions. He wanted to place them, and show how his work was reacting to an academic debate, but that this debate was part of what was studied (see Box 9.8). Here he was inspired by the first chapter of Malcolm Ashmore's (1989) *Reflexive Thesis*, called 'The fiction of the lecturer', in which the reader is invited to read the text of a lecture addressing the question 'What is the sociology of scientific knowledge'. This works nicely as an introduction to the SSK literature but what Mike liked the most was the question and answer session at the end. Ashmore 'populates' his lecture theatre with the core set of sociologists of scientific knowledge, and constructs a fictional dialogue between them. The debate starts with a 'Professor Geezer' pointing out that, among other things, 'Having deconstructed scientific knowledge,' these sociologists 'insist that we accept their arguments because they have been scientifically demonstrated' (Ashmore 1989: 15). What Ashmore then does is to stage a discussion defending (t)his position involving these sociologists, which is based on properly referenced fragments: including quotations from their letters to him, interviews with them and their publications. An entirely new fictional scenario is created in which to stage a dialogue that never happened, but perhaps could and should have.

And this shows the potential of mixing principles from autoethnographic and montage writing – i.e. it's a creative use of proper research data, or fictional writing strategies made out of bits – to make valid and convincing arguments.

Box 9.8: Mike Making Conversation (Crang 1995: 315)

What follows is taken from about halfway through chapter X of Mike's thesis, where he was looking at living history. After reading 'the literature' on this topic, he felt that the 'psychologisation' of re-enactors by historians who had never done an ethnography with these people meant their comments needed to be set in context – i.e. challenged and made 'disputable'.

———

[Being a scholarly debate in which various critics put forward their commentaries for the benefit of the reader.]

Peter Fowler: 'Much in vogue today is playing at the past: Britaineering, Sealed Knottery, Druidic dressings up and mediaeval quaffing and wenchery. [. . .] It is probably kinder to regard such goings-on as illustrative of the stimulus of the past rather than decry them as the prostitution of history itself. The only danger is that participants and watchers dupe themselves into thinking that what they are doing is history.' (1992: 14)

Mike Crang: You say 'kinder', I wonder if you'd like to elaborate on that? What would be your harsher verdict?

Peter Fowler: 'All this activity, far from illuminating the past, is actually saying something profound and poignant about the present. A radio programme featuring the participants at 'Tudor' Kentwell (BBC Radio 4, 29 December) illustrated the pathos and very necessary therapy behind the fun and pretence. An individual dissatisfaction with unimportant and uncolourful lives is a fairly obvious part explanation' (1992: 14–15)

Mike Crang: But Peter you know this is too glib. You heard about Kentwell Hall as a first person 'recreation' on the radio, you never actually say you visited the place. That aside are you suggesting that there is some sort of contemporary psychological need to find some non-modern, real – yes colourful – fantasy of self-importance or chance to be a hero in your own 'movie' that re-enactment affords these people? . . .

Box 9.8: continued

Peter Fowler:	'To dress up seems a natural urge, indulged in from childhood and nothing more than a physical expression of personal fantasy, of wishing, but perhaps not too seriously, to be someone else. The experience is temporary, enjoyed knowing you can return.... A possible danger when grown-ups do it is that they do take it too seriously. The proverbial 'little man', perhaps trapped during the week in anonymous routine work on the assembly line or office desk, can release his self not only by imagining that he is a named pikeman in Cromwell's New Model Army for the purposes of an evening's re-enactment; he can go on to delude himself that he has actually become that person and is engaged in an authentic reliving of a real, historic event.' (1992: 15)
Mike Crang:	Aren't you being a bit OTT here? I mean most pikemen I met were damn clear that it was fun – in fact you'll no doubt be horrified to learn – rather like rugby. I suppose that sort of 'fun' re-creation is just what scares you Kevin?
Kevin Walsh:	'these events are nothing but mere titillation, meaningless amateur dramatics, promoting the post-modern simulacrum, a hazy image of a manipulated and trivialised past... many such events contribute to the destruction of place. More often than not the events will not depict occurrences from the past of the locality being used, but there will be, perhaps, a set piece, an imaginary battle that moves from one locality to another each weekend.' (1993: 102–04)
Mike Crang:	But aren't you ending up in exactly the Quixotic quest Richard Handler speaks about , whereby a re-enactment on original topography (how near? have the fields the same crops? the same uniforms? same numbers?) is tolerable, is real history – but the idea of groups portraying the American Revolution in Britain is beyond the pale. So you define what is a 'real' recreation by its relation to the past instead of looking on them all as dramatic acts with present educational force....
Richard Handler:	'living history is as much about the present as the past. Inevitably, living history is shot through with the sentiments of modern culture. As analysts of reconstructed traditions have pointed out, the very attempt to relive the past entails a distinctive consciousness – of the past as a past worthy of being relived...' (1987: 340)

Mike Crang:	Look I like the point about the impossibility but it seems to me that we can't yet square this circle of wanting to laugh at their buffoonery, pathologise their motivations and say they create a sham while at the same time having to admit their meticulous attention to detail.
Tom Woods:	'These living history pioneers orchestrated re-enactments of historical events which have been and in many instances still are characterised by a sophisticated antiquarian concern for detail wedded to a kind of playful dramatic recreation' (1989: 43)
Mike Crang:	Exactly we have to include that sense of historical fastidiousness – that was what took me aback. What I want to do is to keep that duality alive – both the commitment to authenticity and its acknowledged impossibility. …I still found people doing their damnedest to be 'academic' and re-enactors read lots of 'legitimate' works yet still are damned for both any inaccuracies and their attention to accuracy. I keep feeling they are caught in the middle, David you were pretty scathing about Peter Fowler's analysis – what had he written?
David Lowenthal:	'"Pulling crowds to olde-tyme happenings, tourneys, jousts and pseudo-gunfire in the lawn-precious precincts of ruinous castles sanctions false images of the past, as jousting itself is demeaned by 'contamination' with showbiz, its ersatz medievalism"…and, needless to say, the fact that it enjoys neither posh followers nor participants. Not only inauthentic, in short, but vulgar' (1989a: 23)

Second, Mike also wanted to address the visual culture of heritage – an issue building through his thesis. From the literal highlighting of monuments to endless postcards and photographs he wanted to do more than just 'textual' accounts. He had started with the notion of dialectical images – those with different parts whose contrast, when put together, should reenergise both images. However, the field was replete with these already – pictures of happy children in a street of the 1930s and then juxtaposed a soulless roundabout, or pithead gear and now a park. Mike therefore began to look at how he could work through the accretion of images. Box 9.9 thus illustrates how he started putting together pages of

Box 9.9: A Dialectical Image: Photomontage of Bristol Historic Docks'

Mike here brought together two archival pictures (bottom and left) showing the docks and Bristol as scenes of industry, where in the left picture the now high-lighted and persevered church is obscured by activity and in the bottom ships are loading from what is now an Arts cinema, with his own contemporary picture (right) of the now unused but preserved dock.

———

multiple images, each inflecting the other. Not always contrasting or undercutting, but qualifying or elaborating. Sometimes even, just trying to make the point that these images were often seen in collections or in large numbers rather than as solitary objects of contemplation. In the end he continued working through this material to publish a paper (Crang 1996a) trying to argue though the different logics of visual combination representing history in a city. Which begins to suggest that, but of course, we should not restrict this account to purely verbal and textual ways of representing our material.

Cinematic montage

As we pointed out in the autoethnography section, Ian didn't submit the 'proper PhD' whose data construction and analysis have been illustrated throughout this book. After being awarded his PhD, however, he did go back to this data and begin to make sense of it as he should have. This section will be based around a recently published journal article called 'Follow the thing: papaya' (Cook et al. 2004a), which is perhaps closest to what parts of that 'proper PhD' would have looked like. Maybe. Ian's PhD research had been designed to defetishise a commodity through researching the hidden human (and other) relations that got it from one part of the world, in that condition, at that price, onto those shelves, in another part of the world. As illustrated in section two, this research had involved a variety of methods: participant observation on the farm, (serial) interviews and diaries with people on the farm and along the chain and visual/textual analysis of bits and bobs looked for and found by accident in various offices, shops and libraries along the way. It had also been undertaken in/between a number of different locales: most of the research was undertaken on one Jamaican papaya farm and at three UK supermarket headquarters, but lots of other people and places also got wrapped up in the research along the way. So, this was far from the kind of single locale, systematic, comparative study that seemed to have worked so neatly in his MA research.

While doing this proper PhD fieldwork, Ian found that he could more or less make sense of the part he was working on at any one time, but when he travelled to the next locale, to do the next piece of research, his understanding unravelled and a new one had to be pieced together, before moving on again, etc. The commodity system he was studying was also far from straightforward or transparent. He kept coming across all kinds of 'impression management' strategies, language games, (double) bluffing, double standards and (deliberate) ignorance, all of which seemed to be essential to the more or less efficient flow of fresh papayas from field to shelf. And there were a lot of overlaps between the bits studied 'separately' as, for example, Jamaican farmers visited UK supermarket buyers, and as UK-based importers visited farmers, to keep alive important business relationships. At the time, the best way that Ian could describe his research experience was that he'd done it in a hall of mirrors. So, how could he make an overall sense of this, in a proper thesis style? He couldn't even begin to imagine how he could write a coherent, linear narrative to make them work together or to make overall judgements about the people or processes involved. One of his supervisors suggested that he write through a time-line, in which what people were doing in various parts of the papaya chain at the same time formed the structure of the argument (e.g. 'as Mina the supermarket fruit buyer is fast asleep at home in Kent, Pru the fruit packer is rushing to pack the final boxes of papaya due to leave Jamaica on BA's late flight from Montego Bay....').[12] Apart from this interesting idea, however, he was really stuck. He couldn't find any ethnographic accounts of such multi-locale, commodity-based research to imagine what his thesis could look like as a whole.[13]

Around the same time, Ian's other supervisor told him about a documentary s/he had seen at a Bristol arts cinema called *Ananas (Pineapple)* (1983) that had uncanny parallels with his papaya research. *Ananas* was based on the travels of an Israeli filmmaker, Amos Gitai, who had tried to follow a tin of Dole pineapple rings from San Francisco to the pineapple fields of Hawaii and of the Philippines. He had interviewed company agronomists, plantation managers, an heir to the Dole family fortune, religious leaders, farm workers and many others along the way. This was an ethnographic film, in the sense that Gitai tried to find out about the lives of many of the people involved in this trade through talking with them in the places where they lived and worked, and letting them show him what they did. Together, the lives and stories hidden in the tin were starkly different. Gitai seemed to have anticipated and found a way to work through the contradictions in his multi-locale fruit-following research through cinematic montage. Luckily, an *Ananas* video was available to hire from the British Film Institute and Gitai's work had been analysed and discussed in great detail by film theorists. So Ian could learn a great deal about these montage techniques and their intended effects in this film (see Cook and Crang 1996). And, after being asked to write a short book chapter on his proper PhD research in 2001, Ian returned to this film and related montage literature to help him to get his head around how to write and illustrate this. The main thing he had to figure out was if and how he might use *Ananas* to develop 'a sort of cinematic imagination geared to writing' (Marcus 1994: 45).

Amos Gitai had been interviewed about his cinematic imagination on many occasions, and had also spelled this out in detail in his films' published funding proposals and other behind-the-scenes documents (see BFI 1985; Willemen 1993). Here, this imagination seemed to have four main elements. First, Gitai seemed to think of himself as the architect of cinematic spaces in which, he wrote:

> There's the spine, and the walls and the beams…and you can see them but they don't interfere with the inner spaces of the building or the film. So you have a structure which allows you to read into the building or the film, but it does-n't over-interpret the inner spaces; each one has a kind of cumulative effect, like when you walk through a space and each corridor or room or window gives you another view of it, but you will know it's a continuous structure (in Rosen 1990: 49).

Second, when shaping *Ananas*, he wanted the key theme in its cinematic space to be a 'juxtaposition of major profits on one hand, and political and economic repression on the other, seen through a single delicatessen product – sliced pineapple' (in BFI 1985: 43). But, he didn't want to simply berate people over this. Rather, he wanted to work more loosely in order to be open to surprises because 'sometimes people give you a sort of jewel and they reveal something you didn't know or express it in an incredibly compact way' (BFI 1985: 43). So, he wrote, 'Our over-all approach is that each time we see something that bears on the subject, we will film it. We will film in the same way that one would use a fishing net: trawling' (in BFI 1985, 41). And this approach would rely on uninter-rupted scenes lasting up to several minutes and often involving silences and the questions and physical presence of the film crew that, once edited into the final film, would allow audiences not only to see people, events and filmmaking in context, but also the time to think about what was going on in the film (MacDougall 1992; Willemen 1992; Williams 1993).

Finally, in Gitai's *Ananas* plan, he also envisaged how he could construct a film so that what it was 'about' – within the bounds of its architecture – would be worked out by its audiences, who could also critically question the way the film had been put together (Rabinowitz 1993; Stewart 1985). The ways in which his shots would be edited together were, therefore, crucial. He wrote that:

> Although each shot will be complete in itself, the 'capsules' will also cause one or more arguments to emerge through the way they are linked to the preceding or the following shot. In this way, the overall movement and structure of the film will be built up gradually and cumulatively. Through these sequence shots and by establishing a dialectical relation between image and sound, the documentary *Pineapple* will reflect the nature of the subject, attempting to grasp the contradictions inherent in the production process.…Instead of constructing a linear story, we will juxtapose the elements of the film.…(in BFI 1985: 40).

Ananas would, therefore, have nothing like the traps of familiar 'realist' documentaries in which an authoritative narrator tells the audience what the film is about, and the footage is filmed and edited to illustrate this (as discussed in chapter 7). Instead, as one reviewer put it, the film 'addresses its subject with a tone of casual innocence startling the viewer expecting a film about imperialism and exploitation. It pretends not to know the story it is about to unfold. It demands that the viewer watch with the naivety of the supermarket customer' (Dubrule in BFI 1985: 46). *Ananas* starts off much like a more conventional documentary with the authoritative account of an American agronomist who has been 'in the business' for most of his life. However, after it cuts to the home of a descendant of the Dole family who began the pineapple trade in Hawaii, 'the film apparently takes a course organised more by visual or aural association, than by any strict narrative link. The hook of an authorised storyline has for the moment disappeared from view' (Dubrule in BFI 1985: 47). From this point on, viewers had some sense-making to do. As one reviewer explained, the editing together of the film's 'capsules' meant that:

> The authority of each interviewee's overview of the story is persistently undercut, either by the material which precedes it or follows, or by formal devices within the shot. The whispering vocals of the music track which runs continuously throughout the film interfere with the synchronous sounds, suggesting a voice alternative to the momentum of the Company which is insistent but difficult to hear. Its persistent tropical rhythms link the disparate scenes in a way which emotively contradicts and threatens the Western viewpoint of the (Dole) Success Story. The spectator is not allowed to accept the documentary evidence at face value. ... These formal effects are manipulated to produce an anti-tourist's eye view: the external determining factors of the evidence must be recognised in order to understand its meaning.
>
> The narrative dynamic is made understandable by an accumulation of these circumstantial interconnections, collected en route by the spectator. The different levels of discourse in the film, whether in the historical data of the intertitles or in the information presented in the interviews themselves, are juxtaposed with one another to trace a network of overlapping associations far broader in its implications than the simple itinerary proposed at the outset. What emerges is the description of an object which otherwise thrives in its invisibility: the interlocking and interdependent systems of multi-national corporate power. Across histories of agronomics, technology, politics and religion, a logic is seen to operate, shaping the course of events in areas of economy and society which appear mutually independent. The focal point of this Success Story logic is shown to be the extreme exploitation and subjugation of the Filipino worker (Dubrule in BFI 1985: 49–50; MacDougall 1992).

This is, of course, just one detailed interpretation of *Ananas*. But there could be more. And that's the point. There's plenty for viewers to latch on to, because 'the film does not shrivel into empty rhetoric if we disagree with aspects of the argument: we can still work with the materials presented to formulate other arguments, other "senses"' (Willemen 1992: 19).

Now is the time to go back to Marcus' (1994: 45) question about how ethnographers could develop 'a sort of cinematic imagination geared to writing'. If you found a film that portrayed what you had studied better than a similar piece of writing, how could you learn something from it to try to achieve a similar effect in your writing? How about writing a 'compositional checklist'? If Ian had had to write one based on *Ananas*, it might have looked something like this:

- See your writing as a form of 'architecture' (i.e. as a way to create 'spaces for imagination').
- Decide on a key, underlying theme for your paper to explore, but don't say very much about it in your preface, introduction or abstract: multi-site research usually involves 'putting questions to an emergent object of study whose contours, sites, and relationships are not known beforehand' (Marcus 1995: 102), so it's appropriate to ask readers to expect their understandings to emerge through a similar process.
- Find academic justification(s) for *this way of doing things* in 'the literature', and include this in your preface, introduction, or abstract: your readers will probably need something to situate your work.
- Plan your sequence of capsules or 'scenes' which will be quite detailed stories in themselves, but will also touch on/elaborate/twist around issues that were part of previous capsules, and/or introduce new issues to be touched on, etc. in later capsules.
- Include at least one 'jewel' from your research data in each capsule; as mentioned earlier, empirical vignettes can offer points of revelation, clarity or challenge.
- As with autoethnographic writing, think of ways in which your reader may be able to identify or otherwise engage in the stories being told: e.g. as Gitai's consumer – or offer multiple points of identification throughout the text e.g. via tourist knowledge, consumer behaviour, work experience, etc.
- Again as with autoethnographic writing, find ways in which you can introduce your academic arguments in such a way that they are part of, rather than hovering outside and above the narrative that's unfolding.
- Give your writing a structure that starts somewhere and ends somewhere, but also mixes things up: multi-site ethnographic research requires writing that conjures up a sense of processes that are taking place in 'transcultural space, in different locales at once, in parallel, separate but simultaneous worlds' (Marcus 1994: 40), so why not, for example, occasionally place next to each other capsules that – geographically or otherwise – are great distances apart, rather than travelling short distances, capsule by capsule, on a gradual, linear journey from shelf to farm?

- Finally, don't expect to be able to write in such a way that you will be in control of all the possible permutations of meaning that your paper contains: use your writing to think things through, revisit your data, rewrite and reorganise your chapter/paper, over and over until it feels right, imaginatively, academically, politically, emotionally and so on.

This is the kind of advice that would perhaps have been useful before writing but Ian didn't write a checklist before he wrote his papaya paper. Much of this section is based on a paper he co-wrote in 1996 that argued that people doing research into the 'geographies of food' could learn a lot from watching *Ananas* (see Cook and Crang 1996).[14] If it hadn't been co-authored, and he'd had much longer to write his PhD, it could have been another thesis chapter.[15] The papaya paper certainly followed on from it, and it was read and reread as that papaya paper was written. This should be apparent in the extract quoted below (in Box 9.10). But, the proof of this kind of pudding is in its eating. So, the question to ask here is what can you as a reader make of this extract?

Box 9.10: Ian's Fruit Montage (from Cook et al. 2004a: 642–47)

The extract below is taken from the first few pages of Ian's papaya paper. It illustrates how he justified this style of writing for publication in a journal called *Antipode*: how the narrative kicked off, how it was (dis)organised and how it started to unfold. What this extract shows is, first, a structure in which, after the first scene-setting capsule ('Producing Papaya'), an alternation between capsules that are primarily single locale ethnographic descriptions of one character's life and work in the chain, and capsules that are primarily about trans-local processes that (dis)connect them. Second, the paper includes a sense of story-boarding by having each ethnographic capsule begin with a raw quotation from an interview with each character, and each process capsule begin with between one and three photos of places, things, paintings, maps, advertising etc. taken or gathered during the research process to encourage a visual imagination of the bits, bobs, voices, processes and scenes entangled in the paper. Third, the paper wasn't an attempt to bring separate elements or disciplines together, but to show how they comprised the same trans-national/trans-local time–space papaya thing (Gille 2001). Fourth, it was written in a choppy and often ungrammatical style that was initially intended to allow as much detail as possible to be squashed within the standard journal word limit, but also doubled as the kind of literary device that could encourage readers to engage more in the paper by, perhaps, filling in the holes, trying to work out what's actually being said and so on (see Richardson 2002).[a] Finally, we have to point out that all individuals in this paper were anonymised through the changing of proper names and, in places, through the creation of composite characters.

[a] One of the *Antipode* reviewers, however, argued that this made the paper 'almost unreadable'.

FOLLOW THE THING: PAPAYA

[Abstract]
In a recent round table about *Antipode's* radical geographies, contributors argued that the journal needed more papers which stimulated debate, were accessible to academics and non-academics alike, didn't 'preach to the cognoscenti', were written to fit into radical teaching agendas, and were diverse and eclectic in style (Waterstone 2002: 663; Hague 2002). This paper has been written to fit this bill. It outlines the findings of multi-locale ethnographic research into the globalization of food, focusing on a supply chain stretching from UK supermarket shelves to a Jamaican farm, and concluding in a North London flat. It addresses perspectives and critiques from the growing literature on the geographies of commodities, but presents these academic arguments 'between the lines' of a series of overlapping vignettes about people who were (un)knowingly connected to each other through the international trade in fresh papaya, and an entangled range of economic, political, social, cultural, agricultural and other processes also shaping these connections in the early 1990s. The research on which it is based was initially energized by David Harvey's (1990, 422) call for radical geographers to 'get behind the veil, the fetishism of the market', to make powerful, important, disturbing connections between Western consumers and the distant strangers whose contributions to their lives were invisible, unnoticed, and largely unappreciated. Harvey argued that radical geographers should attempt to de-fetishise commodities, re-connect consumers and producers, tell fuller stories of social reproduction, and thereby provoke moral and ethical questions for participants in this exploitation who might think they're decent people. This paper has been written to provoke such questions, to provide materials to think through and with, for geography's ongoing debates about the politics of consumption.

The Idea

. . . . if we accept that geographical knowledges through which commodity systems are imagined and acted upon from within are fragmentary, multiple, contradictory, inconsistent and, often, downright hypocritical, then the power of a text which deals with these knowledges comes not from smoothing them out, but through juxtaposing and montaging them . . . so that audiences can work their way through them and, along the way, inject and make their own critical knowledges out of them (Cook and Crang 1996: 41).

Box 9.10: continued

The Thing

The Following

Producing papaya:

FIGURE 1.   Left: 30 foot trees. Right: packing papaya.

Once they're picked, they start to die. Twisted off the stem. Just as they have 'turned'. From fully green, to green with a yellow streak. By farm workers. Men. Walking slowly along an avenue of 'trees'. Alongside a trailer, full of green plastic crates. Pulled by a tractor. Work that's undertaken in the hot sun. But they're shaded by the leaves splaying out from the tree top. Leaves that shade the fruit growing around that column. 'Turning' fruits at the bottom and flowers at the top. These 'trees' are perhaps ten feet tall. And eight months old. Picking is easy. But, in the next field, the 'trees' are eighteen months old. Thirty feet tall. And soon to be felled. The leaves finally succumbing to 'bunchy top'. The sprayer can't reach them. But, picking is still going on there. Thirty feet up. On a platform made from scaffolding. Welded to another trailer. Pulled slowly along by another tractor. Wheels following undulating tracks in the baked mud. Eight pickers leaning precariously off that platform. Four a side. Jerked about. Slowly moving. Looking for those colour changes. Cupping the bottom of the 'turning' fruits. Carefully twisting them off. Each a good handful. Placing them in crates for the packing house, where they're washed, weighed, graded, trimmed, wrapped and packed neatly in boxes. Primarily by women. All trying to prevent the white latex oozing from the fruits' peduncles from dripping onto *their* skin. It's nasty. We're on a papaya farm. Picking for export. To the USA and Europe. *Fresh.* Sold in mainstream supermarkets. 'Product of Jamaica'.

The papaya buyer:

> *I know that if I was going to buy, you know, mangoes (or) papayas, I wouldn't go into (my stores). But then I wouldn't go into (our competitors') either.... 'Ethnic' shops...have a lot of good lines. So I'd probably go there 'cause I know it would be a lot cheaper (laughs).... I know my mum would never go into (my stores) to buy mangoes. I don't think I would either, purely because it's an image that we've created in the supermarkets. Everything's got to look perfect. But, just the fact that it's got a blemish in there, I mean, it's edible.*

In 1992, Mina had been a speciality fruit and veg buyer for eight years. Buyers don't usually last that long in one department. She worked at a supermarket HQ just outside London. Most of this work revolved around her phone and computer. Keeping tabs on the market. What crops had done well in which parts of the world. That month or week. And how this should influence their supply and price. All of her produce came via three big suppliers. Never directly. Each supplier able to offer her a wide range of produce. From huge volumes of mainstream fruits like pineapples, to dozens of boxes of obscure fruits like Sapodillas. People in the trade expected papaya to go mainstream. Soon. Alongside mangoes. Following Kiwi Fruits before them. Broken into the market through promotions: low prices

Box 9.10: continued

and high volumes. £1 per fruit too expensive for the consumer. A psychological barrier. But 99p was good value. She said.

There was a weekly rhythm to Mina's work. Early in the week, she got a 'feel' for the market. What's out there. What's coming 'on line' from where, when. At what price and quality. To keep everything on the shelves year round. Regardless of season. And how had sales gone, line by line, during previous week? What were the figures from checkout scanning? Each fruit was bar-coded, or had an ID photo at the till. To accurately register sales. She placed her orders every Tuesday. Set her prices that day. What she was going to pay her suppliers. What she was going to charge her consumer. To achieve a 37–38% profit margin. Which she wouldn't make overall. Because of wastage. Manky or unwanted fruits left on the shelf. Damaged, rotting or past their sell-by dates. Their shelf lives. Perhaps only three days long. One of her rivals placed his orders on Thursdays. His company had better computers. So he could buy stock closer to the day it reached the shelf. Keeping his money for a couple more days. New stock started to arrive on the shelves on Sundays. In all supermarkets. They'd be on sale for the same price. For seven days. Changing the following Sunday.

Supermarket shoppers usually pass through the fresh fruit and veg first. Not pet food. Those colours. Shapes. Smells. Textures. Mundane, strange and plain weird. From all around the world. Questions were being asked in the trade press. Was the speciality or exotic produce there to make money? Or was it a statement about supermarkets' global reach and sophistication? Photographs of exotic fruits were used in annual reports and promotional materials. To symbolise something. The decreasing cost and increasing popularity of package holidays to the tropics meant first hand exposure for many British consumers. To fruits in their 'natural' settings. And what about those Indian, Chinese, and other so-called 'ethnic' restaurants in the UK where this took place closer to home for many more people? Mina assumed that these two exposures were responsible for 90% of her sales. Consumers wanting to recreate at home what they had experienced elsewhere. The rest were probably impulse buys. But how did her new product development work? How did she change her offering? Suppliers would offer something new at the right price and volumes. She'd take a sample and try it out with a 'taste panel': made up of her work mates, other buyers, secretaries, cleaners. She'd get a home economist to prepare it fresh, or in a recipe. Then ask what her panel thought about it. Would they actually buy it? For how much? £1? They had kept prickly pears and tamarillos off her shelves. They didn't like them. The seeds in one were annoying. And the other looked great, but tasted like an unripe tomato. To them.

This is obviously a very specific piece of montage writing that was inspired by a very specific film, whose key themes were broken down above into a highly specific checklist. Obviously, however, there are many more ways of writing multi-site, 'follow the thing' ethnographies,[16] and of writing ethnographies inspired by techniques of cinematic montage. The way that we hope this subsection has been more widely useful is to show how the creation of a checklist can be a useful guide for unfamiliar (montage) writing, especially if you have been inspired by something that is not academic writing. To take things further, this also means that you should consider a) including research-relevant ethnographies *and* novels, films, art exhibitions, etc. as part of your 'proper' reading throughout your project, and b) if you decide that there's one or more that you want to write like, do a detailed academic analysis of how you (other writers, and the author/director/artist if you're lucky) believe it works. This could be included as a thesis chapter that could help direct subsequent supervisory and other feedback towards if and how these principles work in practice, and what adjustments could be made.

The ends of montages

It's important to say, at this point, that this fragmentation/montage approach is not suited for every topic, nor easy to adopt successfully. Done badly, it can seem like an excuse for unsorted lists of empirical vignettes. Benjamin's friend, the critical theorist Theodor Adorno, accused his style of standing at the crossroads of positivism and mysticism. And this approach does not absolve the researcher of making hard and careful choices. As Benjamin put it, there is all the difference in the world between the presentation of confusion and a confused presentation. It is then a creative act. Kamberelis, using Denzin and Lincoln (2000: 4), suggests that thinking through these aesthetic categories of 'Montage and pentimento, like jazz which is improvisation, create the sense that images, sounds and understandings are blending together, overlapping, forming a composite, a new creation' (2003: 677). A good montage, however, treads a fine line between being too smooth, linear and easy to navigate and being too bitty, incoherent and distracting to make much sense to its audiences (Beach 2001; Marcus 1994). So adopting this approach is not simply a matter of deciding that your material is 'too complicated' and abandoning your critical faculties. Rather, it can be an effective way for you to make your materials speak in new ways by intervening in how they might conventionally be presented, by looking at their connections with different aesthetic forms or textual styles from documentary or fiction. Thus the sociologist Howard Becker (2001) drew inspiration from the writer George Perec's works documenting urban life as found scenarios – whose mundane juxtapositions showed up the surprising textures of life. Perec in his book *Attempt at a Description of a Place in Paris* [*Tentative d'épuisement d'un lieu parisien*] (1975) addresses this where he outlines species of spaces, through observations of what he intended to be twelve locations to talk of the feel of the city, with multiple moments interlaced without really a strong narrative. We might look at this flow from ethnography to fiction, in the way Amitav Ghosh turned his PhD into a novel – and was thus able to place an autobiographical persona at the centre of the account and undercut the authoritative persona developed in his thesis by making a 'braided narrative' alternating the story of fieldwork and a mediaeval history – bringing in mediaeval slave trades to set the 'village' in long-standing transnational networks (Srivastava 2001). In so doing, he worked to produce parallel histories where his fictional slave characters challenged the way they tended to be written out, literally silent, in Western histories (Mondal 2003: 22–23). However, again this is no 'magic bullet' or solution. It may not work. Perec abandoned one attempt to catalogue urban memory as just too vast to contain, and Benjamin never finished his arcades project. If your 'architecture' does not carry you through, then just creating a collage is unlikely to succeed.

FINISHING: CONCERNS AND CRITERIA?

This has been quite a mammoth chapter. We have argued throughout this book that we co-constitute the field with our informants. So we have tried to suggest and show ways of representing those entanglements through three sorts of styles of writing. Narayan (1993: 672) for instance calls for the 'enactment of hybridity' that shows the researcher as at least belonging to both the world of scholarship and everyday life, and there are other styles used by other people – Kamberelis (2003: 676) invokes the Amerindian character of the 'Trickster' to suggest that given the kind of methodological syncretism we have advocated and the fact that 'research activity is always implicated in and partially constitutes the people and events researched' then what we should be aiming for is 'the production of open, nonrepresentational texts', i.e. texts that perform their own knowledge and show their own production. So we do not want this to seem like an attempt to close down options, but to show how choices are grounded.

We want to finish it, however, with two concerns, and a discussion of the criteria by which we might hope our research/writing would be judged. Our first major concern is that we probably haven't given enough attention to the process, i.e. the pains and pressures of writing.

Much ethnographic research is about leaving the people and places we know, getting to know others elsewhere, risking and altering our sense of self in the process, and then returning to what used to be familiar circumstances to do the bulk of our writing. All of these moves and changes, Vincent Crapanzano (1977: 70–71) argues:

> may be very disturbing to the individual. He [sic.] may be flooded with vague anxieties, specific, even paranoid fears, resentments, feelings of stubbornness, of anger, of cruelty even, of inadequacy, impotence, worthlessness, and of depersonalization and loss of identity...At home he must be his old self again, must adopt the standpoint of those significant within his own socio-historical horizon. He requires reaffirmation – reconstitution – and this he tries to accomplish in many ways, including, most notably, the writing of ethnography, which will also 'free' him to be a professional again (see also Bennett and Shurmer-Smith 2001: 260).

Reestablishing and validating your research through writing is very stressful. This might be because, for example:

- our readers (particularly supervisors and imagined examiners) can scare us (if they think our work is crap, we're screwed!),
- we might be 'encouraged' or feel compelled to write in ways that we're not comfortable with or confident about,[17]
- we might choose to write defensively and maybe hide behind certain kinds of writing (i.e. writing things that are a lot like a lot of other accounts can be a relatively safe option),
- these and other pressures might paralyse us for weeks or months (sitting around the place totally stressed out, drinking lots of coffee, pacing around, doing bits of dusting, realising that our total achievement for the day has been to write one hundred words and delete two hundred) and/or
- we might try to avoid these pressures by following that 'good advice' to keep writing and getting feedback on working papers from the various parts of our research, only later to get conflicting advice that they need total rewriting because they don't fit together as a whole.

Most of these symptoms of 'writing hell' may be caused, at least in part, by too close an adherence to that sequential read-do-write model of academic research. Here, 'writing up' is something that's done at the end, when we start to think what our research might look like as a whole 'submitable' thing. But what if our undergraduate dissertation supervisors had recommended that we read a variety of good undergraduate dissertations *at the start of our projects*, to get us to think about what ours could look like in the end? What if our Masters or PhD thesis supervisors did the same? And/or what if, having done enough preliminary mixed-up reading, doing and writing to have a good idea what our projects' focus will be and how it might progress, we and our supervisors met to discuss how we were going to write that thesis? We're not just talking here about the chapter outlines that students are often asked to come up with, but the writing styles and genres that we have been getting into as part of our 'reading', and thinking about in relation to your study. Like any aspect of anyone's research at this stage, this may change. But sometimes an early choice – for example to write a thesis on plant hunting a bit like a 'how to' gardening book[18] – might just stick, and help us to decide what research training courses we need to sign up for in order to get the material we will need for the sort of finished product we want. Even if we don't attain such clarity of thought so early on, it surely makes sense to read about writing and to look for inspiration for writing in our subject area (in novels, plays, films, wherever) right from the start of our projects.

Our second concern is whether this chapter has achieved the right balance between offering advice suitable for readers undertaking all kinds of projects, and illustrating how things can work in practice through drawing upon three highly specific postgraduate theses that we have researched and written. We don't want to suggest that this is a reflection on what all ethnographers are, or should be, doing. In fact for many of us, we will not do just 'one thing' at all. Many pages of our theses read as conventional academic argument, with citations, cautionary epithets ('tend to', 'are likely', etc.). There can be good reasons for those too. In this chapter, we're concerned that this might give the impression that we think that code-writing is kind of boring and standard (yawn), and autoethnography and montage writing are exciting and 'cutting edge' (whoopee!). We have, after all, presented a 'writing styles' section here in which three out of the four (sub)sections explain and illustrate the latter, more 'experimental' forms of writing. What we hope is that these examples show how the stories our three very different projects involved writing choices that made sense under their different circumstances. There were always quite grounded reasons for the choices we made throughout our projects, as there no doubt will be in yours. You won't be doing your research in the same circumstances as we did ours, so you won't end up making the same kinds of choices and mistakes. You'll make plenty of your own, and that's normal. What we have been trying to provide throughout this book, however, is a feel for how things *can and do* come together in a research project, *often unexpectedly*. Doing research is a matter of not only following instructions and making logical choices, but also of casting nets quite widely, following hunches, looking for inspiration, being lucky now and again, seizing opportunities, thinking laterally, trying things out, and trusting that all will probably work out in the end if you know roughly what to expect about your research process at the start. The exploration of ideas, connections and possibilities is not just confined to the fieldwork.

So, finally, if this all seems a bit too loose a conclusion for your liking, let's get to those specific writing and assessment criteria we promised at the start. To an extent, we have already provided guidelines for 'good' writing in some of the previous (sub)sections. But given our need to provide advice not only on the kinds of writing that we have done, but also on the kinds that you might do, we need to provide some more general criteria. In very basic terms, ethnographic writing is supposed to be not only 'scientific', 'academic', 'true to the world', 'rigorous', 'full of 'facts' and 'concrete details', but also 'literary', 'evocative', 'engaging', 'imaginative', 'accessible' and full of 'flesh and blood emotions' and 'feelings' (Bochner 2000: 267; Richardson 2000b: 253; Wogan 2004: 138). Writing that more or less touches all of these bases should be properly ethnographic in that it 'capture[s] a segment of time in the lives of those we are observing and describes it in a way that allows others to understand what is happening' (Berger 2001: 507; Wogan 2004). As Peter Wogan (2004: 138) argues, producing such a list may only be 'mak[ing] explicit the criteria that have been used all along in judging ethnographies...' But lists of one-word and short-phrase-criteria still seem a bit vague, and reviewers of ethnographic manuscripts have been reluctant to go in more detail (partly because of concerns that this might standardise writing and hamper innovation: Bochner 2000). However, given the increasing amount of experimental writing – which many consider as going beyond the bounds of proper ethnography – more detailed criteria have been flushed out.[19] Perhaps most direct, here, is Laurel Richardson's (2000b: 254) list of five reviewing criteria that she uses to hold 'all ethnography to high and difficult standards':

1. *Substantive contribution:* Does this piece contribute to our understanding of social-life? Does the writer demonstrate a deeply grounded (if embedded) human-world understanding and perspective?
2. *Aesthetic merit:* Does this piece succeed aesthetically? Does the use of creative analytical practices open up the text, invite interpretive responses?
3. *Reflexivity:* How did the author come to write this text? How was the information gathered? Ethical issues? How has the author's subjectivity been both a producer and a product of this text? Is there adequate self-awareness and self-exposure for the reader to make judgements about the point of view? Do authors hold themselves accountable to the standards of knowing and telling of the people they have studied?
4. *Impact:* Does this affect me? Emotionally? Intellectually? Generate new questions? Move me to write? Move me to try new research practices? Move me to action?

5. *Express a reality*: Does this text embody a fleshed out, embodied sense of lived-experience? Does it seem 'true' – a credible account of a cultural, social, individual or communal sense of the 'real'?

What's useful about such detailed lists is that, if they are known to be held in common by writers and assessors, then they can give the former a much clearer impression of their audience's expectations. But, how many of us are likely to have our theses examined or papers reviewed by Laurel Richardson? What detailed criteria – however explicit or implicit – are other assessors using?[20] How similar and/or different might they be? Supposing our supervisors and assessors don't do this kind of work themselves? What kind of criteria will they be using? How open-minded are they? If assessors' criteria could be so very different, what's the use in talking about criteria at all? Here, there's a simple answer: set your own criteria early on in terms of the 'aims' of your research: e.g. 'to use [this form of writing] to achieve [these sorts of effects]'. Then invite your reader to judge what follows accordingly (see Griffiths 2004).

10 Go Forth and Do...?

'my thoughts were soon crippled if I forced them on in any single direction against their natural inclination. And this was of course, connected with the very nature of the investigation. For this compels one to travel over a wide field of thought criss-cross in every direction. The philosophical remarks in this book are, as it were, a number of sketches of landscapes which were made in the course of these long and involved journeyings' (Wittgenstein, Philosophical Investigations (page ix in Bolter 1991: 115)).

We hope that this book will encourage students to do a variety of ethnographies. As a first-time ethnographer or otherwise, we hope that it will give you enough of a start so that you can get an idea of the sorts of issues which you are likely to encounter. We do not expect it to have exhausted all or any of these, but do hope that it will both answer some of the questions which often concern first-timers and provide access to materials that may enable the study of further issues in more depth. As such, this book is very much an overview or a port of first call. We have attempted to write about how ethnographies can actually work out as contingent constructions, rather than to succumb to a temptation to make the contingencies of doing ethnographic work appear as theoretical advances anticipated from the start. Taking this latter approach here would have been, we suggest, a misguided attempt to emulate the appearances of a 'scientific' model which has either never existed (Knorr-Cetina 1981b) or at least represents an unhelpful mystification of the social processes involved in doing all research (Lowe 1992; Strauss 1987).

Instead of 'pure' knowledge carved out back in the academy we have tried to suggest a deeply entangled set of relationships between field and academy, between our wish to know about issues driven by our understandings of other academics, which lead to our wish to know about respondents' understandings of the world, which produce our interpretations of their interpretations of our requests. Current philosophy of science uses geographical metaphors to grapple with this epistemology that 'envisions localized elements of knowledge through a language of paths, routes movements and planes and maps' and a 'spatial language of writing the world' (Harari and Bell 1982: xxi). Michel Serres suggests research requires a spatial sensitivity, that sees '[t]he space of knowledge, indeed space itself, [is] not...homogeneous or rigidly bound together' and that 'the real is not cut up into regular patterns, it is sporadic, spaces and ties with straits and passes' (1982: xii) leaving more fluctuating and shifting patterns than nice neat divisions of field and academy. The knowledge produced might be seen then as 'islands sown in archipelagos on the noisy, poorly-understood disorder of the sea' where our work can form only 'sporadic rationalities'. The archetypal figure for this process of making and transmitting knowledge is not the inventor Prometheus, but Hermes, the guide, who keeps moving and connects, disconnects and reconnects the endless variety of spaces that he traverses. The thinker is not a solitary recluse but a weaver of spaces (1982: xxxiii). This ethnographic spatial imaginary then acknowledges the complex links binding the local and global, near and far, present and absent in 'a topological way of thinking and philosophy of mixed bodies' (Polizzi 2000: 253). That is a way of thinking that bends spaces to see what we often think of separate as connected or sharing outlines and places, while also differentiating what might appear to be similar. We have tried to show this sense of entangled moments from preparing to doing to making sense offers a way of thinking through doing ethnographies – a way that acknowledges complexity rather than hiding it, that utilises partiality rather than being threatened by it, that mixes creativity with rigour and serendipity with preparation.

Some readers may be discouraged by how we have outlined the possible pitfalls, the fragility of our interpretations and the wide range of complex issues which inevitably become part of doing an ethnography. It may appear to some that ethnographies are impossible to 'get right'. This may be true, and neither of us feels that we have ever fully succeeded in doing our own 'properly'. However, it is far more satisfying to feel that you have addressed these issues rather than tried to avoid them under some quantitative epistemology. Ethnographies may lack the apparently 'concrete' results of other methods (with hypotheses proven or not), but an honest and serious engagement with the world is not a failure because it admits that things are messier than that and tries to think through the various complexities and entanglements involved rather than to deny them. We would encourage any such effort.

ABOUT THE AUTHORS

Ian's PhD studentship at the University of Bristol ran out in 1993 and, just in time, fortune favoured him with a Lectureship in Human Geography at the University of Wales, Lampeter. In 1999, he moved to the School of Geography at the University of Birmingham, where he is now a Senior Lecturer in Human Geography. For a number of years, he ran an *Advanced Qualitative Research* module on Birmingham's MA Social Research and MSc Research in Human Geography, and he still runs a final year undergraduate module on the *Geographies of Material Culture*. Post-PhD, he has researched and written about food geographies within and between the Caribbean and the UK (with Phil Crang, Mark Thorpe, Michelle Harrison and Shelley Sacks), about cyborg- and other 'border pedagogies' (with Tim Angus, James Evans, Helen Griffiths et al.) and about process-oriented approaches to research and teaching as 'Ian Cook et al.' He co-edited *Cultural Turns / Geographical Turns: Perspectives on Cultural Geography* (with David Crouch, Simon Naylor and James Ryan for Pearson, 2000), co-wrote *Practising Human Geographies* (with Paul Cloke, Phil Crang, Mark Goodwin, Joe Painter and Chris Philo for Sage, 2004), is the Cultural Geography subeditor of *Geography Compass* (Oxford: Blackwell) and currently serves on the editorial boards of *Qualitative Research* (London: Sage) and *Acme: an Online Journal of Critical Geographies* (www.acme-journal.org).

Mike left Bristol in 1994 to start a Lectureship in Human Geography at the University of Durham, where, showing a spectacular lack of imagination, he has stayed ever since and where he is now a Reader in Geography. While there, he has taught undergraduate modules on IT skills, qualitative research methods, thought and practice in geography, identity politics, gender and geography, consumption and production, cultural and historical geography, representing cities and a range of Masters classes on European cities, methods and research design, and philosophy in geography. Post-PhD, he has done more field research in the UK, Greece, Singapore and Sweden, and continues to write about qualitative methods, heritage, memory, identity and tourism but has added new work on electronic media. He has contributed analysis chapters to some recent collections on qualitative research in geography; edited *Virtual Geographies* (with Phil Crang and Jon May for Routledge, 1999), *Thinking Space* (with Nigel Thrift for Routledge, 2000) and *Tourism: Between Place and Performance* (with Simon Coleman, for Berghahn, 2002). He also edits *Time and Society* (London: Sage), *Tourist Studies* (London: Sage) and serves on the editorial boards of *Environment and Planning A* and the international journal of *Social and Cultural Geography*; and is currently writing a second edition of his *Cultural Geographies* textbook (for Routledge).

Notes

Chapter 1

1 In this quotation, words in bold type are those that the person stressed in her speech. The sequences of three dots indicate where speech has been edited out and, here, most often indicates Ian's interjections such as 'yeah', 'right' and so on.

Chapter 2

1 The concept of power/knowledge will be used throughout this book to stress that power is inescapably bound up with the production of knowledge and, therefore, that the production of ethnographic knowledge is an inherently political act (see in particular chapter 9). For the genealogy of this concept, see Foucault (1977, 1980).

Chapter 3

1 George Marcus (1998), for example, argued that too many exemplars of such multi-sited ethnography are limited by the narrow linguistic capabilities of researchers. At the time he was writing, most such studies, like Ian's, had only made connections between English-speaking people across the world. Thus, he argued, multi-lingual researchers were therefore required to take multi-sited work off in new directions.

2 In Jamaica, for example, the official language is Standard English, which is spoken as a first language by perhaps only 1% of the population (Turriff 2002). There has been a longstanding campaign to make the language that the majority do speak – Jamaican English (or Jamaican) – the official language instead (Bryan 2004). This campaign has involved considerable amounts of linguistic research whose aim has been to turn an oral into a written language, with its own rules of grammar, dictionaries and so on (see Cassidy 1961). When Ian interviewed the workers on the papaya farm, they spoke in a language that he found difficult to understand. As a result, he felt that he could not translate the recordings of these conversations into Standard English and so, instead, employed a linguist to transcribe these interviews into this not (yet) official Jamaican language. Armed with a copy of the *Dictionary of Jamaican English* (Cassidy and Le Page 1982), he was not only better able to understand what these conversations had been about, but was also able to include interview quotations in his thesis and subsequent publications. These quotations showed conversations between people speaking in/between different 'Englishes'.

3 See McDowell (1992b) and Schoenberger (1991, 1992) for a different angle on this.

4 On the papaya farm where he worked, Ian was similarly described by management as a 'Spy for Tesco's', one of the UK retailers they supplied.

5 There are many more extensive 'codes of conduct' that you may choose to adopt or that you may have to abide by depending on national, disciplinary and/or institutional contexts. Each will be inspired by different traditions and goals and will be anticipating different research processes. For example, the codes set out by the Social Research Association (www.the-sra.org/Ethicals. htm) and the Association of Social Anthropologists (www.theasa.org/ethics. htm) are about attitudes and the bigger picture of what research might achieve; the British Sociological Association (www.britsoc.org.uk/about/ethic. htm) provides 61 points of advice on researcher practices; the EU's RESPECT code for social research in the Information Society (www.respectproject.org) addresses issues that may be mediated or involve technical monitoring; the Norwegian *Guidelines for Research Ethics in the Social Sciences, Law and the Humanities* 2001 (www.etikkom.no/Engelsk/NESH/Publications/ NESHguide) pay special attention to societal benefit and the need to pass results back to participants and the Tri-Council Statement on Ethics for Research by Canadian Research Councils 2003 (www.pre.ethics.gc.ca/english/ policystatement/policystatement. cfm) is a more general multidisciplinary code of ethics.

6 Given that Ian's first publications from his PhD did not name or describe this fruit (e.g. Cook 1994, 1995), readers used their imaginations, usually assuming that he was talking about bananas.

Chapter 4

1 This was an opportunity that didn't work out. The buyer who promised to arrange this *after* Ian returned from his Jamaican fieldwork was made redundant while Ian was away. He got this news from Jim, the papaya farm's manager.

2 For other accounts of this kind, see Howard (1994), Mullings (1999) and Skelton (2001).

3 See chapter 3, footnote 5.

4 See Howard (1994) and Robson (1994) for examples of photography making a difference.

Chapter 5

1 However, once underway it is quite possible for a meeting to go on for two or three hours. If this is a good interview, check with your interviewee that it's OK to continue, don't call time yourself, let them do it and always make sure you have the recording equipment to carry on (e.g. extra tapes and batteries).

2 In using such examples here we by no means wish to imply that female researchers should only consider interviewing women, or that male researchers should only consider interviewing men.

3 See also Laurier and Philo's in-car ethnographies of mobile office workers (e.g. 2003).

4 This may also be known as an 'interview schedule', 'interview prompt' or 'topic guide'.

5 Although, see Nash (1979) for her *serial* corporate interviewing.

6 Ian now wishes that someone had told him about the Institute for Grocery Distribution information unit in Radlett, Hertfordshire in the UK. This allows students free access to its food trade publication cuttings service where a 'fruit file', for example, can be quickly and easily located, photocopied and taken home for careful perusal. Here, several weeks' worth of research can be done in an afternoon. He could, however, have found out about this in the reference section of his university library where books detailing specialist libraries in the UK and around the world can be found. Readers are therefore advised to try to find such books in their libraries. Whatever topic you have chosen, it is likely that there is a library somewhere that specialises in it. University libraries also subscribe to information services, where official reports can be easily accessed on-line. Many organisations and government agencies also openly publish their reports on-line.

7 This may be enabled by the fact that many executives have, at one time or another, worked for their current competitors.

8 In practice, friendship and other relationships (from the most personal to the most businesslike) may also develop between researchers and researched as they get to know each other well, and these often carry on once the research is officially over.

9 Here, it is important to point out that, although Oakley conducted most of these interviews herself, she was able to employ a research assistant – something which most readers of this booklet will no doubt be unable to afford.

10 In both of Ian's projects, in the course of the daily diary discussions these tables were either filled in by the participant and then annotated by him, or he filled them out entirely.

11 They may also be treated as a table of information that can, for example, be used to construct time–space diagrams of people's everyday activities (see Rose 1993; Thrift 1983).

12 Ian has found that diaries lasting longer than a week tended to become increasingly repetitive and chore-like for both parties.

13 All three participants who took part in the formal research were male (see earlier).

14 In the following excerpt, Jim's words are *like this(in italics)*, Ian's are like this (in roman) and those of a woman they met on the way are **like this (in bold)**. Square brackets indicate where names have been changed to preserve anonymity, and curly brackets contain comments typed while transcribing to indicate why there were gaps in the transcript. To explain the uses of two full stops at the end and beginnings of some words, in the second line – *You know . . . Yeah . . . .three and a half* – Ian agreed 'Yeah' while Jim was still talking, but in the sixth line – *I used to work there before.. Yeah . . . and, we sell to* – Jim's sentence tailed off, Ian said "yeah" and Jim then continued. This notation was more or less invented by Ian, but standard notations may also be worth using. See later.

15 Both Mike and Ian, for example, used Sony Professional cassette tape recorders for their PhD interviews that, they understood, were 'industry standard' for radio broadcasting at the time. Throughout this section, we will therefore refer to this equipment, its tapes, microphones and batteries. But, of course, we also need to acknowledge that many researchers are now using minidisk recorders,

memory sticks, iPods, laptops and other digital recorders that have much greater capacities than 45-minutes per side audio-cassette tapes. If you have gone digital, please translate this advice to fit the hardware and software that you plan to use where, for instance, mini-disks may need checking or file or folder sizes may need specifying and a memory card of 64Mb should be able to hold 10 hours of recording. Digital recording is now developing very quickly, and you may want to think whether a memory stick might suffice for one-to-one chats or recording your own notes, or a minidisk player, or even if you have a laptop into which you can record directly through a microphone. When weighing up these options we urge you to think of a couple of issues that follow from these choices. First, think of how you will back up and make copies of the material – laptops are prime targets for being stolen, while water or heat can ruin tapes and minidisks. So think how you will make and store reserve copies of materials. It may be as online files of network space which is a good option and digital recording does enable a much easier and quicker backing up of interview recordings, or it may be physical tapes which offer more security for you. Second, before deciding on which recording mechanism carefully check out what transcription facilities you may have. Even prosaic things such as finding that you have used ordinary cassettes but the transcribers use mini-tapes can derail projects, while if you are using digital media, check what transcription software you can access that will allow you to play back and up/down load audio files, and even if there is voice recognition software (though typically you have to train it to specific voices, so you end up listening to recordings and then repeating them yourself, then trawling for errors after that).

16 This is a conventional transcription where the discussion is presented like the text of a play. Here, the notation – see later – is a combination of that described in footnote one of chapter 1 and footnote 14 of this chapter. In addition, above, square brackets contain clarifications of the meanings of words that changed with JD's tone of voice. So, for example, sometimes when he said what could be transcribed as "Uh huh", it meant "no". This notation is therefore essential if the transcript is to show what was said.

17 Transcriber is designed for long speech recordings (like interviews or off-air recordings) and allows you to break them up and label sections, and even to analyse intonation and level via graphical displays. It can be downloaded at www.etca.fr/CTA/gip/Projets/Transcriber/

Chapter 6

1 In this excerpt, speakers are denoted before the colon and curly brackets contain words that could be heard during transcription but which could not be easily attributed to an individual. This whole interchange lasted 20 seconds.

2 Here, italics indicate words that were stressed by the interviewee.

Chapter 7

1 This includes freeware such as Anvil (Annotation of Video and Spoken Language) that allows you to manipulate video, annotate frames and so forth just as you might annotate transcripts (Loehr and Harper 2003) See the next chapter for more on this process.

2 To convert video tape to digital material for editing video capture boards for the computer costs less than a £100. Do though be aware that say a fifteen-minute video, uncompressed, could quite happily use more than 6 gigabytes of memory. You can use compression filters called 'codecs' (compression-decompression) that can reduce this by a factor of nine while maintaining fair quality.

Chapter 8

1 It's also worth noting here that systematic research may itself get disrupted and prove impossible. This was the case with Ian's papaya farm interview series, for example, where the interviews were completed but only a minority were transcribed in Jamaican because the devaluation of £ Sterling in September 1992 made the cost of doing this in J$ unaffordable, overnight. So, he ended up developing a more process-oriented analysis/writing used for his PhD thesis (see chapter 9).
2 Microsoft Word, for example, will do this for you if you click through the following: Format -> Document -> Layout -> Line numbers -> Add Line Numbering.

Chapter 9

1 Rose's specific moment of indeterminacy, however, may illustrate the differences between the depth of interpersonal understanding that can develop through one-off versus serial interviews (where questions arising from one interview can be raised in the next).
2 See also Leigh Berger's (2001) account of the experiences and interests that led her to research the Dalet Shalom Messianic Congregation, 'where congregants believe that cultural and ethnic ties to Judaism can be retained while recognising that Jesus (to whom they refer in Hebrew as *Yeshua*) is the Messiah' (508); and Rachel Saltmarsh's (2001) account of how her experience of higher education led her to write about, and research, her working class origins in a former pit village in the North of England. For a wider justification for relating the personal and the profession in these ways, see Agger (2002).
3 Other authors have argued that it's not just a research topic that can be so closely related to personal experiences. Academic theories are often taken on board by researchers not only because they 'make sense' intellectually, but also because they 'feel right' in the context of their wider life: as Joseph Bristow has put it for instance, 'humanist traditions within Marxism, . . . find their ground, not in theories of political economy, but in a feeling of injustice (capitalism is wrong because we *feel* it is wrong and, equally, *rationalise* it as wrong)' (1991: 117–18).
4 This may be possible through, for example, putting detailed academic and/or methodological discussions in footnotes or endnotes that don't need to be read (e.g. Mitchell 2002 which Barnes (2004: 315) describes as 'Written for academics, [but]. . .not necessarily an academic book': Wogan 2004; Payne 2005), and/or including encounters with key readings as part of your autoethnographic narrative (as in Box 9.5) and/or through staging the research journey as a rolling conversation between fictionalised, and more and less,

academic actors (e.g. Latour 1996, see Laurier and Philo 1999; Miller 1997) and/or directing inquisitive readers to a longer version available on a website (Agger 2002: 451).

5 Here, just as it is necessary with research participants, you may have to take great care about what you choose to reveal about yourself. As Behar (1996: 13) says, revelation is a double risk since 'a boring self-revelation, one that fails to move the reader, is more than embarrassing, it is humiliating'. As a researcher you too need to think what you should keep private and how much is none of our readers' business (Bennett and Shurmer Smith 2001; Payne 2005).

6 Whatever you decide to do, it's important to avoid authority claims that 'nurture our own individuality and at the same time lay claim to "knowing" something' (Richardson 2000a: 925), claiming some extra-specialness of intellect, introspection or suffering. Open narratives are less 'me-me-me-me-me-me-me' and more 'it-me-them-you-here-me-that-you-there-her-us-then-so-...' (Cook 2001: 120).

7 Ian, for example, has supervised a number of undergraduate dissertations where best laid plans have unravelled but a great deal has been learned in the process. Thus, instead of handing in what might be called methodology-oriented dissertations (where things turned out more or less as planned), he advised them to hand in autoethnographic, process-oriented dissertations (where readers are invited to join students on their journey of discovery).

8 Most accounts of the techniques and politics of montage mention their influential use by Russian filmmakers such as Sergei Eisenstein from this time onwards (e.g. Marcus 1994).

9 This is why Ian sometimes writes as 'Ian Cook et al.': see his/their (1998, 2004a, 2004b and 2005) papers.

10 The precise number depended on which bits might eventually make it into the thesis.

11 These books of old pictures often included 'now' and 'then' juxtapositions to illustrate change. So, to respond to what appeared to be one way his participants were representing the world, Mike felt he had to adopt a similar strategy (drawing on Benjamin's writing to do so).

12 This is the kind of montage writing that George Marcus (1994) praised in David Lodge's (1985) academic novel *Small World*.

13 In his 1995 review of the literature on multi-locale ethnographies, George Marcus stated that at that time there were 'no ethnographies in the genre traditionally associated with studies of contemporary capitalist political economy that literally take a thing-oriented approach' (107).

14 Ian would like to thank the co-author of that paper – Phil Crang – for permission to steal and adapt bits of their argument here.

15 Something like his autoethnography chapter (in Box 9.5) could also have been in that PhD.

16 See, for example, Nancy Scheper-Hughes' (2004) excellent and very different paper about her research on the international (and often illegal) trade in fresh human kidneys for transplant operations. This multi-locale, thing-following research is presented as one long, rolling narrative with all kinds of twists and turns, leaps from place to place, sharp illustrations, reflections on positionality and research ethics, juxtapositions and so on woven into it.

17 This, of course, may well include being encouraged to write through autoethnography and/or montage.

18 This example is taken from a discussion about writing and chapter structures with Emily Quinton, a PhD student whom Ian is currently co-supervising (see www.emilyquinton.com for details of the project).

19 See, for example, the 'Special Focus' section of *Qualitative inquiry* on 'Assessing alternative modes of qualitative and ethnographic research: How do we judge? Who judges?' (2000, Volume 6, Number 2, 251–91).

20 Compare, for example, Richardson's (2000b) list with Bochner's (2000: 270–71).

References

Abu-Lughod, L. (1990) Can there be a Feminist Ethnography? *Women & Performance: a Journal of Feminist Theory* 5(1): 7–27.

Agar, M. (1980) *The Professional Stranger: An Informal Introduction to Ethnography*. New York: Academic Press.

Agar, M. (1986) *Speaking of Ethnography*. London/Newbury Park/Delhi: Sage.

Agger, B. (2002) Sociological Writing in the Wake of Postmodernism. *Cultural Studies <=> Critical Methodologies* 2(4): 427–59.

Ahmet, A. (2003) Gender and Bodily Performance in the Department Store, in A. Blunt, P. Gruffud, J. May, M. Ogborn and D. Pinder (eds) *Cultural Geography in Practice*. London: Arnold, pp. 251–54.

Aitken, S. and Wingate, J. (1993) A Preliminary Study of Self-Directed Photography of Middle-Class, Homeless and Mobility Impaired Children. *Professional Geographer* 45(1): 65–72.

Alleyne, M. (1988) *Roots of Jamaican Culture*. London: Pluto Press.

Anderson, J. (2004) Talking Whilst Walking: A Geographical Archaeology of Knowledge. *Area* 36(3): 254–61.

Asch, A. and Sacks, L.H. (1983) Lives Without, Lives Within: Autobiographies of Blind Women & Men. *Journal of Visual Impairment & Blindness* 77(6): 242–47.

Ashcroft, B. Griffiths, G. and Tiffin, H. (1989) *The Empire Writes Back: Theory and Practice in Post-Colonial Literatures*. London: Routledge.

Ashmore, M. (1989) *The Reflexive Thesis: Wrighting Sociology of Scientific Knowledge*. Chicago, IL: University of Chicago Press.

Atkinson, P. (1990) *The Ethnographic Imagination: Textual Constructions of Reality*. London: Routledge.

Aufderheider, P. (1993) Latin American Grassroots Video: Beyond TV. *Public Culture* 5: 579–92.

Axelrod, M. (1979) The Dynamics of the Group Interview, in J. Higginbotham and K. Cox (eds) *Focus Group Interviews*. Chicago, IL: American Marketing Association, pp. 75–80.

Bærenholdt, J.O., Haldrup, M., Larsen, J. and Urry, J. (2004) *Performing Tourist Places*. Andover, MA: Ashgate.

Bailey, C., White, C. and Pain, R. (1999) Evaluating Qualitative Research, Dealing with the Tensions between 'Science' and 'Creativity'. *Area* 31: 169–83.

Ball, M. and Smith, G. (1992) *Analysing Visual Data*. London/Newbury Park/Delhi: Sage.

Banks, M. (2001). *Visual Methods in Social Research*. London: Sage.

Barley, N. (1984) *Adventures in a Mud Hut: an Innocent Anthropologist Abroad*. New York: Vanguard.

Barnes, T. (2004) Review of *Rules of Experts: Egypt, Techno-Politics, Modernity* by Timothy Mitchell. *Environment and Planning D: Society and Space* 22: 315–16.

Baxter, J. and Eyles J. (1997) Evaluating Qualitative Research in Social Geography: Establishing 'Rigour' in Interview Analysis. *Transactions of the Institute of British Geographers* 22: 505–25.

Beach, D. (2001) Artistic Representation and Research Writing. *Reflective Practice* 2(3): 313–29.

Becker, H. (2001) Georges Perec's Experiments in Social Description. *Ethnography* 2(1): 63–76.

Becker, K. (2000) Picturing a Field: Relationships between Visual Culture and Photographic Practice in a Fieldwork Setting, in P. Anttonen (ed.) *Folklore, Heritage Politics and Ethnic Diversity*. Stockholm, Sweden, Botkyrka Multicultural Centre, pp. 100–21.

Becker Ohrn, K. (1975) The Photoflow of Family Life. *Folklore Forum* 13: 27–36.

Bedford, T. and J. Burgess (2001). The Focus-Group Experience, in M. Limb and C. Dwyer (eds) *Qualitative Methodologies for Geographers: Issues and Debates*. London: Arnold, pp. 121–35.

Behar, R. (1996) *The Vulnerable Observer: Anthropology that Breaks your Heart*. Boston, MA: Beacon Press.

Behar, R. and Gordon, D. (eds) (1995) *Women Writing Culture*. Berkeley, CA: University of California Press.

Bellenger, D., Bernhardt, K. and Goldstucker, J. (1979) Qualitative Research Techniques: Focus group Interviews, in J. Higginbotham and K. Cox (eds) *Focus Group Interviews*. Chicago, IL: American Marketing Association, pp. 71–75.

Benjamin, W. (1999) *The Arcades Project*. Cambridge, MA: Harvard University Press.

Bennett, K. (2000) Inter/Viewing and Inter/Subjectivities: Powerful Performances, in A. Hughes, C. Morris and S. Seymour (eds) *Ethnography and Rural Research*. Cheltenham: Countryside and Community Press, pp. 120–35.

Bennett, K. and Shurmer-Smith, P. (2001) Writing Conversation, in M. Limb and C. Dwyer (eds) *Qualitative Methodologies for Geographers*. London: Arnold, pp. 81–93.

Berg, L. and Mansvelt J. (2000) Writing In, Speaking Out: Communicating Qualitative Research Findings, in I. Hay (ed.) *Qualitative Research Methods in Human Geography*. Oxford/Melbourne: Oxford University Press, 161–82.

Berger, L. (2001) Inside Out: Narrative Autoethnography as a Path Toward Rapport. *Qualitative inquiry* 7(4): 504–18.

Berko, L. (1992) Surveiling the Surveiled: Video, Space & Subjectivity. *Quarterly Review of Film and Video* 14(1–2): 61–92.

Bers, T. (1989) The Popularity and Problems of Focus Group Research. *College & University* 64(3): 260–68.

BFI (1985) *The Films of Amos Gitai*. London: British Film Institute.

Blumenthal, D. (1999) Representing the Divided Self. *Qualitative inquiry* 5(3): 377–92.

Blunt, A., Gruffudd, P., May, J., Ogborn, M. and Pinder, D. (eds) (2003) *Practising Cultural Geography*. London: Arnold.

Bochner, A. (2000) Criteria Against Ourselves. *Qualitative Inquiry* 6(2): 266–72.

Bogdan, R. and Taylor, S. (1984) *Introduction to Qualitative Methods: The Search for Meanings*. Chichester: Wiley.

Bolter, J.D. (1991) *Writing Space: The Computer, Hypertext and the History of Writing*. New Jersey: Lawrence Erlbaum.

Bondi, L. (1999) Stages on Journeys: Some Remarks About Human Geography and Psychotherapeutic Practice. *Professional Geographer* 51(1): 11–24.

Bondi, L. and Domosh, M. (1992) Other Figures in Other Places: on Feminism, Postmodernism and Geography. *Environment & Planning D: Society & Space* 10: 199–213.

Borchgrevink, A. (2003) Silencing Language: of Anthropologists and Interpreters. *Ethnography* 4(1): 95–121.

Borland, K. (1991) 'That's Not What I Said': Interpretive Conflict in Oral Narrative Research, in Gluck, S. and Patai, D. (eds) *Women's Words: the Feminist Practice of Oral History*. London: Routledge, pp. 63–75.

Bosk, C. and de Vries, R. (2004) Bureaucracies of Mass Deception: Institutional Review Boards and the Ethics of Ethnographic Research. *Annals of the American Academy of Political and Social Sciences* 595: 249–63.

Bourdieu, P. (1984) *Distinction: A Critique of the Judgement of Taste*. London: Routledge.

Bourdieu, P. (1988) *Homo Academicus*. Cambridge: Polity Press.

Bourdieu, P. (1990a) *In Other Words: Essays Towards a Reflexive Sociology*. Cambridge: Polity Press.

Bourdieu, P. (1990b) *Photography: A Middle-Brow Art*. Cambridge: Polity Press.

Bourdieu, P. (2003) Participant Objectivation. *Journal of the Royal Anthropological Institute* NS 9: 281–94.

Bradshaw, M. (2001) Contracts and Member Checks in Qualitative Research in Human Geography: Reason for Caution? *Area* 33(2): 202–11.

Branthwaite, A. and Lunn, T. (1985) Projective Techniques in Social and Market Research, in Walker, R. (ed.) *Applied Qualitative Research*. Aldershot: Gower, pp. 101–28.

Bringer, J., Johnston, L. and Brackenridge, C. (2004) Maximizing Transparency in a Doctoral Thesis: The Complexities of Writing about the Use of QSR*NVIVO within a Grounded Theory Study. *Qualitative Research* 4(2): 247–65.

Bristow, J. (1991) Life Stories: Carolyn Steedman's History Writing. *New Formations* 13: 113–31.

Brown, B. and Laurier, E. (2004) *Maps and Journeys: an Ethnomethodological Investigation*. www.geog.gla.ac.uk:443/publications/elaurier/olpapers (last accessed 4 January 2005).

Bryan, B. (2004) Jamaican Creole: in the Process of Becoming. *Ethnic and Racial Studies* 27(4): 641–59.

Burgess, J. (1992a) The Art of Interviewing, in Rogers, A., Viles, H. and Goudie, A. (eds) *The Student's Companion to Geography*. Oxford: Blackwell, pp. 207–12.

Burgess, J. (1992b) The Cultural Politics of Nature Conservation and Economic Development, in Anderson, K. and Gale, F. (eds) *Inventing Places: Studies in Cultural Geography*. Melbourne: Wiley, pp. 235–51.

Burgess, J. (1999) The Genesis of in-Depth Discussion Groups: A Response to Liz Bondi. *Professional Geographer* 51(3): 458–60.

Burgess, J. and Gold, J. (eds) (1985) *Geography, the Media and Popular Culture*. London: Croom Helm.

Burgess, J., Limb, M. and Harrison, C. (1988a) Exploring Environmental Values through the Medium of Small Groups: 1 Theory and Practice. *Environment & Planning A* 20: 309–26.

Burgess, J., Limb, M. and Harrison, C. (1988b) Exploring Environmental Values through the Medium of Small Groups: 2. Illustrations of a Group at Work. *Environment & Planning A* 20: 457–76.

Burgess, J., Harrison, C. and Maiteny, P. (1991) Contested Meanings: The Consumption of News about Nature Conservation. *Media, Culture & Society* 13: 499–519.

Burgess, R. (1986) Being a Participant Observer. in J. Eyles (ed.) *Qualitative Approaches in Social and Geographical Research. Occasional Paper 26.* London: Department of Geography and Earth Science, Queen Mary College, University of London, pp. 47–66.

Burgin, V. (ed.) (1987) *Thinking Photography.* London: Macmillan.

Butz, D. (2001) Autobiography, Autoethnography, and Intersubjectivity: Analyzing Communication in Northern Pakistan, in Moss, P. (ed.) *Placing Autobiography in Geography.* Syracuse, NY: Syracuse University Press, pp. 149–66.

Butz, D. and Besio, K. (2004) The Value of Autoethnography for Field Research in Transcultural Settings. *Professional Geographer* 56(3): 350–60.

Callaway, H. (1992) Ethnography and Experience: Gender Implications in Fieldwork and Texts, in J. Okely and H. Callaway (eds) *Anthropology and Autobiography.* London: Routledge, pp. 29–49.

Cameron, J. (2001) Focussing on the Focus Group, in I. Hay (ed.) *Qualitative Research Methods in Human Geography.* Oxford/Melbourne: Oxford University Press, pp. 83–102.

Cassell, J. (ed.) (1987) *Children in the Field.* Philadelphia, PA: Temple University Press.

Cassell, J. (1988) The Relationship of Observer to Observed when Studying Up. *Studies in Qualitative Methodology* 1: 89–108.

Cassidy, F.G. (1961) *Jamaica Talk: Three hundred years of the English language in Jamaica.* London: Macmillan & Co.

Cassidy, F.G. and Le Page, R. (eds) (1982) *Dictionary of Jamaican English* (Second edition). Cambridge: Cambridge University Press.

Chalfen, R. (1987) *Snapshot versions of life.* Bowling Green, OH: Bowling Green State University Popular Press.

Cintron, R. (1993) Wearing a Pith Helmet at a Sly Angle: or, Can Writing Researchers do Ethnography in a Postmodern Era? *Written Communication* 10(3): 371–412.

Clifford, J. (1986) Introduction: Partial Truths, in J. Clifford and G. Marcus (eds) *Writing Culture: the Poetics and Politics of Ethnography.* Berkeley, CA: University of California Press, pp. 1–26.

Clifford, J. (1992) Traveling Cultures, in L. Grossberg, C. Nelson and P. Treichler (eds) *Cultural Studies.* London: Routledge, pp. 96–116.

Clifford, J. (1997) Spatial Practices: Fieldwork, Travel and the Disciplining of Anthropology, in J. Clifford (ed.) *Routes: Travel and Translation in the Late Twentieth Century.* London: Harvard University Press, pp. 52–91.

Clifford, J. and Marcus, G. (eds) (1986) *Writing Culture: the Poetics and Politics of Ethnography.* Berkeley, CA: University of California Press.

Cloke, P., Cook, I., Crang, P., Goodwin, M., Painter, J. and Philo, C. (2004) *Practising Human Geographies.* London: Sage.

Cochrane, A. (1998) Illusions of Power: Interviewing Local Élites. *Environment and Planning A* 30: 2121–32.

Cohen, E., Nir, Y. and Almagor, U. (1992) Stranger–Local Interaction in Photography. *Annals of Tourism Research* 19(2): 213–33.

Collier, M. (2000) Approaches to Analysis in Visual Anthropology, in T. van Leeuwen and C. Jewitt (eds) *Handbook of Visual Analysis.* London: Sage, pp. 35–60.

Collier, J. and Collier, M. (1986) *Visual Anthropology: Photography as a Research Method*. Albuquerque, NM: University of New Mexico Press.

Comaroff, J. and Comaroff, J. (2003) Ethnography on an Awkward Scale: Postcolonial Anthropology and the Violence of Abstraction. *Ethnography* 4(2): 147–80.

Conquergood, D. (1991) Rethinking Ethnography: Towards a Critical Cultural Politics. *Communication Monographs* 58: 179–94.

Cook, I. (1992) *Drowning in See-World? Critical Ethnographies of Blindness*. Unpublished MA thesis, University of Kentucky.

Cook, I. (1993) Constructing the Exotic: The Case of Tropical Fruit. Paper presented at the Institute of British Geographers Annual Conference, Royal Holloway and Bedford New College, Egham, Surrey: 5–8 January.

Cook, I. (1994) New Fruits and Vanity: The Role of Symbolic Production in the Global Food Economy, in A. Bonanno, L. Busch, W. Friedland, L. Gouveia and Mignione, E. (eds) *From Columbus to ConAgra: The Globalization of Agriculture and Food*. Lawrence, KS: University of Kansas Press, pp. 232–48.

Cook, I. (1995) Constructing the Exotic: The Case of Tropical Fruit, in J. Allen and D. Massey (eds) *Geographical worlds*. Oxford: Oxford University Press, pp. 137–42.

Cook, I. (1997a) *A Grumpy Thesis: Geography, Autobiography, Pedagogy*. Unpublished PhD thesis, University of Bristol.

Cook, I. (1997b) Participant Observation, in R. Flowerdew and D. Martin (eds) *Methods in Human Geography: a Guide for Students doing Research Projects*. Harlow: Longman, pp. 127–49.

Cook, I. (2000) 'Nothing can Ever be a Case of Us and Them Again': Exploring the Politics of Difference through Border Pedagogy and Student Journal Writing. *Journal of Geography in Higher Education* 24(1): 13–27.

Cook, I. (2001) 'You Want to be Careful You don't End up like Ian. He's all over the Place': Autobiography in/of an Expanded Field, in Pamela Moss (ed.) *Placing Autobiography in Geography*. Syracuse, NY: Syracuse University Press, pp. 99–120.

Cook, I. and Crang, M. (1995) *Doing Ethnographies*. CATMOG 58. London: Institute of British Geographers.

Cook, I. and Crang, P. (1996) *Commodity Systems, Documentary Filmmaking and New Geographies of Food: Amos Gitai's 'Ananas'*. (www.gees.bham.ac.uk/downloads/gesdraftpapers/iancook-pineapple.htm last accessed 6 June 2006)

Cook et al, I. (1998) *You Want to be Careful You don't End up like Ian. He's all over the Place': Autobiography in/of an Expanded Field (the Director's Cut)*. Falmer: University of Sussex Research Papers in Geography No. 34.

Cook et al, I. (2004a) Follow the Thing: Papaya. *Antipode* 36(4): 642–64.

Cook et al, I. (2004b) Trade, in S. Harrison, S. Pile and N. Thrift (eds) *Patterned Ground: Ecologies of Culture and Nature*, London: Reaktion, pp. 124–26.

Cook et al, I. (2005) Positionality/Situated Knowledge, in D. Atkinson, P. Jackson, D. Sibley and N. Washbourne (eds) *Cultural Geography: a Critical Dictionary of Key Ideas*. London: IB Tauris, pp. 14–24.

Cooper, C. (1993) *Noises in the Blood: Orality, Gender and the 'Vulgar' Body of Jamaican Popular Culture*. Basingstoke: Macmillan.

Crang, M. (1992) Academe Rules! Studying Sideways, Studying Under. *Praxis* 25: 20–23.

Crang, M. (1995) *The Production of Spaces for the Past: a Cultural Geography of the Heritage Industry in England*. Unpublished PhD thesis, University of Bristol.

Crang, M. (1996a) Envisioning Urban Histories: Bristol as Palimpsest, Postcards, and Snapshots. *Environment & Planning A* 28(3): 429–52.

Crang, M. (1996b) Living History: Magic Kingdoms or a Quixotic Quest for Authenticity? *Annals of Tourism Research* 23(2): 415–31.

Crang, M. (1997a) Analyzing Qualitative Materials, in R. Flowerdew and D. Martin (eds) *Methods in Human Geography: A Guide for Students Doing a Research Project*. London: Longman, pp. 183–96.

Crang, M. (1997b) Picturing Practices: Research through the Tourist Gaze. *Progress in Human Geography* 21(3): 359–74.

Crang, M. (2000) Playing Nymphs and Swains in a Pastoral Idyll? in A. Hughes, C. Morris and S. Seymour (eds) *Ethnography & Rural Research*. Cheltenham: Countryside and Community Press, pp. 158–78.

Crang, M. (2001) Filed Work: Making Sense of Group Interviews, in M. Limb and C. Dwyer (eds) *Qualitative Methods for Geographers*. London: Arnold, pp. 215–33.

Crang, M. (2002) Qualitative Methods: The New Orthodoxy? *Progress in Human Geography* 26(5): 647–55.

Crang, M. (2003) Telling Materials, in M. Pryke, G. Rose and S. Whatmore (eds) *Using Social Theory*. London: Sage, pp. 127–44.

Crang, M., Hudson, A., Reimer, S. and Hinchliffe, S. (1997) Software for Qualitative Research: 1 Prospectus and Overview. *Environment and Planning A* 29: 771–87.

Crang, P. (1992) The Politics of Polyphony: Reconfigurations in Geographical Authority. *Environment & Planning D: Society & Space* 10: 527–49.

Crang, P. (1994) It's Showtime: on the Workplace Geographies of Display in a Restaurant in Southeast England. *Environment & Planning D: Society & Space* 12: 675–704.

Crapanzano, V. (1977) On the Writing of Ethnography. *Dialectical Anthropology* 2: 69–73.

Crapanzano, V. (1986) Hermes' Dilemma: The Masking of Subversion in Ethnographic Description, in J. Clifford and G.E. Marcus (eds) *Writing Culture: The Poetics & Politics of Ethnography*. Los Angeles and Berkeley, CA: University of California Press, pp. 51–76.

Crawford, P. and D. Turton (eds) (1992) *Film as Ethnography*. Manchester: Manchester University Press.

Crick, M. (1992) Ali and Me: An Essay in Street Corner Anthropology, in J. Okely and H. Callaway (eds) *Anthropology & Autobiography*. London: Routledge, pp. 175–92.

Csikzsentmihalyi, M. and Rochberg-Halton, E. (1981) *The Meaning of Things: Domestic Symbols and the Self*. Cambridge: Cambridge University Press.

Cupples, J. (2002) The Field as a Landscape of Desire: Sex and Sexuality in Geographical Fieldwork. *Area* 34(4): 382–90.

Cupples, J. and S. Kindon (2003) Far from Being 'Home Alone': The Dynamics of Accompanied Fieldwork. *Singapore Journal of Tropical Geography* 24(2): 211–28.

Curry, M. (1996) *The Work in the World: Geographical Practice and the Written Word*. Minneapolis, MN: Minnesota University Press.

Dann, G. (1996) The People of Tourist Brochures, in T. Selwyn (ed.) *The Tourist Image: Myths and Myth Making in Modern Tourism*. Chichester: Wiley, pp. 61–82.

Dant, T. (1999) *Material Culture in the Social World*. Buckingham: Open University Press.

Davies, G. (2003) Researching the Networks of Natural History Film-making, in A. Blunt, P. Gruffudd, J. May, M. Ogborn and D. Pinder (eds) *Cultural Geography in Practice*. London, Arnold, pp. 202–17.

Delaney, C. (1988) Participant-Observation: The Razor's Edge. *Dialectical Anthropology* 13: 291–300.

Delph-Janiurek, T. (2001) (Un)Consensual Conversations: Betweenness, 'Material Access', Laughter and Reflexivity in Research. *Area* 33(4): 414–21.

Denzin, N. and Lincoln, Y. (eds) (2000) *The Handbook of Qualitative Research* (second edn) London: Sage.

Derrida, J. (1999) Word Processing. *Oxford Literary Review* 21: 3–17.

Desforges, L. (2001) Tourism Consumption and the Imagination of Money. *Transactions, Institute of British Geographers* 26: 353–64.

DeVita, P. (ed.) (1992) *The Naked Anthropologist: Tales from Around the World.* Belmont, CA: Wadsworth.

Dewdney, A. and Lister, M. (1988) *Youth Culture and Photography.* London: Macmillan.

Dodman, D.R. (2003) Shooting in the City: An Autophotographic Exploration of the Urban Environment in Kingston, Jamaica. *Area* 35(3): 293–304.

Doel, M. and Hubbard, P. (2002) Taking World Cities Literally: Marketing the City in a Global Space of Flows. *City* 6(3): 351–68.

Douglas, J. (1976) *Investigative Social Research: Individual and Team Field Research.* London/Newbury Park/Delhi: Sage.

Dowler, L. (2001) Fieldwork in the Trenches: Participant Observation in a Conflict Area, in M. Limb and C. Dwyer (eds) *Qualitative Methodologies for Geographers: Issues and Debates.* London: Arnold, pp. 153–64.

Dowmunt, I. (ed.) (1992) *Channels of Resistance: Global TV and Local Empowerment.* London: Channel 4/British Film Institute.

Duncan, J. (1981) The Problems and Perils of the Superorganic in Cultural Geography. *Annals of the Association of American Geographers* 70: 181–90.

Duneier, M. (2001) *Sidewalk.* New York: Farrar Straus Giroux.

Dunn, K. (2000) Interviewing, in I. Hay (ed.) *Qualitative Research Methods in Human Geography.* Oxford/Melbourne: Oxford University Press, p. 50–82.

Dwyer, K. (1977) On the Dialogic of Field Work. *Dialectical anthropology* 2: 143–51.

Edwards, E. (1992) *Anthropology and Photography, 1860–1920.* New Haven, CT and London: Yale University Press.

Edwards, E. (2001) *Raw Histories: Photographs, Anthropology and Museums.* Oxford: Berg.

Ellis, C. (1999) Heartful Autoethnography. *Qualitative health research* 9(5): 669–83.

Ellis, C. (2000) Creating Criteria: An Ethnographic Short Story. *Qualitative Inquiry* 6(2): 273–77.

Ellis, C. and Bochner, A. (2000) Autoethnography, Personal Narrative, Reflexivity: Researcher as Subject, in N. Denzin and Y. Lincoln (eds) *The Handbook of Qualitative Research* (second edn) London: Sage, pp. 733–68.

Elwood, S. and Martin, D. (2000) 'Placing' Interviews: Location and Scales of Power Inqualitative Research. *Professional Geographer* 52: 649–57.

Emerson, R.M., Fretz, R. and Shaw, L. (1995) *Writing Ethnographic Fieldnotes.* Chicago, IL: University of Chicago Press.

Emmison, M. and Smith, P. (2000) *Researching the Visual: Images, Objects, Contexts and Interactions in Social and Cultural Inquiry.* London: Sage.

England, K. (1994) Getting Personal: Reflexivity, Positionality, and Feminist Research. *Professional Geographer* 46(1): 80–89.

England, K. (2001) Interviewing Elites: Cautionary Tales About Researching Women Managers in Canada's Banking Industry, in P. Moss (ed.) *Feminist Geography in Practice: Research and Methods.* Oxford: Blackwells, pp. 200–13.

Evans-Pritchard, E.E. (1940) *The Nuer: a Description of the Modes of Livelihood and Political Institutions of a Nilotic People*. Oxford: Oxford University Press.

Falconer Al-Hindi, K. and Kawabata, H. (2002) Toward a More Fully Reflexive Feminist Geography, in Moss, P. (ed.) *Feminist Geography in Practice: Research and Methods*. Oxford: Blackwell, pp. 103–15.

Fetterman, D.M. (1989) *Ethnography: Step by Step*. London/Newbury Park/Delhi: Sage.

Fielding, N. and Lee, R. (1991) *Using Computers in Qualitative Research*. London/Newbury Park/Delhi: Sage.

Fielding, N.G. and Lee R.M. (1998) *Computer Analysis and Qualitative Research*. London: Sage.

Fine, E. (1984) *The Folklore Text: From Performance to Print*. Bloomington, IN: Indiana University Press.

Fine, G. (1993) 10 Lies of Ethnography – Moral Dilemmas of Field-Research. *Journal of Contemporary Ethnography* 22(3): 267–94.

Fine, G. (2003) Towards a Peopled Ethnography: Developing Theory from Group Life. *Ethnography* 4(1): 41–60.

Flowerdew, R. and Martin, D. (eds) (1997) *Methods in Human Geography: a Guide for Students doing Research Projects*. Harlow: Longman.

Foucault, M. (1977) *Discipline and Punish*. London: Allen Lane.

Foucault, M. (1980) *Power/Knowledge*. New York: Pantheon.

Fusco, C. (1994) The Other History Of Intercultural Performance. *The Drama Review* 38(1): 143–67.

Fyfe, N. (1992) Observations on Observations. *Journal of Geography in Higher Education* 16(2): 127–33.

Garfinkel, H. (1984) *Studies in Ethnomethodology*. Cambridge: Polity.

Garlick, S. (2002) Revealing the Unseen: Tourism, Art and Photography. *Cultural Studies* 16(2): 289–305.

Gatson, S. and Zweerink, A. (2004) Ethnography Online: 'Natives' Practising and Inscribing Community. *Qualitative research* 4(2): 179–200.

Geertz, C. (1973) *The Interpretation of Cultures*. New York: Basic Books.

Geiger, S. (1986) Women's Life Histories: Method and Content. *Signs: a Journal of Women in Culture & Society* 11(20): 334–51.

Geiger, S. (1990) What's so Feminist about Women's Oral History? *Journal of Women's History* 2(1): 169–82.

Giddens, A. (1984) *The Constitution of Society: Outline of the Theory of Structuration*. Cambridge: Polity.

Giddens, A. (1991) *Modernity & Self-Identity: Self & Society in the Late Modern Age*. Cambridge: Polity.

Gille, Z. (2001) Critical Ethnography in the Time of Globalization: Toward a New Concept of Site. *Cultural Studies <=> Critical Methodologies* 1(3): 319–34.

Gilroy, P. (1987) *There Ain't no Black in the Union Jack: The Cultural Politics of Race and Nation*. London: Hutchinson.

Gilroy, P. (1992) Cultural Studies and Ethnic Absolutism, in L. Grossberg, C. Nelson and P. Treichler (eds) *Cultural Studies*. London: Routledge, pp. 187–98.

Gilroy, P. (1993a) *The Black Atlantic: Modernity and Double Consciousness*. London: Verso.

Gilroy, P. (1993b) *Small Acts: Thoughts on the Politics of Black Cultures*. London: Serpent's Tail.

Ginsburg, F. (1991) Indigenous Media: Faustian Contract or Global Village? *Cultural Anthropology* 6(1): 94–114.

Ginsburg, F. (1993) Aboriginal Media and the Australian Imaginary. *Public Culture* 5: 557-78.

Gluck, S. and Patai, D. (eds) (1991) *Women's Words: The Feminist Practice of Oral History*. London: Routledge.

Goffman, E. (1977) *Gender Advertisements*. New York: Harper & Row.

Gold, L. (2002) Positionality, Worldview and Geographical Research: A Personal Account of a Research Journey. *Ethics, Place and Environment* 5(3): 223-37.

Gómez, R. (2003) Magic Roots: Children Explore Participatory Video. In (ed.) S. White. *Participatory Video: Images That Transform and Empower*. London, Sage: 215-31.

Gordon, D. (1988) Writing Culture, Writing Feminism: The Poetics and Politics of Experimental Ethnography. *Inscriptions* 3(4): 7-24.

Gordon, E. (2003) Trials and Tribulations of Navigating IRBs: Anthropological and Biomedical Perspectives of 'Risk' in Conducting Human Subjects Research. *Anthropological Quarterly* 76(2): 299-320.

Green, J. and Hart, L. (1999) The Impact of Context on Data, in R.S. Barbour and J.Kitzinger (eds) *Developing Focus Group Research: Politics, Theory and Practice*. London: Sage.

Greenbaum, T. (1988) *The Practical Handbook and Guide to Focus Group Research*. Lexington: Lexington Books.

Griffiths, H. (2004) *Funky Geography: Paulo Friere, critical pedagogy and school geography*. Unpublished MSc Thesis. School of Geography, Earth and Environmental Sciences, The University of Birmingham, Birmingham (www.gees.bham.ac.uk/people/phd.asp?offset = 20&ID = 479; last accessed 5 July 2005).

Grimshaw, A. (1992) *Servants of the Buddha: a Winter in the Himalayas*. London: Open Letters Press.

Grimshaw, A. (2001) *The Ethnographer's Eye: Ways of Seeing in Modern Anthropology*. Cambridge: Cambridge University Press.

Guba, E. and Lincoln, Y. (2005) Paradigmatic Controversies, Contradictions and Emerging Confluences, in N. Denzin and Y. Lincoln (eds) *The Sage Handbook of Qualitative Research* (third edn) London: Sage, pp. 191-216.

Gustavson, L. and Cytrynbaum, J. (2003) Illuminating Spaces: Relational Spaces, Complicity and Multisited Ethnography. *Field Methods* 15(3): 252-70.

Hall, C. (1992) *White, Male and Middle Class: Explorations in Feminism and History*. Cambridge: Polity.

Hall, S. (1991) Old and New Identities, Old and New Ethnicities, in King, A.D. (ed.) *Culture, Globalization and the World System*. Basingstoke: Macmillan pp. 41-68.

Hallett, L. (2001) *The Production of Jam in Southern Coastal Maine: A Sense-of-Place Study*. Unpublished MA Thesis: University of Kansas.

Hannerz, U. (2003) Being There . . . And There . . . And There! Reflections on Multi-Site Ethnography. *Ethnography* 4(2): 201-16.

Harari, J. and Bell, D.F. (1982) *Journal À Plusieurs Voies. Hermes: Literature, Science, Philiosophy*. M. Serres. Baltimore, MD: Johns Hopkins University Press, pp. ix-xl.

Haraway, D. (1988) Situated Knowledges: The Science Question in Feminism and the Privilege of Partial Perspective. *Feminist Studies* 14(3): 575-99.

Harper, D. (2002) Talking about Pictures: A Case for Photo Elicitation. *Visual Studies* 17(1): 13-26.

Harper, D. (2003) Framing Photographic Ethnography: A Case Study. *Ethnography* 4(2): 241-66.

Hastrup, K. (1992) Anthropological Visions: Some Notes on Textual and Visual Authority, in P. Crawford and D. Turton (eds) *Film as Ethnography*. Manchester, NH: Manchester University Press, pp. 9–22.

Hay, I. (ed.) (2000) *Qualitative Research Methods in Human Geography*. South Melbourne: Oxford University Press.

Hebdige, D. (1990) Digging for Britain: An Excavation in Seven Parts, in D. Strinati and S. Wagg (eds) *Come on Down? Popular Media Culture in Post-War Britain*. London: Routledge, pp. 325–77.

Hedges, A. (1985) Group Interviewing, in R. Walker (ed.) *Applied Qualitative Research*. Aldershot: Gower, pp. 71–91.

Herbert, S. (2000) For Ethnography. *Progress in Human Geography* 24(4): 550–68.

Herod, A. (1993) Gender Issues in the Use of Interviewing as a Research Method. *Professional Geographer* 45(3): 305–17.

Herod, A. (1999) Reflections on Interviewing Foreign Elites: Praxis, Positionality, Validity and the Cult of the Insider. *Geoforum* 30: 313–27.

Heyman, R. (2000) Research, Pedagogy and Instrumental Geography. *Antipode* 32(3): 292–307.

Highmore, B. (2004) Homework: Routine, Social Aesthetics and the Ambiguity of Everyday Life. *Cultural Studies* 18(2/3): 306–27.

Hinchliffe, S., Hudson, A., Crang, M. and Reimer, S. (1997) Software for Qualitative Research: 2 Some Thoughts on Aiding Analysis. *Environment and Planning A* 29: 1109–24.

Hine, C. (2004) Social Research Methods and the Internet: a Thematic Review. *Sociological research online* 9(2). www.socresonline.org.uk/9/2/hine.html (last accessed 29 March 2005).

Hirsch, J. (1981) *Family Photographs: Content, Meaning and Effect*. Oxford: Oxford University Press.

Hitchings, R. and Jones, V. (2004) Living with Plants and the Exploration of Botanical Encounter within Human Geographic Research Practice. *Ethics, place & environment* 7(1–2): 3–18.

Hochschild, A.R. (1983) *The Managed Heart: Commercialization of Human Feeling*. Berkeley, CA, London: University of California Press.

Hoggart, K., Lees, L. and Davies, A. (2002) *Researching Human Geography*. London: Arnold.

Holbrook, B. and Jackson, P. (1996) Shopping Around: Focus Group Research in North London. *Area* 28(2): 136–42.

Holland, P. (1991) History, Memory and the Family Album, in J. Spence and P. Holland (eds) *Family Snaps: The Meanings of Domestic Photography*. London: Virago, pp. 1–14.

Hollander, J. (2004) The Social Contexts of Focus Groups. *Journal of Contemporary Ethnography* 33(5): 602–37.

Holliday, R. (2000) We've Been Framed: Visualising Methodology. *Sociological Review* 48(4): 503–22.

Howard, S. (1994) Methodological Issues in Overseas Research: Experiences from Nicaragua's Northern Atlantic Coast, in E. Robson and K. Willis (eds) *Postgraduate Fieldwork in Developing Areas: a Rough Guide*. London: Institute for British Geographers, pp. 19–35.

Hughes, A. and Reimer, S. (2005) Guest Editorial: Publishing Commodity Chains. *Geoforum* 36(3): 273–75.

Hughes, A., Morris, C. and Seymour, S. (eds) (2000) *Ethnography and Rural Research*. Cheltenham: Countryside and Community Press.

Hunt, J. (1989) *Psychoanalytic Aspects of Fieldwork*. London/Newbury Park/Delhi: Sage.

Hyams, M. (2004) Hearing Girls' Silences: Thoughts on the Politics and Practices of a Feminist Method of Group Discussion. *Gender, Place & Culture* 11(1): 105–19.

Ingersoll, F. and Ingersoll, J. (1987) Both a Borrower and Lender Be: Ethnography, Oral History and Grounded Theory. *Oral History Review* Spring 15: 81–102.

Jackson, J. (1995) 'Déjà Entendu': The Liminal Qualities of Anthropological Fieldnotes, in J. van Maanen (ed.) *Representation in Ethnography*. London: Sage, pp. 36–78.

Jackson, P. (1983) Principles and Problems of Participant Observation. *Geografiska Annaler, Series B* 64(1): 39–46.

Jackson, P. (1985) Urban Ethnography. *Progress in Human Geography* 9(2): 157–76.

Jackson, P. (1989) *Maps of Meaning*. London: Unwin Hyman.

Jackson, P. (2001) Making Sense of Qualitative Data, in M. Limb and C. Dwyer (eds) *Qualitative Methodologies for Geographers: Issues and Debates*. London: Arnold, pp. 199–214.

Jackson, P. and Smith, S. (1984) *Exploring Social Geography*. Hemel Hempstead: Unwin Hyman.

Jacobs, D. (1981) Domestic Snapshots towards a Grammar of Motives. *Journal of American Culture* 4(1): 93–105.

James, W. (1992) Migration, Racism and Identity: The Caribbean Experience in Britain. *New Left Review* 193: 15–55.

Jeater, D. (1992) Roast Beef and Reggae Music: The Passing of Whiteness. *New Formations* Winter: pp. 107–21.

Johnson, J. (1983) Trust and Personal Involvements in Fieldwork, in Emerson, R. (ed.) *Contemporary Field Research*. Boston, MA: Little Brown, pp. 203–15.

Johnson, M. (1992) A Silent Conspiracy? Some Ethical Issues of Participant Observation in Nursing Research. *International Journal of Nursing Studies* 29(2): 213–23.

Jones, J.P. and Natter, W. (1993) Pets or Meat: Class, Ideology and Space in Roger and Me. *Antipode* 25(2): 140–58.

Jones, S. (1985) The Analysis of Depth Interviews, in Walker, R. (ed.) *Applied Qualitative Research*. Aldershot: Gower, pp. 56–70.

Jones, S. (1988) *Black Culture, White Youth: The Reggae Tradition from JA to UK*. Basingstoke: Macmillan.

Jordan, S.A. (2002) Ethnographic Encounters: The Process of Cultural Translation. *Language and Intercultural Communication* 2(2): 96–110.

Kamberelis, G. (2003) Ingestion, Elimination, Sex, and Song: Trickster as Premodern Avatar of Postmodern Research Practice. *Qualitative Inquiry* 9(5): 673–704.

Katz, C. (1992) All The World is Staged: Intellectuals and The Projects of Ethnography. *Environment and Planning D: Society and Space* 10: 495–510.

Katz, C. (1994) Playing the Field: Questions of Fieldwork in Geography. *Professional Geographer* 46(1): 67–72.

Katz, J. (2001) From How to Why: On Luminous Description and Causal Inference in Ethnography (Part I). *Ethnography* 2(4): 443–73.

Katz, J. (2002) From How to Why: On Luminous Description and Causal Inference in Ethnography (Part 2). *Ethnography* 3(1): 63–90.

Keith, M. (1992) Angry Writing: (Re)Presenting the Unethical World of the Ethnographer. *Environment & Planning D: Society & Space* 10: 551–68.

Kenney, K. (1993) Using Self-portrait Photographs to Understand the Self-Concepts of Chinese and American University Students. *Visual Anthropology* 5(3–4): 245–69.

Kindon, S. (2003) Participatory Video in Geographic Research: A Feminist Practice of Looking? *Area* 35(2): 142–53.

Kittler, F. (1999) *Gramophone, Film, Typewriter*. Stanford, CA: Stanford University Press.

Kneafsey, M. (2000) Changing Roles and Constructing Identities: Ethnography in the Celtic Periphery, in A. Hughes, C. Morris and S. Seymour (eds) *Ethnography and Rural Research*. Cheltenham: Countryside and Community Press, pp. 52–65.

Knorr-Cetina, K. (1981a) Introduction, in K. Knorr-Cetina and A. Cicourel (eds) *Advances in Social Theory and Methodology: Towards an Integration of Macro-Sociology and Micro-Sociology*. Andover: Routledge and Kegan Paul, pp. 1–45.

Knorr-Cetina, K. (1981b) *The Manufacture of Knowledge: An Essay on the Constructivist and Contextual Nature of Science*. Oxford: Pergamon.

Kobayashi, A. (1994) Coloring the Field: Gender, 'Race' and the Politics of Fieldwork. *Professional Geographer* 46(1): 73–80.

Kong, L. (1998) Refocusing on Qualitative Methods: Problems and Prospects for Research in a Specific Asian Context. *Area* 30(1): 79–82.

Krueger, R. (1988) *Focus Groups: A Practical Guide for Applied Research*. London/Newbury Park/Delhi: Sage.

Krueger, R. and Casey, M. (2000) *Focus Groups: A Practical Guide for Applied Research*. Thousand Oaks, CA: Sage.

Kusenbach, M. (2003) Street Phenomenology: The Go-Along as Ethnographic Research Tool. *Ethnography* 4(3): 455–85.

Lacan, J. (1977) *Ecrits: Selected Writings*. London: Routledge.

La Pelle, M. (2004) Simplifying Qualitative Data Analysis Using General Purpose Software Tools. *Field Methods* 16(1): 85–108.

Latour, B. (1996) *Aramis, or the Love of Technology*. Cambridge: Harvard University Press.

Laurier, E. and Philo, C. (1999) X-morphising: Review Essay of Bruno Latour's *Aramis, or the Love of Technology*. *Environment & planning A*, 31: 1047–71.

Laurier, E. and Philo, C. (2003) The Region in the Boot: Lone Subjects and Multiple Objects. *Environment and Planning D: Society and Space* 21: 85–106.

Law, J. and Urry, J. (2004) Enacting the Social. *Economy & society* 33(3): 390–410.

Lawson, V. (2000) Arguments Within Geographies of Movement: The Theoretical Potential of Migrants' Stories. *Progress in Human Geography* 24(2): 173–89.

Lesy, M. (1980) *Time Frames: The Meaning of Family Pictures*. New York: Pantheon.

Lewins, A. and Silver, C. (2005) *Choosing a CAQDAS Package* (third edn) http://caqdas.soc.surrey.ac.uk/ChoosingLewins&SilverV3Nov05.pdf (last accessed December 2005).

Ley, D. (1974) *The Black Inner City as Frontier Outpost: Images and Behaviour of a Philadelphia Neighbourhood*. Washington, DC: Association of American Geographers.

Ley, D. (1988) Interpretive Social Research in the Inner City, in J. Eyles (ed.) *Research in Human Geography: Introductions and Investigations*. Oxford: Blackwell, pp. 121–38.

Ley, D. (1992) Qualitative Methods: Reshaping a Tradition. *Journal of Geography in Higher Education* 16(2): 167–70.

Lie, S. (1988) Pour une lecture féminine? in S. Sellers (ed.) *Writing Differences: Readings from the Seminar of Hélène Cixous*. Milton Keynes: Open University Press, pp. 196–203.

Lieber, E., Weisner, T. and Presley, M. (2003) Ethnonotes: An Internet-Based Field Note Management Tool. *Field Methods* 15(4): 405–25.

Limb, M. and Dwyer, C. (2001) Introduction: Doing Qualitative Research in Geography, in M. Limb and C. Dwyer (eds) *Qualitative Methodologies for Geographers: Issues and Debates.* London: Arnold, pp. 1–22.

Limb, M. and Dwyer, C. (eds) (2001) *Qualitative Methodologies for Geographers: Issues and Debates.* London: Arnold.

Linebaugh, P. (1982) All the Atlantic Mountains Shook. *Labour/Le travailleur* 10: 87–121.

Linebaugh, P. and Rediker, M. (1990) The Many-Headed Hydra: Sailors, Slaves, and the Atlantic Working Class in the Eighteenth Century. *Journal of Historical Sociology* 3(3): 225–52.

Lodge, D. (1985) *Small World.* Harmondsworth: Penguin.

Loehr, D. and Harper, L. (2003) Commonplace Tools for Studying Commonplace Interactions: Practitioners' Notes on Entry-Level Video Analysis. *Visual Communication* 2(2): 225–33.

Lomax, H. and Casey, N. (1998) Recording Social Life: Reflexivity and Video Methodology. *Sociological Research Online* 3(2).(http://www.socresonline.org.uk/socresonline/3/2/1.html last accessed 6 June 2006).

Longhurst, R. (1996) Refocusing Groups: Pregnant Women's Geographical Experiences of Hamilton, New Zealand/Aotearoa. *Area* 28(2): 143–49.

Lowe, M. (1992) Safety in Numbers? How to Teach Qualitative Geography? *Journal of Geography in Higher Education* 16(2): 171–75.

Lutz, C. and Collins, J. (1993) *Reading National Geographic.* Chicago, IL: Chicago University Press.

MacDougall, D. (1992) When Less is Less: the Long Take in Documentary *Film Quarterly* 46 (2): 36–46.

Madge, C. (1993) Boundary Disputes: Comments on Sidaway (1992). *Area* 25(3): 294–99.

Magolda, P. (2000) Accessing, Waiting, Plunging in, Wondering, and Writing: Retrospective Sense-Making of Fieldwork. *Field Methods* 12(3): 209–34.

Mandel, J. (2003) Negotiating Expectations in the Field: Gatekeepers, Research Fatigue and Cultural Biases. *Singapore Journal of Tropical Geography* 24(2): 198–210.

Mann, M. (1986) *Sources of Social Power 1.* Cambridge: Cambridge University Press.

Maranhao, T. (1986) The Hermeneutics of Participant Observation. *Dialectical Anthropology* 10(3–4): 291–309.

Marcus, G.E. (1986) Contemporary Problems of Ethnography in the Modern World System, in J. Clifford and G.E. Marcus (eds) *Writing Culture: The Poetics and Politics of Ethnography.* Los Angeles and Berkeley, CA: University of California Press, pp. 165–93.

Marcus, G.E. (1992) Past, Present and Emergent Identities: Requirements for Ethnographies of Late Twentieth-Century Modernity Worldwide, in S. Lasch and J. Friedman (eds) *Modernity and Identity.* Oxford: Blackwell, pp. 309–30.

Marcus, G.E. (1994) The Modernist Sensibility in Recent Ethnographic Writing and the Cinematic Metaphor of Montage, in Taylor, L (ed.) *Visualising Theory: Selected Essays from V.A.R. 1990–1994.* London: Routledge, pp. 37–53.

Marcus, G.E. (1995) Ethnography in/of the World System: the Emergence of Multi-Sited Ethnography. *Annual Review of Anthropology* 24: 95–117.

Marcus, G.E. (1998) *Ethnography Through Thick and Thin.* Princeton, NJ: Princeton University Press.

Marcus, G.E. and Clifford, J. (eds) (1986) *Writing Culture: The Poetics and Politics of Ethnography*. Los Angeles and Berkeley, CA: University of California Press.

Marcus, G.E. and Cushman, D. (1982) Ethnographies as Texts. *Annual Review of Anthropology* 11: 25–69.

Marcus, G.E. and Fischer, M.M.J. (1986) *Anthropology as Cultural Critique: an Experimental Moment in the Human Sciences*. Chicago, IL: University of Chicago Press.

Markwell, K. (1996) Dimensions of Photography in a Nature-Based Tour. *Annals of Tourism Research* 24(1): 131–55.

Markwell, K. (2000) Photo-Documentation and Analyses as Research Strategies in Human Geography. *Australian Geographical Studies* 38(1): 91–98.

Markwell, K. (2001) 'An Intimate Rendezvous with Nature'? Mediating the Tourist–Nature Experience at Three Tourist Sites in Borneo. *Tourist Studies* 1(1): 39–58.

Markwick, M. (2001) Postcards from Malta – Image, Consumption, Context. *Annals of Tourism Research* 28(2): 417–38.

Marshall, C. and Rossman, G. (1989) *Designing Qualitative Research*. London/Newbury Park/Delhi: Sage.

Marshall, P. (2003) Human Subjects Protections, Institutional review Boards and Cultural Anthropological Research. *Anthropological Quarterly* 76(2): 269–85.

Mascia-Lees, F.E., Sharpe, P. and Ballerino Cohen, C. (1989) The Postmodern Turn in Anthropology: Cautions from a Feminist Perspective. *Signs: Journal of Women in Culture and Society* 15(1): 7–33.

Massey, D. (1991) A Global Sense of Place. *Marxism Today* June: 24–29.

McCracken, G. (1988a) *Culture and Consumption: New Approaches to the Symbolic Character of Consumer Goods and Activities*. Bloomington, IN: Indiana University Press.

McCracken, G. (1988b) *The Long Interview*. London/Newbury Park/Delhi: Sage.

McDowell, L. (1992a) Doing Gender: Feminism, Feminists and Research Methods in Human Geography. *Transaction of the Institute of British Geographers* 17: 399–416.

McDowell, L. (1992b) Valid Games? A response to Erica Schoenberger. *Professional Geographer* 44(2): 212–15.

McDowell, L. (1993) Power and Masculinity in City Work Spaces. Paper presented at the Institute of British Geographers Annual Conference, Royal Holloway and Bedford New College, Egham, Surrey: 5–8 January.

McDowell, L. (1994) Polyphony and Pedagogic Authority. *Area* 26(3): 241–48.

McDowell, L. (1998) Elites in the City of London: Some Methodological Considerations. *Environment and Planning A* 30: 2133–46.

Michael, M. (2000) *Reconnecting Culture, Technology and Nature: From Society to Heterogeneity*. London: Routledge.

Miles, M. and Crush, J. (1993) Personal Narratives as Interactive Texts: Collecting and Interpreting Migrant Life-Histories. *Professional Geographer* 45(1): 95–129.

Miles, M. and Huberman, M. (1984) *Qualitative Data Analysis*. London/Newbury Park/Delhi: Sage.

Miller, D. (1987) *Material Culture and Mass Consumption*. Oxford: Blackwell.

Miller, D. (1998a) *Material Culture: Why Some Things Matter*. London: UCL Press.

Miller, D. (1998b) A Theory of Virtualism, in J. Carrier and D. Miller (eds) *Virtualism: a New political Economy*. Oxford: Berg, pp. 187–215.

Miller, D. (2000) Virtualism – the Culture of Political Economy, in I. Cook, D. Crouch, S. Naylor and J. Ryan (eds) *Cultural Turns / Geographical Turns: Perspectives on Cultural Geography*. Harlow: Prentice Hall, pp. 196–213.

Miller, D. and Slater, D. (2001) *The Internet: an Ethnographic Approach*. Oxford: Berg.

Miller, P. (1997) The Multiplying Machine. *Accounting, Organisations and Society* 22(3): 355–64.

Mitchell, D. (1995) There's No Such Thing as Culture: Towards a Reconceptualisation of the Idea of Culture in Geography. *Transactions, Institute of British Geography* 20: 102–16.

Mitchell, T. (2002) *Rule of Experts: Egypt, Techno-Politics, Modernity*. Berkeley, CA: University of California Press.

Mohammad, R. (2001) 'Insiders' and/or 'Outsiders': Positionality, Theory and Praxis, in M. Limb and C. Dwyer (eds) *Qualitative Methodologies for Geographers: Issues and Debates*. London: Arnold, pp. 101–20.

Mondal, A. (2003) Allegories of Identity: 'Postmodern' Anxiety and 'Postcolonial' Ambivalence in Amitav Ghosh's in an Antique Land and the Shadow Lines. *Journal of Commonwealth Literature* 38(3): 19–36.

Moore, S. (1988) Getting a Bit of the Other – the Pimps of Postmodernism, in Chapman, R. and Rutherford, J. (eds) *Male Order: Unwrapping Masculinity*. London: Lawrence & Wishart, pp. 165–92.

Morgan, D. (1988) *Focus Groups as Qualitative Research*. London/Newbury Park/Delhi: Sage.

Morgan, D. (1995) Why Things (Sometimes) go Wrong in Focus Groups. *Qualitative Health Research* 5: 516–23.

Morley, D. (1991) Where the Global Meets the Local: Notes from the Sitting Room. *Screen* 32(1): 1–15.

Moss, P. (ed.) (2002) *Feminist Geography in Practice: Research and Methods*, London: Blackwell.

Mountz, A., Miyares, I., Wright, R. and Bailey, A. (2003) Methodologically Becoming: Power, Knowledge and Team Research. *Gender, Place & Culture* 10(1): 29–46.

Mullings, B. (1999) Insider or Outsider, Both or Neither: Some Dilemmas of Interviewing in a Cross-Cultural Setting. *Geoforum* 30: 337–50.

Murphy, M. (1992) On Jogging with Fascists and Strolling with Reds: Ethnoethnography and Political Polarisation in an Andalucian Town, in P. DeVita (ed.) *The Naked Anthropologist: Tales from Around the World*. Belmont, CA: Wadsworth, pp. 173–83.

Murphy, P. (1999) Doing Audience Ethnography: a Narrative Account of Establishing Ethnographic Identity and Locating Interpretive Communities in Fieldwork. *Qualitative inquiry* 5(4): 479–504.

Murphy, P. (2002) The Anthropologist's Son (or, Living and Learning in the Field). *Qualitative Inquiry* 8(2): 246–61.

Musello, C. (1980) Studying the Home Mode. *Studies in Visual Communication* 6(1): 23–42.

Myerhoff, B. (1982) Life History among the Elderly: Performance, Visibility and Re-Membering, in J. Ruby (ed.) *A Crack in the Mirror: Reflexive Perspectives in Anthropology*. Philadelphia, PA: University of Pennsylvania Press, pp. 99–120.

Nader, L. (1974) Up the Anthropologist – Perspectives Gained from Studying Up, in D. Hymes (ed.) *Reinventing Anthropology*. New York: Vintage, pp. 284–311.

Nagar, R. (1997) Exploring Methodological Borderlands through Oral Narratives, in J.P. Jones III, H. Nash and S. Roberts (eds) *Thresholds in Feminist Geography*. Oxford: Roman and Littlefield, pp. 203–24.

Narayan, K. (1993) How Native Is a 'Native' Anthropologist? *American Anthropologist* 95(3): 671–86.

Nash, J. (1979) Anthropology of the Multinational Corporation, in G. Huizer and B. Mannheim (eds) *The Politics of Anthropology: from Colonialism and Sexism Toward a View from Below.* Paris: Mouton, pp. 421–46.

Nast, H. (1994) Opening Remarks on 'Women in the Field'. *Professional Geographer* 46(1): 54–66.

Neumann, M. (1999) *On the Rim: Looking for the Grand Canyon.* Minneapolis, MN: Minnesota University Press.

Oakley, A. (1981) Interviewing Women: a Contradiction in Terms, in H. Roberts (ed.) *Doing Feminist Research.* London: Routledge, pp. 30–61.

Oinas, P. (1999) Voices and Silences: The Problems of Access to Embeddedness. *Geoforum* 30: 351–61.

Oliver, M. (1992) Changing the Social Relations of Research Production? *Disability, Handicap & Society* 7(2): 101–14.

Oliver, S. (2003) Geography's Difficult Engagement with the Psychological Therapies. *Social and Cultural Geography* 4(3): 313–21.

Ostrander, S.A. (1993) 'Surely You're Not in This Just to be Helpful': Access, Rapport and Interviews in Three Studies of Élites. *Journal of Contemporary Ethnography* 22(1): 7–27.

Paerregard, K. (2002) The Resonance of Fieldwork. Ethnographers, Informants and the Creation of Anthropological Knowledge. *Social Anthropology* 10(3): 319–34.

Parr, H. (2002) New Body-Geographies: The Embodied Spaces of Health and Medical Information on the Internet. *Environment & Planning D: Society and Space* 20: 73–95.

Patton, M. (1980) *Qualitative Evaluation Methods.* London/Newbury Park/Delhi: Sage.

Payne, R. (2005) *Writing to Recover: A conversation with the (bulimic) Self: Exploring the Promises and Limits of Autoethnography.* Unpublished Manuscript, School of Geography, Earth and Environmental Sciences, University of Birmingham.

Personal Narratives Group (eds) (1989) *Interpreting Women's Lives: Feminist Theory & Personal Narratives.* Bloomington, IN: Indiana University Press.

Pfaffenberger, B. (1989) *Microcomputer Applications in Qualitative Research.* London/Newbury Park/New Delhi: Sage.

Pile, S. (1991) Securing the Future: Survival Strategies Amongst Somerset Dairy Farmers. *Sociology* 25(2): 255–74.

Pile, S. (1993) Human Agency and Human Geography Revisited: a Critique of 'New Models' of the Self. *Transactions of the Institute of British Geographers,* NS 18(1): 122–39.

Pile, S. and Thrift, N. (1995) Mapping the subject, in S. Pile and N. Thrift (eds) *Mapping the Subject: Geographies of Cultural Transformation.* London: Routledge, pp. 13–51.

Pink, S. (2001) *Doing Visual Ethnography: Images, Media and Representation in Research.* London: Sage.

Pink, S. (2001) More Visualising, More Methodologies: On Video, Reflexivity and Qualitative Research. *Sociological Review* 49: 586–99.

Pinney, C. (1992) The Lexical Spaces of Eye-Spy, in P. Crawford and D. Turton (eds) *Film as Ethnography.* Manchester, NH: Manchester University Press.

Plattner, S. (2003) Human Subjects Protection and Cultural Anthropology. *Anthropological Quarterly* 76(2): 287–97.

Pluciennik, M. and Q. Drew (2000) 'Only Connect': Global and Local Networks, Contexts and Fieldwork. *Ecumene* 7(1): 67–105.

Polizzi, G. (2000) Hermeticism, Messages, and Angels. *Configurations* 8: 245–69.

Pollner, M. and Emerson, R. (1983) The Dynamics of Inclusion & Distance in Fieldwork Relations, in R. Emerson (ed.) *Contemporary Field Research*. Boston, MA: Little Brown, pp. 235–52.

Portelli, A. (1981) The Peculiarities of Oral History. *History Workshop Journal* 12: 96–107.

Pratt, G. (2001) Studying Immigrants in Focus Groups, in P. Moss (ed.) *Feminist Geography in Practice: Research and Methods*. Oxford: Blackwell, pp. 214–29.

Pratt, M.L. (1986) Fieldwork in Common Places, in J. Clifford and G.E. Marcus (eds) *Writing Cultures: The Poetics and Politics of Ethnography*. Berkeley and Los Angeles, CA: University of California Press, pp. 27–50.

Pred, A.R. (1995) *Recognizing European Modernities: A Montage of the Present*. London: Routledge.

Pred, A.R. (2000) *Even in Sweden: Racisms, Racialized Spaces, and the Popular Geographical Imagination*. Berkeley, CA, London: University of California Press.

Price, M. (2001) The Kindness of Strangers. *Geographical Review* 91(1–2): 143–50.

Pryke, M., Rose, G. and Whatmore, S. (eds) (2003) *Using Social Theory*. Milton Keynes: Open University Press.

Punch, M. (1986) *The Politics and Ethics of Fieldwork*. London/Newbury Park/Delhi: Sage.

Rabinowitz, P. (1993) Wreckage upon Wreckage: History, Documentary and the Ruins of Memory. *History and Theory* 32: 119–37.

Radway, J. (1988) Reception Studies: Ethnography and the Problem of Dispersed Audiences and Nomadic Subjects. *Cultural Studies* 2(3): 359–76.

Rapport, N. (1993) *Diverse World Views in an English Village*. Edinburgh: Edinburgh University Press.

Rediker, M. (1987) *Between the Devil and the Deep Blue Sea: Merchant Seaman, Pirates and the Anglo-American Maritime World, 1700–1750*. Cambridge: Cambridge University Press.

Reme, E. (1993) Every Picture Tells a Story: Wall Decorations as Expressions of Individuality, Family Unit and Cultural Belonging. *Journal of Popular Culture* Spring: pp. 19–38.

Rennie, D. (1998) Grounded Theory Methodology: The Pressing Need for a Coherent Logic of Justification. *Theory and Psychology* 8: 101–19.

Richards, L. and Richards, T. (1994) From Filing Cabinet to Computer, in A. Bryman and R. Burgess (ed.) *Analysing Qualitative Data*. London: Routledge, pp. 147–72.

Richardson, L. (2000a) Writing: a Method of Inquiry, in N. Denzin and Y. Lincoln (eds) *The Handbook of Qualitative Research* (second edn). London: Sage, pp. 923–48.

Richardson, L. (2000b) Evaluating Ethnography. *Qualitative Inquiry* 6(2): 253–55.

Richardson, L. (2002) Writing Sociology. *Cultural Studies <=> Critical Methodologies* 2(3): 414–22.

Richardson, M. (2004) Polemical Posturing Versus Feigned Naivety in Documentary. *The film journal*, www.thefilmjournal.com/issue9/polemic.html (last accessed 4 January 2005).

Robson, E. (1994) From Teacher to Taxi Driver: Reflections on Research Roles in Developing Areas, in E. Robson and K. Willis (eds) *Postgraduate Fieldwork in Developing Areas: a Rough Guide. IBG Developing Areas (IBG Developing Areas Research Group Monograph 8)*. London: IBG, pp. 36–59.

Rogoff, I. (2000) *Terra Infirma: Geography's Visual Culture*. London: Routledge.

Rony, F.T. (2003) The Quick and the Dead: Surrealism and the Found Ethnographic Footage Films of Bontoc Eulogy and Mother Dao: The Turtlelike. *Camera Obscura* 18(1): 128–55.

Rosaldo, R. (1989) *Culture and Truth: The Remaking of Social Analysis*. Boston, MA: Beacon Press.

Rose, G. (1993) *Feminism and Geography: The Limits of Geographical Knowledge*. Cambridge: Polity.

Rose, G. (1997) Situating Knowledges: Positionality, Reflexivity and Other Tactics. *Progress in Human Geography* 21(3): 305–20.

Rose, G. (2000) Practising Photography: An Archive, a Study, Some Photographs and a Researcher. *Journal of Historical Geography* 26(4): 555–71.

Rose, G. (2001) *Visual Methodologies: An Introduction to the Interpretation of Visual Materials*. London: Sage.

Rose, G. (2003) On the Need to Ask How, Exactly, Is Geography 'Visual'? *Antipode* 35(2): 212–21.

Rose, G. (2004) 'Everyone's Cuddled up and it Just Looks Really Nice': the Emotional Geography of some Mums and their Family Photos. *Social and Cultural Geography*, 5: 549–64.

Rose, G. (forthcoming) 'You Just Have to Make a Conscious Effort to Keep Snapping Away, I Think': a Case Study of Family Photos, Mothering and Familial Space', in S. Hardy and C. Wiedmer (eds) *Mothering and Space*. Palgrave Macmillan.

Rosen, M. (1990) The Architecture of Documentary Film: an Interview with Amos Gitai. *Cineaste* 17(3): 48–50.

Routledge, P. (2002) Travelling East as Walter Kurtz: Identity, Performance, and Collaboration in Goa, India. *Environment & Planning D: Society and Space* 20(4): 477–98.

Rowles, G.D. (1978a) *Prisoners of Space? Exploring the Geographical Experience of Older People*. Boulder, CO: Westview.

Rowles, G.D. (1978b) Reflections on Experiential Fieldwork, in M. Samuels and D. Ley (eds) *Humanistic Geography: Prospects and Problems*. Chicago, IL: Maaroufa, pp. 173–93.

Rowles, G.D. (1980) Growing Old 'Inside': Aging and Attachment to Place in an Appalachian Community, in N. Datan and N. Lohmann (eds) *Transitions of Aging*. New York: Academic Press, pp. 152–70.

Rowles, G.D. (1983) Place and Personal Identity in Old Age: Observations from Appalachia. *Journal of Environmental Psychology* 3: 299–313.

Ruby, J. (1991) Speaking For, Speaking About, Speaking With, Speaking Alongside – an Anthropological and Documentary Dilemma. *Visual Anthropology Review* 7(2): 50–66.

Russell, C. (1999) *Experimental Ethnography: The Work of Film in the Age of Video*. Durham, NC: Duke University Press.

Ryan, G. and Bernard, H.R. (2003) Techniques to Identify Themes. *Field Methods* 15(1): 85–109.

Sacks, S. and Cook, I. (2000) *Social Sculpture and Connective Aesthetics: a Discussion* (www.gees.bham.ac.uk/downloads/gesdraftpapers/iancook-shelleysacks.htm last accessed 3 June 2006).

Saltmarsh, R. (2001) A Journey into Autobiography: a Coal Miner's Daughter, in P. Moss (ed.) *Placing Autobiography in Geography*. Syracuse, NY: Syracuse University Press, pp. 138–48.

Sanjek, R. (ed.) (1990) *Fieldnotes: The Makings of Anthropology*. Ithaca, NY: Cornell University Press.

Scheper-Hughes, N. (2004) Parts Unknown: Undercover Ethnography of the Organs-Trafficking Underworld. *Ethnography* 5(1): 29–73.

Schoenberger, E. (1991) The Corporate Interview as a Research Method in Economic Geography. *Professional Geographer* 43(2): 180–89.

Schoenberger, E. (1992) Self-Criticism and Self-Awareness in Research: a Reply to Linda McDowell. *Professional Geographer* 44(2): 215–18.

Schrager, S. (1983) What is Social in Oral History? *International Journal of Oral History* 4(2): 76–98.

Schrijvers, J. (1991) Dialectics of a Dialogical Ideal: Studying Down, Studying Sideways and Studying Up, in L. Nencel and P. Pels (eds) *Constructing Knowledge: Authority and Critique in Social Science*. London: Sage, pp. 162–79.

Schrijvers, J. (1993) Motherhood Experienced and Conceptualised: Changing Images in Sri Lanka and the Netherlands, in D. Bell, P. Caplan and W. Karim (eds) *Gendered Fields: Women, Men and Ethnography*. London: Routledge, pp. 143–58.

Schutz, A. (1967) *Phenomenology of the Social World*. Chicago, IL: Northwestern University Press.

Schwartz, D. (1989) Visual Ethnography: Using Photography in Qualitative Research. *Qualitative Sociology* 12(2): 119–54.

Schwartz, J. and Ryan, J. (eds) (2003) *Picturing Place: Photography and the Geographical Imagination*. London: I.B. Tauris.

Seamon, D. (1979) *A Geography of the Lifeworld: Movement, Rest and Encounter*. New York: St. Martin's Press.

Seamon, D. and Nordin, H. (1980) Marketplace as Place Ballet. *Landscape* 24(3): 35–41.

Seidel, J. (1991) Method and Madness in the Application of Computer Technology to Qualitative Data Analysis, in N.G. Fielding and R.M. Lee (eds) *Using Computers in Qualitative Research*. Beverly Hills, CA: Sage, pp. 107–16.

Sekula, A. (1995) *Fish Story*. Dusseldorf: Richter Verlag.

Shokeid, M. (1997) Negotiating Multiple Viewpoints: The Cook, the Native, the Publisher and the Ethnographic Text *Current anthropology* 38(4): 631–45.

Shostak, M. (1981) *Nisa: The Life and Words of a !Kung Woman*. Cambridge: Harvard University Press.

Shurmer-Smith, P. (1998) Becoming a Memsahib: Working with the Indian Administrative Service. *Environment and Planning A* 30: 2163–79.

Shurmer-Smith, P. (ed.) (2002) *Doing Cultural Geography*. London: Sage.

Sidaway, J. (1992) In Other Worlds: on the Politics of Research by 'First World' Geographers in the 'Third World'. *Area* 24(4): 403–08.

Sidaway, J. (2000a) Photography as Geographical Fieldwork. *Journal of Geography in Higher Education* 26(10): 95–103.

Sidaway, J. (2000b) Recontextualising Positionality: Geographical Research and Academic Fields of Power. *Antipode* 32: 260–70.

Silverman, D. (1993) *Interpreting Qualitative Data*. London: Sage.

Sin, C.H. (2003) Interviewing in 'Place': The Socio-Spatial Construction of Interview Data. *Area* 35: 305–12.

Skeggs, B., Moran, L., Tyrer, P. and Binnie, J. (2004) Queer as Folk: Producing the Real of Urban Space. *Urban Studies* 41(9): 1839–56.

Skelton, T. (2001) Cross-Cultural Research: Issues of Power, Positionality and 'Race', in M. Limb and C. Dwyer (eds) *Qualitative Methodologies for Geographers: Issues and Debates*. London: Arnold, pp. 87–100.

Smith, L.T. (1999) *Decolonizing Methodologies: Research and Indigenous Peoples*. London: Zed Books.

Smith, S. (2001) Doing Qualitative Research: from Interpretation to Action, in M. Limb and C. Dwyer (eds) *Qualitative Methodologies for Geographers: Issues and Debates*. London: Arnold, pp. 23–40.

Spaul, M. (nd) *Structuring a Flash Animation – Some Preliminary Theory*. (www. geocities.com/Athens/Atrium/6237/notesite/imd/imdgz4.htm last accessed 3 June 2006).

Spencer, J. (1989) Anthropology as a Kind of Writing. *Man*, New Series 24: 145–64.

Spradley, J.P. (1979) *The Ethnographic Interview*. London: Holt, Rinehart & Winston.

Spry, T. (2001) Performing Autoethnography: An Embodied Methodological Praxis. *Qualitative Inquiry* 7(6): 706–32.

Srivastava, N. (2001) Amitav Ghosh's Ethnographic Fictions: Intertextual Links between In An Antique Land and His Doctoral Thesis. *Journal of Commonwealth Literature* 36(2): 45–64.

Stacey, J. (1988) 'Can there be a Feminist Ethnography?' *Women's Studies International Forum* 11: 21–27.

Stephen, A. (1995) Familiarising the South Pacific, in A. Stephen (ed.) *Pirating the Pacific: Images of Travel, Trade and Tourism*. Sydney: Powerhouse Publishing, pp. 60–77.

Stewart, D. and P. Shamdasani (1990) *Focus Groups: Theory and Practice*. London/Newbury Park/Delhi: Sage.

Stewart, J. (1985) Introduction. In BFI *The films of Amos Gitai*. London: British Film Institute, pp. 1–3.

Strathern, M. (1989) The Limits of Auto-Anthropology, in A. Jackson (ed.) *Anthropology at Home*. London: Tavistock, pp. 16–37.

Strauss, A. (1987) *Qualitative Analysis For Social Scientists*. Cambridge: Cambridge University Press.

Swenson, J., Griswold, W. and Kleiber, P. (1992) Focus Groups: Method of Inquiry/Intervention. *Small Group Research* 23(4): 459–74.

Taussig, M. (1987) *Shamanism, Colonialism and the Wild Man: a Study in Terror and Healing*. Chicago, IL: Chicago University Press.

Taussig, M. (1992) *The Nervous System*. London: Routledge.

Taussig, M. (1993) *Mimesis and Alterity: A Particular History of the Senses*. London: Routledge.

Taylor, L. (ed.) (1994) *Visualising Theory: Selected Essays from Visual Anthropology Review*. London: Routledge.

Taylor, T. and Cameron, D. (1987) *Analysing Conversation: Rules and Units in the Structure of Talk*. Oxford: Pergamon.

Taylor, Y. (2004) Negotiation and Navigation – an Exploration of the Spaces/ Places of Working-Class Lesbians. *Sociological Research Online* 9(1). (http:// www.socresonline.org.uk/9/1/taylor.html)

Tedlock, B. (1991) From Participant Observation to the Observation of Participation. *Journal of Anthropological Research* 47(1): 69–94.

Temple, B. and Young, A. (2004) Qualitative Research and Translation Dilemmas. *Qualitative research* 4(2): 161–78.

Templeton, J. (1987) *Focus Groups: a Guide for Marketing and Advertising Professionals*. Chicago, IL: Probus.

Tesch, R. (1990) *Qualitative Research: Analysis Types and Research Tools*. California: Falmer.

Thede, N. and Ambrosi, A. (eds) (1991) *Video the Changing World*. New York: Basic Books.

Thomas, J. (1993) *Doing Critical Ethnography*. London/Newbury Park/Delhi: Sage.

Thomas, N. (1991) *Entangled Objects: Exchange, Material Culture, and Colonialism in the Pacific*. London: Harvard University Press.

Thomas, N. (1994) *Colonialism's Culture: Anthropology, Travel and Government*. Cambridge: Polity.

Thomas, N. (1995) The Beautiful and the Damned in A. Stephen (ed.) *Pirating the Pacific: Images of Travel, Trade and Tourism*. Sydney: Powerhouse Publishing, pp. 42–60.

Thomas, R. (1993) Interviewing Important People in Big Companies. *Journal of Contemporary Ethnography* 22(1): 80–96.

Thornton, S. (2000) An Academic Alice in Adland: Ethnography and the Commercial World. *Critical Quarterly* 41(1): 57–68.

Thrift, N.J. (1983) On the Determination of Social Action in Time and Space. *Environment & Planning D: Society & Space* 1: 23–57.

Thrift, N.J. (1995) Classics in Human Geography Revisited, Thrift, N. 'On the Determination of Social Action in Space and Time': Author's Response. *Progress in Human Geography* 19(4): 528–30.

Thrift, N.J. (2000a) Non-representational Theory, in R. Johnston, D. Gregory, G. Pratt and M. Watts (eds) *The Dictionary of Human Geography* (fourth edn) Oxford: Blackwell, p. 556.

Thrift, N.J. (2000b) Still Life in Nearly Present Time: The Object of Nature. *Body & Society* 6(3–4): 34–57.

Thrift, N.J. (2003) Practising Ethics, in M. Pryke, G. Rose and S. Whatmore (eds) *Using Social Theory*. London: Sage.

Thrift, N.J. (2004) Intensities of Feeling: Towards a Spatial Politics of Affect. *Geografiska Annaler B* 86(1): 57–78.

Throop, C.J. (2003) Articulating Experience. *Anthropological Theory* 3(2): 219–41.

Tillmann-Healy, L. (2003) Friendship as Method. *Qualitative Inquiry* 9(5): 729–49.

Torgovnick, M. (1990) *Gone Primitive: Savage Intellects, Modern Lives*. Chicago, IL: University of Chicago Press.

Trinh, T. M.-h. (1989) *Woman, Native, Other: Writing Postcoloniality and Feminism*. Bloomington, IN: Indiana University Press.

Turner, T. (1991) Social Dynamics of Video Media in an Indigenous Society: The Cultural Meaning and Personal Politics of Video Making in Kayapo Communities. *Visual Anthropology Review* 7(2): 68–76.

Turriff, C. (2002) Jamaica Debates 'Queen's English' *Education Guardian* 22 March, www.EducationGuardian.co.uk (last accessed 11 August 2004).

Twyman, C., Morrison, J. and Sporton, D. (1999) The Final Fifth: Autobiography, Reflexivity and Interpretation in Cross-Cultural Research *Area* 31(4): 313–25.

Underwood, C. and Jabre, B. (2003) Arab Women Speak Out: Self-Empowerment Via Video, in S. White (ed.) *Participatory Video: Images That Transform and Empower*. London: Sage, pp. 235–51.

Valentine, G. (1993a) Negotiating and Managing Multiple Sexual Identities: Lesbian Space–Time Strategies. *Transactions of the Institute of British Geographers* 18(2): 237–48.

Valentine, G. (1993b) Desperately Seeking Susan: a Geography of Lesbian Friendships. *Area* 25(2): 109–16.

Valentine, G. (1999) Doing Household Research: Interviewing Couples Together and Apart. *Area* 31: 67–74.

Valentine, G. (2002) People Like Us: Negotiating Sameness and Difference in the Research Process, in P. Moss (ed.) *Feminist Geography in Practice: Research and Methods*. Oxford: Blackwell, pp. 116–26.

van der Ploeg, J.D. (1986) The Agricultural Labour Process and Commoditization, in N. Long, J.D. van der Ploeg, C. Curtin and L. Box (eds) *The Commoditization Debate: Labour Process, Strategy and Social Network*. Papers of the Departments of Sociology 17, Agricultural University Wageningen, pp. 24–57.

van Leeuwen, T. (2000) Semiotics and Iconography, in T. van Leeuwen and C. Jewitt (eds) *Handbook of Visual Analysis*. London: Sage, pp. 92–118.

van Leeuwen, T. and Jewitt, C. (eds) (2000) *Handbook of Visual Analysis*. London: Sage.

Van Maanen, J. (1988) *Tales of the Field: On Writing Ethnography*. Chicago, IL: University of Chicago Press.

van Vleet, K. (2003) Partial Theories: On Gossip, Envy and Ethnography in the Andes. *Ethnography* 4(4): 491–519.

Wade, J. (1984) Role Boundaries and Paying Back: 'Switching Hats' in Participant Observation. *Anthropology and Education Quarterly* 15(3): 211–24.

Waitt, G. and Head, L. (2002) Postcards and Frontier Mythologies: Sustaining Views of the Kimberley as Timeless. *Society & Space* 20: 319–44.

Walker, A. and Moulton, R. (1989) Photo Albums: Images of Time and Reflections of Self. *Qualitative Sociology* 12(2): 155–82.

Wax, M. (1980) Paradoxes of 'Consent' to the Practices of Fieldwork. *Social Problems* 27(30): 272–83.

Wax, R. (1983) The Ambiguities of Fieldwork, in R. Emerson (ed.) *Contemporary Field Research*. Boston, MA and Toronto: Little Brown & Co, pp. 191–202.

Weitzman, E.A. and Miles, M.B. (1995) *Computer Programs for Qualitative Data Analysis: A Software Sourcebook*. Thousand Oaks, CA: Sage.

Wellings, K., Branigan, P. and Mitchell, K. (2000) Discomfort, Discord and Discontinuity as Data: Using Focus Groups to Research Sensitive Topics. *Culture, Health & Sexuality* 2: 255–67.

Western, J. (1981) *Outcast Cape Town*. Minneapolis, MN: University of Minnesota Press.

Western, J. (1996) Qualitative Research and the Language Trap. *Area* 28(2): 234–38.

White, S. (ed.) (2003) *Participatory Video: Images That Transform and Empower*. London: Sage.

Whitehead, T. (1986) Breakdown, Resolution and Coherence: The Fieldwork Experiences of a Big, Brown, Pretty Talking Man in a West Indian Community, in T. Whitehead and M. Conaway (eds) *Self, Sex and Gender in Cross-Cultural Fieldwork*. Urbana and Chicago, IL: University of Illinois Press, pp. 213–39.

Whyte, W. (1955) *Street Corner Society: The Social Structure of an Italian Slum*. Chicago, IL: Chicago University Press.

Willemen, P. (1992) *Bangkok-Bahrain* to *Berlin-Jerusalem:* Amos Gitai's Editing. *Screen* 33(1): 14–26.

Willemen, P. (ed.) (1993) *The Films of Amos Gitai, a Montage*. London: British Film Institute.

Williams, L. (1993) Mirrors Without Memories: Truth, History and the New Documentary. *Film Quarterly* 46(3): 9–21.

Williams, M., Mason, B. and Renold, E. (2004) Using Computers in Qualitative Research: a Review of Software Packages. *Building research capacity* 7: 4–7.

Willis, P. (1977) *Learning to Labour: how Working Class Kids Get Working Class Jobs*. New York: Columbia University Press.

Willis, P. and Trondman, M. (2000) A Manifesto For Ethnography. *Enthnography* 1: 5–16.

Wogan, P. (2004) Deep Hanging Out: Reflections on Fieldwork and Multisited Andean Ethnography. *Identities: Global Studies in Culture and Power* 11: 129–39.

Wolfinger, N. (2002) On Writing Fieldnotes: Collection Strategies and Background Expectancies. *Qualitative Research* 2(1): 85–95.

Worth, S. (1981) *Studying Visual Communication: Selected Writings*. Philadelphia, PA: University of Pennsylvania Press.

Worth, S. and Adair, J. (1972) *Through Navajo Eyes: An Exploration in Film Communication and Anthropology*. Bloomington, IN: Indiana University Press.

Young, L. and Barrett, H. (2001) Adapting Visual Methods: Action Research with Kampala Street Children. *Area* 33(2): 141–52.

Zeigler, D.J., Brunn, S.D. and Johnson, J. (1996) Focusing on Hurricane Andrew through the Eyes of the Victims. *Area* 28(2): 124–29.

Ziller, R. (1990) *Photographing the Self*. London/Newbury Park/Delhi: Sage.

Ziller, R. and Smith, D. (1977) A Phenomenological Utilisation of Photographs. *Journal of Phenomenological Psychology* 7: 172–85.

Index